JOHN MARSTON

a reference guide

A
Reference
Guide
to
Literature

Lawrence S. Thompson
Editor

JOHN MARSTON

a reference guide

KENNETH TUCKER

G.K.HALL&CO.

70 LINCOLN STREET, BOSTON, MASS.

Library of Congress Cataloging in Publication Data

Tucker, Kenneth.
    John Marston : a reference guide.

    (A Reference guide to literature)
    Bilbiography: p.
    Includes index.
    1. Marston, John, 1575?-1634—Bibliography. I. Title.
II. Series.
    Z8551.38.T83   1985   [PR2696]   016.822'3   85-941
    ISBN 0-8161-8355-4

This publication is printed on permanent/durable acid-free paper
MANUFACTURED IN THE UNITED STATES OF AMERICA

Contents

The Author

Kenneth Tucker was born in Louisville, Kentucky, in
1940. He received his B.A. and M.A. degrees from the
University of Louisville in 1963 and 1965, respectively.
In 1970 the University of Kentucky awarded him his
Ph.D. Since that year he has taught at Murray State
University, Murray, Kentucky, where he is a professor
of English. His specialties are Shakespeare and
Elizabethan-Jacobean drama.

Preface

This bibliography lists not only books and articles written about Marston but editions of Marston's works. It, moreover, cites references to and discussions of Marston in histories of English drama and literature as well as in books and articles upon Elizabethan drama and culture. Items are arranged chronologically.

I have attempted to consult each item listed. Of course, this was not always possible, as in cases of works published in limited editions. When I could not obtain a copy of a work or, in the case of dissertations, gain reliable information as to the contents, I have placed an asterisk before the entry number and in lieu of an annotation have cited the source mentioning the item.

Reprints of items are cited in the entries for those items. When listing an often reprinted work, such as Sir Paul Harvey's Oxford Companion to English Literature, I have tended to cite only the original publication and a recent or important reprint. Revisions, however, are given a separate citation and are cross-referenced with the original entry.

In the annotations I have tried to express the essence of each piece of writing while keeping the annotation brief. When the item presents general, fundamental, or commonly known information, I have written simply "Discusses" the subject considered. Thus a notation that the writing "Discusses Marston's quarrel with Hall" indicates that the item provides basic information. When the book or article presents new facts or interpretations, I have provided a summary of its contents. Besides annotating the entries, I have also indicated which works of Marston have numerous mentions or detailed and emphatic treatment in a book or article. To do so I have listed the titles of these works beneath the annotation when the annotation itself does not mention the work. My practice does not preclude the possibility that the author might have made passing comments on other works by Marston. My purpose is simply to guide the reader to meaningful treatments of the works being studied.

A word also needs to be said about the cross-referencing of editions. Since the editions of Marston's writings appear in the bibliography in two categories, collected editions and single editions of works, I have used the following means of citing editions. For collections of Marston's writings I have written Collected Edition before the year and item number. Thus, if the reader finds in an annotation mention of Bullen's edition of Marston's works, in parentheses beside the reference he will find Collected Edition 1887.1. This would refer him to the collected edition section of the bibliography. He would then turn to the year (1887) and the item number (1) in order to find bibliographical data and the annotation for Bullen's edition. In cases of single editions of the plays and poetry, I have simply written the work's title before the year and item number. If in a cross-reference, the reader should see <u>Antonio and Mellida</u> 1907.1, he would turn to <u>Antonio and Mellida</u> in the single edition section and then find the year entry (1907) and the item entry (1). Cross-referencing for articles and books is similar. For instance, a cross reference to 1947.3 would refer the user to entries for 1947. The 3 following would indicate the third item under 1947.

In listing the early editions of the works of Marston and others, I have included the item numbers from A.W. Pollard and R.G. Redgrave's <u>A Short-Title Catalogue of Books Printed in England, Scotland and Ireland</u> . . . 1475-1640 and Donald Wing's <u>A Short-Title Catalogue of Books Printed in England, Scotland, Ireland, Wales and British Columbia</u> . . . 1641-1700. In doing so, I have used volume I-Z of the revised Pollard and Redgrave by W.A. Jackson, F.S. Ferguson, and Katherine F. Pantzer and the A-England volume of the revised Wing, the only volumes of the new editions available at the time of the bibliography's compilation. For the numbers of items whose titles begin with letters from other portions of the alphabet, I have used the earlier editions of these reference tools.

A few other notes of guidance. Book reviews are given as separate articles. Numerous cross-references are used to lead users to reprints, reviews, and major treatments of selected subjects, such as discussions of particular texts. The index lists authors and editors cited in the entries, titles of book-length studies of Marston, and editions and discussions of Marston's writings. Also given are persons and some literary works cited in the annotations as well as selected subject headings.

A project of this scope could not have been completed without the help of many persons. Gratefully remembered are the contributions of the following persons who filed cards, Xeroxed materials, checked entries and alphabetizings, and typed portions of the manuscript: Carolyn Beadle, Melody Bucy, Frances Jane Monroe, Claudia Moore, and Laura Trouvé. Especial thanks goes to Jamie Helton, who typed the final version of the manuscript.

Deeply remembered is the valuable assistance of Mrs. Betty Hornsby of the Murray State Library staff, who patiently labored to obtain for me Xerox reproductions of numerous articles and copies of rarely seen books. I owe an especial debt to my colleague Mrs. Helen Roulston, who proofread my manuscript several times and offered helpful criticism. Especial thanks are due to James Harner of Bowling Green State University, who carefully read the initial manuscript and made numerous suggestions and Ms. Janice Meagher of G.K. Hall, who likewise gave helpful advice. Again I am deeply grateful to Professor Lawrence Thompson of the University of Kentucky, who guided me through this project as well as through the completion of my John Ford and Cyril Tourneur bibliographies. He has done much to make this project a reality.

Introduction

Since the romantics revived interest in Shakespeare's fellow
dramatists, critics on the whole have treated John Marston as the
social outcast, if not indeed the village idiot, of Elizabethan
drama. Almost in unison Victorian scholars decried him as an obnox-
ious individual given to writing obscenity and as an unskilled dramatist, whose works are marred by incoherences in plotting, strained
diction, unnatural characters, and his inability to unify his plays
into satisfying works of art. Early twentieth-century scholars
easily followed in the wake of their Victorian predecessors, particularly in judging Marston a ramshackle dramatist. Indeed the general
critical judgment for many decades was that Marston's major contribution to English letters resided in the light he shed upon such
skilled and sensitive contemporaries as Shakespeare and Jonson.

Marston's name, nevertheless, remained in histories of English
drama. Whereas few Victorian or early modern scholars cared to
devote numerous pages to such Renaissance dramatists as Thomas Nabbes
and Robert Davenport, critics through the years continued to read
Marston. Historians and enthusiasts of Elizabethan drama debated the
purposes of his techniques and the character of his works, almost as
though the poet evoked an uncanny spell, even upon the psyches of
those who condemned him most. True, of course, not all Victorian
and early twentieth-century appraisals of Marston were negative.
Here and there such critics as Algernon Charles Swinburne and G.B.
Harrison praised him. Others, like Theodore Spencer and T.S. Eliot,
have with reservation found Marston a source of interest and merit.
Until recent years, however, appreciative judgments formed a minority
report. But criticism frequently imitates the pendulum's swing, and
the movement toward a positive evaluation of Marston has come. In-
spired by European avant-garde drama, critics of the 1960s and 1970s
began to paint a new critical portrait of Marston as an acutely
intellectual theatrical experimenter, whose use of dramaturgy and
understanding of the lot of mankind foreshadow those of Beckett,
Ionesco, and other contemporary dramatists.

Before surveying criticism of Marston, however, I should look
at his life and contemporary reputation, for modern criticism of

Marston—now a huge spreading oak—has its roots firmly set in Jacobean soil. The son of a well-known English lawyer and a mother of Italian descent, Marston was born most likely in 1576. In 1594 he graduated from Brasenose College, Oxford. Disinclined to follow his father's profession, he abandoned it for literature and stormed the London literary scene as a self-proclaimed enfant terrible. He displayed the effrontery to launch in his first book The Metamorphosis of Pigmalion's Image and Certain Satires (1598) a forthright attack upon Joseph Hall. The origins of this famous dispute are somewhat obscure. Hall, a Cambridge don, had published a year earlier the first portion of his Virgidemiarum, a collection of Juvenalian satires. Possibly, irked by what seemed to be Hall's arrogance and by his apparent literary limitations, Marston was the initial aggressor. Some evidence suggests that it was Hall himself who retaliated by pasting an epigram insulting to the neophyte satirist in copies of Pigmalion distributed at Cambridge. If so, this was probably Hall's only counterattack. Marston, however, continued his onslaught in The Scourge of Villainy (1598), a collection of trenchant satires. Soon other writers joined in, supporting one or the other of the principals. Although personal antagonism was a major ingredient of this squabble, the quarrel involved literary questions such as those regarding choices of diction and objects of satire. By 1599, the Marston-Hall feud, as well as the Thomas Nashe-Gabriel Harvey fracas, had become so vituperative and, according to Elizabethan views, so potentially subversive of the social order, that the archbishop of Canterbury declared a moratorium on satirical verse. Marston's poems were publicly burnt.

A common opinion holds that this ban forced Marston to turn to the stage in order to vent his spleen. Recently, scholarship has provided evidence that Marston was fascinated by plays before the archbishop's celebrated intervention. Moreover, critics have speculated that he was constructing dramas before the Order for Conflagration. Whatever the reasons, Marston turned to the stage. After a short stint with the Admiral's Men, he began writing for the boys' company at St. Paul's by penning (or revising) Histriomastix (1599). Immediately thereafter he involved himself in his second and possibly more turbulent literary quarrel, that with Ben Jonson, the much discussed War of the Theaters.

The beginnings of this clash are also conjectural. Some critics have seen The Scourge of Villainy's Torquatus as a sniping caricature of Jonson. The majority hold that Marston unintentionally offended Jonson by portraying him as Chrysoganus in Histriomastix. Whatever the offense, Jonson retaliated. He certainly pilloried Marston as Carlo Buffone in Everyman Out of His Humour (1599) and as Crispinus in The Poetaster (1601). Furthermore, Jonson probably intended Hedon of Cynthia's Revels (1600) to be an unflattering likeness of his adversary. Marston, however, was not idle. He burlesqued Jonson as Brabant Senior in Jack Drum's Entertainment (ca. 1601) and as Lampatho Doria in What You Will (ca. 1601). The final skirmish was Satiromastix (1602), a whimsical, but cutting reply to The Poetaster.

Utilizing some of that play's characters, Satiromastix features Horace, Jonson's flattering self-portrait, as an arrogant versifying poseur. Though the work was authored primarily, if not solely, by Thomas Dekker, whom Jonson had also offended, Marston probably contributed choice passages. He almost certainly helped plan the play. Historians of Elizabethan drama differ as to which, if either, dramatist emerged triumphant. Moreover, scholars have disagreed as to the dispute's nature and scope. Some have questioned the feud's sincerity and have seen it as an attention-garnering pose. Others have expanded its boundaries beyond personal pique and judged it part of a larger rivalry between the children's and the adult companies. Still others have singled out competing dramatic theories as the cause of the opposition. All agree, however, that after Satiromastix, the bickering ended. Probably wearied by the fracas, both dramatists were desirous of letting it slip quietly from public attention.

During these years Marston did not expend all his creative energy in sniping at Jonson. Either 1599 or 1600 saw the emergence of his now controversial plays Antonio and Mellida and Antonio's Revenge, the results of respective attempts to write a romantic tragicomedy and a Senecan revenge play. Soon after the quarrel with Jonson he transferred his loyalty to the child actors at Blackfriars and constructed his more celebrated plays, The Malcontent (ca. 1603), The Fawn (ca. 1604), and The Dutch Courtesan (ca. 1604). In 1605, having made peace with Jonson, he joined his former antagonist and George Chapman to draft Eastward Hoe. Unfortunately, the play, a satirical comedy, immediately embroiled the authors in risky controversy. Passages, very likely penned by Marston, ridiculed the Scots, King James, and the monarch's notorious penchant for granting knighthoods in exchange for cash. Court and king were bitterly offended, and the authors were temporarily imprisoned.

Afterward, Marston resumed playwriting with The Wonder of Women or The Tragedy of Sophonisba (ca. 1606), a Senecan tragedy. Although it is seldom read today, Marston believed it his best play. (Some modern readers, most notably T.S. Eliot, have concurred.) This is the last entire drama bequeathed us by Marston's pen. There exists, of course, The Insatiate Countess (ca. 1608), a work partially written by Marston and completed by the actor William Barksted. But estimates differ as to how much of the work as we have it is Marston's.

During the new century's first decade, Marston's personal life took dynamic turns. Perhaps as early as 1605, he married Mary Wilkes, the daughter of an Anglican clergyman. On 8 June 1608, Marston was sentenced to Newgate. The cause of his arrest is uncertain, but some scholars conjecture that it concerned his involvement with another play targeting James I. How long Marston remained incarcerated is unclear, but his imprisonment was most likely brief. On 24 December 1609, he was ordained an Anglican clergyman. Why he deserted the stage for the pulpit is a source of inevitable speculation. Possibly, King James's wrath provoked by the 1608 offense (if there was one) "persuaded" Marston to abandon his dramatic career and steer for safer waters. Also possible is that disillusionment stung him as to his dramatic skills. <u>Or</u>, as Theodore Spencer believed, metaphysical doubts so increasingly beset him that he sought solace and sureness of conviction within the traditions of the church.

In 1616, he became the vicar of Christ's Church, Hampshire. His only child, an infant son, died in 1624. In 1631, he retired from his position. Two years later the London printer William Sheares issued a collection of Marston's plays with the author's name upon the title page. Marston, the clergyman, evidently objected to this public reminder of his earlier reputation as a cynical, risqué, controversial dramatist. Authorial ascription was removed from the second edition. On 17 June 1634, Marston made his will. Certainly extreme illness beset him, for he could not even sign the document. Then on 25 June he died.

This outline of Marston's career points to some directions later criticism would take. To his contemporaries Marston speedily earned notoriety as a "sharp-fanged" satirist, unwavering in his attempt to indict the fads and follies of an age. His quarreling with Hall and Jonson exhibited an acerbic, even vengeful personality. His possible attempts to use drama as a weapon against the king argue for a dynamic, if not reckless, desire to point the finger at supposed incompetence and corruption whatever the cost. Clearly he gained admirers among young intellectuals, such as Everard Guilpin, who shared his critical outlook. Equally sure is that other contemporaries found him offensive. The authors of the anonymous <u>The Return from Parnassus, Part II</u> (a play written and performed by students of St. John's College, Cambridge) used the occasion to drub Marston for his bitterness and scurrility:

> What, Monsieur Kinsayder, lifting up your leg, and
> pissing against the world? put up, man, put up, for
> shame!
> Methinks he is a ruffian in his style,
> Withouten bands or garters' ornament;
> He quaffs a cup of Frenchman's Helicon;
> Then roister doister in his oily terms,
> Cuts, thrusts, and foins, at whomsoever he meets,
> And strews about Ram-Alley meditations.
> Tur, what cares he for modest close-couch'd terms,
> Cleanly to gird our looser libertines?
> Give him plain naked words, stripp'd from their shirts,
> That might beseem plain-dealing Aretine.
> Ay, there is one, that backs a paper steed,
> And manageth a penknife gallantly,
> Strikes his poinardo at a button's breadth,
> Brings the great battering-ram of terms to towns;
> And, at first volley of his cannon-shot,
> Batters the walls of the old fusty world.[1]

The same drama almost certainly burlesques him as the ranting Furor
Poeticus.

His own age, therefore, evidenced two opposing tendencies in
evaluating Marston: one, seeing him as a sharp-witted intellectual,
courageously challenging corruption and vice; the other, judging him
as a crude malcontent, venting exaggerated indignation in jerry-built
verse and inept drama while revealing an offensive personality.
Although undergoing countless minor mutations and shifts of emphasis
since the Renaissance, these two views of Marston have continued.
Indeed they have tinctured much modern discussion of the dramatist,
to which we shall turn.

The criticism of Marston, especially that of the twentieth century, is voluminous, but the major scholarly concerns are as follows:
(1) psychological criticism of Marston, (2) the question of Marston
and literary influences, (3) the nature of Marston's thought, and (4)
the value of Marston's works. Each of these areas shall be discussed
in turn.

PSYCHOLOGICAL CRITICISM OF MARSTON.

Surprisingly enough, despite the twentieth century's long-
enduring infatuation with Freudian psychoanalysis, not many investigations into the intricacies of Marston's personality have made
direct use of depth psychology. We find few excursions into the
bewildering forests of the unresolved Oedipus complex or the swamp of
anxieties produced by unconscious guilt. Although critics have generally shied away from Freudian lingo while probing the dramatist's
personality, they have not hesitated to follow the Freudian trend and
attempt to analyze Marston's apparently obvious conflicts.

Clearly during his literary years, Marston was not at peace with
himself or with Jacobean society. His writings, especially his early
satires, manifest a grim awareness of human depravity and an insistent
anger at vices, treacheries, crimes. To many students of his writings, the intensity of Marston's indignation indicates his emotional
instability. Some have argued that his ire was caused by a violent
attraction toward the very vices he pillories. Others, especially
A. José Axelrad, have posited a morbid fear of sexuality, possibly
induced by an unpleasant erotic initiation, as the root of his
Juvenalian bitterness. Other writers--for instance, Theodore
Spencer--have questioned whether Marston grappled with incipient
psychosis. Although much delving into Marston's psyche has directed
attention to his morbid and splenetic tendencies, other researching
has stressed a humble side that ill accords with the Furor Poeticus
of the Parnassus play.

At times, as in his preface to The Fawn, Marston takes pains to belittle his own literary efforts, to disavow lingering malice on his part, and to extend the handclasp of peace to his detractors. Sometimes, especially in the same play, his satire exhibits more whimsy and tolerance than rancor and spite. Then, too, we might note his delight in including caricatures of himself in his plays, men with reddish hair and short legs, features evidently his own. These observations do not necessarily indicate that we should replace the acerbic Marston with a more genial and well-disposed counterpart. But open-minded research does suggest that Marston was intriguingly complex, often bitter, often egocentric, sometimes self-disparaging, at times kindly, but perhaps predominantly melancholy and skeptical.

Rather than classifying Marston as a narrow-minded misanthrope, we should understand his personality as an unstable fusion of contradictory tendencies and warring emotions, a personality symptomatic of his troubled age.

MARSTON AND THE QUESTION OF LITERARY INFLUENCES.

Marston began his dramatic career when the great age of Elizabethan-Jacobean drama emerged. The fifteen years following the century's birth saw the production of Webster's, Jonson's, and Tourneur's greatest plays as well as much of the best work of Middleton, Chapman, and Shakespeare. It was one of those rare, vital eras when the creative energies of a generation are unleashed, producing numerous works of arresting beauty and tough-minded perception. Both intellectually and theatrically, Marston was at the forefront of this dynamic trend. Modern inquiry has uncovered many philosophical and theological influences upon his understanding of human nature. Calvinism, Stoicism, neo-Stoicism, skepticism have all been shown to be tributaries to Marston's sinister, but challenging view of human existence. A sharply intellectual strain manifests itself in Marston's dramatic sensibility. Ideas, quandaries, theories, ambiguities engrossed him and compelled their expressions in his satires and plays. In so doing, he helped to disseminate daring concepts throughout his intellectual and literary milieu.

Marston, moreover, was an energetic theatrical innovator, experimenting with the facilities of the private theaters and the resources of the boy players. He helped to introduce or spread the use of such dramatic techniques as parody, burlesque, macaronic quips, and aria-like dialogue. Along with Chapman and Jonson, he created an appetite for satiric drama. Quite naturally, much twentieth-century research has labored to trace Marston's influence upon his contemporaries and theirs upon him. Not a few critics have detected Marstonian techniques in the satiric strains of Webster's tragedies. Edward Sharpham's The Fleire owes a direct debt to The Fawn. Indeed The Revenger's Tragedy, ascribed to Tourneur, seems a cousin-german to The Malcontent.

xvi

Many investigations into Marston's relationship with the drama of
his age, however, have emphasized his and Shakespeare's possible
mutual influences. Marston's plays abound with situations and characters similar to those in Shakespeare, as well as echoes of his
greater contemporary's lines. A prominent verdict is that Marston is
indebted to Shakespeare, but not a few writers have suggested that
Shakespeare at times borrowed from Marston. The major controversy
concerning Marston's and Shakespeare's possible mutual influence
centers upon the relationship of <u>Antonio's Revenge</u> and <u>Hamlet</u>. Both
are Senecan revenge plays, written very nearly at the same time, and
include paralleling events and characters. Some researchers have
credited Marston with the first of these two revenge plays and with
revitalizing the flagging Senecan tradition; others ascribe these
achievements to Shakespeare. An increasingly popular theory is that
each writer working independently drew upon the <u>Ur-Hamlet</u> or possibly
the Hamlet story in one or more of its novella forms.

In many cases literary influences, both thematic and technical,
are unfortunately difficult to substantiate. Writer A might have
drawn upon writer B; on the other hand, writer B might have been the
borrower. Or both could have imitated writer C or have drawn from a
common fund of ideas, theories, and techniques. Thus to many readers, studies of influences seem as profitable as a frantic search for
the leprechaun's pot of gold. These studies, nevertheless, have
their value. While rarely guaranteeing answers, they can tell us
much about the literary fashions, techniques, and especially the
zeitgeist of a particular age.

THE NATURE OF MARSTON'S THOUGHT.

The question of the intellectual standpoint of Marston's views
upon man, society, and God has drawn sustained attention. Calvinism,
High Anglicanism, Epicureanism, skepticism, other creeds and intellectual persuasions have garnered adherents who find these beliefs
forming Marston's <u>weltanschauung</u>. Determining the degree to which an
organized system of belief manifests itself in a literary work can be
difficult. Nor is it easy to distinguish the philosophical root of
an author's stance from the writer's own personal reaction to a human
problem. Yet such studies provide us with helpful reference points
for our own excursions into the sometimes enigmatic world of a
writer's mind. And indeed they offer us meaningful, if at times
inexact, labels for ordering our impressions.

A number of inquirers, however, have noted what they believe are
distinct trends or developments in the unfolding of Marston's thought
throughout his literary years. Some have stressed that Marston
progressed from a harsh condemnation of humanity's lapses from virtue
to a broad-minded, if not warmly tolerant, treatment of his species'
proclivity to stumble, especially in erotic misadventures. Adding to

this view, other writers have seen him emerging from a slough of hectoring antisexual feelings to champion the goodness and natural-ness of sexuality and its legitimate expression in marriage.

Other intrigued readers have directed attention upon developments in Marston's career-long love-hate relationship with Stoicism. Accord-ing to this view, the Antonio plays mark a disillusioned departure from the "wisdom" of Seneca and other would-be masters of turbulent emotions. It is suggested that Marston's attitude toward this philo-sophic scheme did not remain statically skeptical, that near the end of his dramatic career, as evidenced by Sophonisba, he experienced a reawakened admiration for some of the Stoical system, namely its emphasis on courage and fortitude. Dissenters from this view specu-late that Stoicism never seemed reasonable enough to Marston to afford him peace and a direction for living; therefore, he sought these in the church.

These are but some of the speculations upon the direction of Marston's thought. That they and other conflicting theories exist argues for two frequently suggested possibilities: (1) that Marston, never able to determine for himself what he believed, remained a wanderer upon his own moor of intellectual confusion; and (2) that Marston, a dedicated seeker of knowledge, grappled with serious moral complexities and would not accept one-dimensional solutions.

Again we see a negative and positive branching of critical opin-ion. Doubtlessly technical weaknesses in Marston's plays account for some of the seeming confusion as to his views. However, to a greater extent than many critics will admit, the question of whether he should be classed as a muddled or keen thinker is a matter of indi-vidual perspective. Like a painting, a concerto, or a woman's face, the value of Marston's thought is subject to varied assessments. To readers who prefer clarity of attitude and vision, Marston's ouevre may seem incredibly incoherent. On the other hand, if the reader is intrigued by Montaignelike skepticism and a sense that life presents us with persistent ambiguities, Marston's works may well be rewarding.

THE VALUE OF MARSTON'S WORKS.

This issue is by far the most vehemently debated in current writings on Marston. As noted earlier, since the sixties a trend has gathered momentum to establish Marston as a bold theatrical experi-menter and an intellectually challenging dramatist. This revisionist theory, associated largely with R.A. Foakes, sees Marston's drama-turgy not as an enfeebled attempt to portray human behavior realis-tically but as an effort to employ irony and burlesque to satirize conventional dramatic genres as well as human nature. Central to this view is the assumption that the child actors performed their roles to mimic and to ridicule adult behavior, thereby to advance a disillusioned, if not indeed a premodern absurdist, view of humanity's confused strivings. Hence, Marston emerges from his reevaluation as a quite contemporary spirit, whose tortured questionings of the meaning of existence foreshadow those of Beckett, Camus, Ionesco, and Arrabal.

This revisionist reading of Marston has not gone unchallenged. Indeed a strong counterreaction has risen to block its advance. Chief among the antagonists of this new assessment is Richard Levin, who has criticized the contemporary trend of finding "good bad dramas" among the yellowing pages of seldom read Elizabethan plays. Accordingly Levin faults critics who find hitherto undisclosed subtleties in works that previous generations accepted at face value and did not award with laurels. Convinced that these modern critics base their interpretations upon insufficient evidence, Levin urges that we should alter the established interpretation of a play only if the critic finds numerous and certain instances of parody and irony. The debate continues and shall probably do so for some years. Obviously some critics have been overly ingenious in detecting irony and burlesque in neglected dramas. But this unhappy error should not blind us to the probability that Marston and his contemporaries did at times employ irony and other not immediately obvious techniques for serious purposes. Perhaps as of the present we do not know enough about the acting styles of the early seventeenth century to render an unimpeachable verdict on this vexing, but important question. A prime goal of future critics should be to examine meticulously the texts of numerous plays to gain a clearer insight into the nature and purposes of Elizabethan dramaturgy.

In closing this introduction, I would underscore that Marston's place in the history of drama is uncertain. Much discussion about his value is evident, but no consensus has been declared. While it is most unlikely that the histories of English drama will elevate him to the rank of Jonson, Webster, and Middleton, he will probably not sink again to the low level to which the Victorians generally relegated him. Marston invites a wide range of opinion; thus concord among students of Renaissance drama as to his significance is unlikely.

What cannot be denied about Marston is that he had a powerful impact upon the drama of his age. And if hard to trace, his influence is pervasive. He could write entertainingly; and though often flawed, his plays do furnish pleasure. He, furthermore, possessed a serious, questing mind, one that grappled with the enigmas of a complex, challenging age--and indeed with the problems endured by all ages in the throes of social, economic, and ideological turmoil. Hence, to read Marston is to acquaint oneself with problems that recurringly beset the human race. These factors indeed make him worthy of careful reading and continued scholarship.

Note

1. The Return from Parnassus, Part II, in A Select Collection of Old English Plays, ed. W.C. Hazlitt (London: Reeves & Turner, 1874; reprint. New York: Benjamin Blom, 1964), 9:116-17.

Abbreviations

AN&Q	American Notes and Queries
AntigR	Antigonish Review
ArielE	Ariel: A Review of International English Literature
BB	Bulletin of Bibliography
CL	Comparative Literature
CompD	Comparative Drama
DUJ	Durham University Journal
EA	Études Anglaises
EAA	Estudos Anglo-Americanos (São Paulo, Brazil)
EETS	Early English Texts Society
EIC	Essays in Criticism (Oxford)
EigoS	Eigo Seinen (Tokyo, Japan)
ELH	English Literary History
ELN	English Language Notes
ELR	English Literary Renaissance
E&S	Essays and Studies
ES	English Studies
Expl.	Explicator
FDT	Fountainwell Drama Texts
HAB	Humanities Association Bulletin (Canada)
HLQ	Huntington Library Quarterly
HussR	Husson Review
JDS	Jacobean Drama Studies
JEGP	Journal of English and Germanic Philology
JWCI	Journal of the Warburg and Courtauld Institute
M&L	Music and Letters
MLN	Modern Language Notes
MLQ	Modern Language Quarterly
MLR	Modern Language Review
MP	Modern Philology
Neophil	Neophilologus
NM	Neuphilologishe Mitteilungen
NMS	New Mermaid Series
NQ	Notes and Queries
Parergon	Bulletin of the Australian and New Zealand Association for Medieval and Renaissance Studies
PBA	Proceedings of the British Academy

PBSA	Papers of the Bibliographical Society of America
PEL	Penguin English Library
PMLA	Publications of the Modern Language Association of America
PQ	Philological Quarterly
QQ	Queen's Quarterly
REL	Review of English Literature
RenD	Renaissance Drama
RenP	Renaissance Papers
RenQ	Renaissance Quarterly
RES	Review of English Studies
RLC	Revue de Littérature Comparée
RN	Renaissance News
RP	Revels Plays
RRDS	Regents Renaissance Drama Series
SAB	Shakespeare Association Bulletin
SB	Studies in Bibliography
SCN	Seventeenth Century News
SEL	Studies in English Literature
SELit	Studies in English Literature (English Literary Society of Japan)
SengL	Studies in English Literature (Hague, Netherlands)
SFQ	Southern Folklore Quarterly
ShS	Shakespeare Survey
SJ	Shakespeare Jahrbuch
SJW	Shakespeare Jahrbuch (Weimer, East Germany)
SNL	Satire Newsletter (State University College, Oneonta, New York)
SP	Studies in Philology
SQ	Shakespeare Quarterly
SR	Sewanee Review
TEAS	Twayne's English Authors Series
ThS	Theatre Survey: The American Journal of Theatre History
TLS	Times Literary Supplement
TN	Theatre Notebook: A Journal of the History and Technique of the British Theatre
TSE	Tulane Studies in English
TSLL	Texas Studies in Literature and Language: A Journal of the Humanities
YES	Yearbook of English Studies

Writings by Marston

1633

*1   The Workes of Mr. Iohn Marston, Being Tragedies and Comedies
     Collected into One Volume. London: W. Sheares, [414] pp.
     (Pollard and Redgrave 17471)
          Cited in Tannenbaum, 1940.5. Discussions: 1927.2; 1928.7.
     Contains Antonio and Mellida, Antonio's Revenge, The Dutch
     Courtezan, The Fawn, Sophonisba, What You Will.

*2   Tragedies and Comedies Collected into One Volume. London:
     Printed by A.M. for William Sheares, [412] pp. (Pollard and
     Redgrave 17472)
          Cited in Tannenbaum, 1940.5. Essentially the same edition
     as Collected Edition 1633.1 with authorial ascription withdrawn,
     apparently at Marston's insistence. Discussions: 1927.2;
     1928.7. Bibliographical information: 1957.13.

1652

*1   Comedies, Tragi-Comedies, & Tragedies: Written by Iohn
     Marston. London. (Wing M 816)
          Cited in Tannenbaum, 1940.5. An exceedingly rare item.
     Only one copy is known to have survived. It has been broken up,
     and the plays have been sold individually. Discussion: 1927.2.
     Bibliographical information: 1957.13. Contains Antonio and
     Mellida, Antonio's Revenge, The Dutch Courtezan, The Fawn, The
     Insatiate Countess, The Malcontent, Sophonisba, What You Will.

1856

1   HALLIWELL, JAMES ORCHARD, ed. The Works of John Marston,
     Reprinted from the Original Editions. 3 vols. London: J.R.
     Smith, 942 pp.

1

Contains <u>Antonio</u> <u>and</u> <u>Mellida</u>, <u>Antonio's</u> <u>Revenge</u>, <u>Certain</u>
<u>Satires</u>, <u>The</u> <u>Dutch</u> <u>Courtezan</u>, <u>Eastward</u> <u>Hoe</u>, <u>The</u> <u>Fawn</u>, <u>The</u>
<u>Insatiate</u> <u>Countess</u>, <u>The</u> <u>Malcontent</u>, <u>The</u> <u>Metamorphosis</u> <u>of</u>
<u>Pigmalion's</u> <u>Image</u>, <u>The</u> <u>Scourge</u> <u>of</u> <u>Villainy</u>, <u>Sophonisba</u>, and
<u>What</u> <u>You</u> <u>Will</u>. Also contains the following minor works: "City
Pageant" and <u>Entertainment</u> <u>of</u> <u>Alice</u>, <u>Dowager-Countess</u> <u>of</u> <u>Derby</u>.
Introduction presents a general discussion of Marston's life and
comments upon his works. Edition has been faulted for simply
copying old editions without attempting to emend textual errors.
Includes explanatory notes. Reviews: 1856.1; 1858.1; 1887.1
(praises Bullen's edition and criticizes Halliwell's); 1943.8.
Suggested emendations: 1856.2; 1858.2; 1862.1.

1887

1   BULLEN, A.H., ed. <u>The</u> <u>Works</u> <u>of</u> <u>John</u> <u>Marston</u>. 3 vols.
    London: J.C. Nimmo, 1195 pp. Reprint. Hildesheim: Georg
    Olms, 1970.
       Contains <u>Antonio</u> <u>and</u> <u>Mellida</u>, <u>Antonio's</u> <u>Revenge</u>, <u>Certain</u>
    <u>Satires</u>, <u>The</u> <u>Dutch</u> <u>Courtezan</u>, <u>Eastward</u> <u>Hoe</u>, <u>The</u> <u>Fawn</u>, <u>The</u>
    <u>Insatiate</u> <u>Countess</u>, <u>The</u> <u>Malcontent</u>, <u>The</u> <u>Metamorphosis</u> <u>of</u>
    <u>Pigmalion's</u> <u>Image</u>, <u>The</u> <u>Scourge</u> <u>of</u> <u>Villainy</u>, <u>Sophonisba</u>, <u>What</u> <u>You</u>
    <u>Will</u>. Also contains the following minor works: "City Pageant,"
    "Comendatory Verses Prefixed to Ben Jonson's <u>Sejanus</u>," Enter-
    tainment <u>of</u> <u>Alice</u>, <u>Dowager-Countess</u> <u>of</u> <u>Derby</u>, and <u>The</u> <u>Mounte-</u>
    <u>bank's</u> <u>Masque</u>, a work once ascribed to Marston. Introduction
    presents a detailed discussion of Marston, drawing upon many
    Jacobean documents and various contemporary references to him.
    Discusses his family, his background, and his literary career.
    Gives detailed attention to his quarrels with Hall and Jonson.
    Though it provides much information, some data has been super-
    seded by later scholarship. Produces text in modern spelling and
    provides textual and explanatory notes. Reviews: 1887.1;
    1921.4. Suggested emendations: 1887.1; 1893.2; 1896.2; 1903.2;
    1906.4; 1908.8; 1943.8, 10; 1948.6. Still considered the stand-
    ard edition by some scholars.

1934

1   WOOD, H. HARVEY, ed. <u>The</u> <u>Plays</u> <u>of</u> <u>John</u> <u>Marston</u>. Vol. 1.
    Edinburgh: Oliver & Boyd, 246 pp.
       Contains <u>Antonio</u> <u>and</u> <u>Mellida</u>, <u>Antonio's</u> <u>Revenge</u>, <u>The</u>
    <u>Malcontent</u>. Reviews: 1934.2; 1935.3, 14.

1938

1   WOOD, H. HARVEY, ed. <u>The</u> <u>Plays</u> <u>of</u> <u>John</u> <u>Marston</u>. Vol. 2.
    Edinburgh: Oliver & Boyd, 360 pp.

Contains The Dutch Courtezan, The Fawn, Sophonisba,
What You Will. Reviews: 1938.1, 5; 1939.3. Emendation to
Sophonisba: 1975.11.

1939

1 WOOD, H. HARVEY, ed. The Plays of John Marston. Vol. 3.
   Edinburgh: Oliver & Boyd, 324 pp.
       Contains The Insatiate Countess, Eastward Hoe, Jack Drum's
   Entertainment, Histriomastix. On pp. lx–xxvii of Vol. 3 appears
   the edition's introduction "John Marston as a Dramatic Author."
   While acknowledging that Marston was never completely successful
   in fashioning satisfying plays, Wood values Marston as a dramatic
   innovator, experimenting with diction, prosody, and stage effects,
   and praises him as a skillful comic writer. Wood's edition
   presents old spelling texts with separate introductions for each
   play. Does not number lines. Edition has been faulted for
   inadequate textual and explanatory notes and for not supplying
   conjectural emendations. Review: 1941.7.

Smaller Collections

1879

*1 GROSART, ALEXANDER B., ed. The Poems of John Marston.
    Blackburn, England: Printed for Subscribers by C.E. Simms,
    Manchester.
        Cited in Tannenbaum, 1940.5.

1961

1 DAVENPORT, ARNOLD, ed. The Poems of John Marston. Liverpool:
   Liverpool University Press, 393 pp.
       Contains Certain Satires, The Metamorphosis of Pigmalion's
   Image, The Scourge of Villainy, as well as the following minor
   works: "City Pageant," Entertainment of Alice, Dowager-Countess
   of Derby, "Commendatory Verses Prefixed to Ben Jonson's Sejanus,"
   and poems from Love's Martyr. Introduction sketches Marston's
   life, outlines his career as a satirist and conflict with Hall,
   speculates upon his psychological makeup, and analyzes intellectual influences upon his Juvenalian stance. Praises Marston's
   influence upon his age and his originality. Also provides bibliographical notes. Presents an old spelling text with numerous
   explanatory notes.

SINGLE EDITIONS

Antonio's Revenge

1602

*1 Antonio's Revenge. The Second Part. Written by I.M. London:
     Printed for Thomas Fisher, [80] pp. (Pollard and Redgrave
     17474)
          Cited in Tannenbaum, 1940.5. Facsimile reprint: Antonio's
     Revenge, 1921.1.

1872

1   Antonio's Revenge. In The Works of the British Dramatists.
     Edited by J.S. Keltie. Edinburgh: W.P. Nimmo, pp. 364-82.
          Introduction provides a general discussion of the play.
     Edition presents a modern spelling text with textual and explana-
     tory notes.

1921

1   Antonio's Revenge. In Antonio and Mellida and Antonio's
     Revenge. Edited by W.W. Greg. Malone Society Reprints.
     London: Malone Society, pp. xii, [152].
          Facsimile of Antonio's Revenge 1602.1. Introduction pro-
     vides bibliographical information.

1965

1   Antonio's Revenge. Edited by G.K. Hunter. RRDS. Lincoln:
     University of Nebraska, pp. ix-xxi, 1-86.
          Points out that the events in Antonio's Revenge both paral-
     lel and contrast with those in Antonio and Mellida. Discusses
     Senecan and Calvinist influences upon the play, suggesting that
     they combine to produce the work's thematic texture. Stresses
     that the play is more concerned with the meaning of revenge than
     probing the motives of the revengers psychologically. Holds that
     the play does not present a clear moral stance on vengeance.
     Rather, sees the act of revenge from conflicting perspectives.
     Concludes by suggesting that Marston was probably imitating the
     Ur-Hamlet rather than Shakespeare's masterpiece. Presents mod-
     ernized text along with numerous explanatory notes.

1978

1   Antonio's Revenge. Edited by W. Reavley Gair. RP.
     Baltimore: Johns Hopkins, 174 pp.
     Discusses early editions, outlines Marston's life, com-
ments upon the date of the play and its sources. Relates
Antonio's Revenge to Hamlet and sees both Shakespeare and
Marston drawing upon the Ur-Hamlet. Surveys criticism of the
play and analyzes its characters. Discusses the way the work
was probably performed by the child actors and sees Antonio's
Revenge as quasi operatic as well as employing mime and other
theatrical techniques. Presents a modern spelling edition with
textual and explanatory notes.

The Dutch Courtezan

1605

*1   The Dutch Courtezan. Written by Iohn Marston. London:
     Printed by T.P. for Iohn Hodgets, [57] pp. (Pollard and
     Redgrave 17475)

1930

1   The Dutch Courtezan. In Early Seventeenth Century Plays,
     1600-1642. Edited by Harold R. Walley and John Harold Wilson.
     New York: Harcourt, Brace, 163-220.
     Sketches Marston's career and comments upon the play's
characterizations, its structure, and the language of Cocledemoy.
Sees The Dutch Courtezan as "Marston's most perfect play." The
collection defines difficult Elizabethan words in the play in a
glossary at the text's end. Modern spelling edition.

1965

1   The Dutch Courtezan. Edited by Martin Wine. RRDS. Lincoln:
     University of Nebraska, pp. xii-xxvii, 1-111.
     Discusses The Dutch Courtezan's stage history and Restora-
tion adaptations of the work and contrasts Marston's play with
its source. Stresses that the role of sexuality in human life is
the play's central concern and sees Malheureux's dilemma as this
theme's focal point. Draws parallels between the plights of
Malheureux and Mulligrub. Judges the play a serious commentary
on humanity, but also sees it as a successful melding of farce
and comedy. Also discusses the text. Presents a modernized
edition with numerous explanatory notes. An appendix lists
Marston's borrowings in the play from Montaigne.

1968

1   The Dutch Courtezan. Edited by Peter Davison. FDT.
Berkeley and Los Angeles: University of California, pp. 1-18,
19-88, 89-103.
      Discusses the influence of Montaigne's essays, especially
"Upon Some Verses of Virgil," upon the play's treatment of sexuality. Sees Marston attempting to dramatize various degrees of
erotic attraction, ranging from idealized love to lustful crav-
ings. Holds that some faults weaken the dramatization of these
concepts. Sees Freevill and Beatrice as inadequate representa-
tions of the ideal and stresses that the play's comic tenor dulls
the tragic edge of Malheureux's dilemma. Provides also a textual
discussion. Old spelling edition with textual notes at the
bottoms of pages and explanatory notes in an appendix.

1975

1   The Dutch Courtezan. In Four Jacobean City Comedies. Edited
by Gāmini Salgādo. PEL. Harmondsworth, Middlesex, England:
Penguin Books, pp. 18-21, 32-108, 413-14.
      Sees the play as an inquiry into the nature of man's sexual
needs and suggests that the drama endeavors to make us aware of
the animal and spiritual in human nature. Provides a modern
spelling edition with explanatory notes at the page bottoms and
in an appendix.

1976

1   The Dutch Courtezan. In Drama of the English Renaissance II:
The Stuart Period. Edited by Russell A. Fraser and Norman
Rabkin. New York: Macmillan, pp. 241-68.
      Rabkin's introduction sketches Marston's life, comments
upon his writings, then discusses The Dutch Courtezan's themes,
faults, and successes. A modern spelling edition with textual
and explanatory notes.

Adaptations of The Dutch Courtezan

1673

*1   ANON. The Cheater Cheated. In The Wits, or Sport Upon Sport:
Being a Curious Collection of Several Kinds of Drolls and
Farces. London: (Wing W 3218)
      A droll based upon the Cocledemoy subplot. Cited in The
National Union Catalogue.

1932

*2   ANON. <u>The</u> <u>Cheater</u> <u>Cheated</u>. In <u>The</u> <u>Wits,</u> <u>or</u> <u>Sport</u> <u>Upon</u> <u>Sport</u>.
      Edited by John James Elson, Jr. Ithaca: Cornell University,
      pp. 346-69.
           A modern edition of <u>The</u> <u>Dutch</u> <u>Courtezan</u> 1673.1.

1680

*1   ANON. <u>The</u> <u>Revenge;</u> <u>or</u> <u>A</u> <u>Match</u> <u>in</u> <u>Newgate</u>. London: Printed
      for W. Cademon, [80] pp. (Wing B 2084)
           This adaptation of <u>The</u> <u>Dutch</u> <u>Courtezan</u> is generally
      ascribed to Thomas Betterton. Some, however, attribute it to
      Aphra Behn. Cited in <u>The</u> <u>National</u> <u>Union</u> <u>Catalogue</u>.

1744

*1   ANON. <u>The</u> <u>Revenge;</u> <u>or</u> <u>A</u> <u>Match</u> <u>in</u> <u>Newgate</u>. In <u>A</u> <u>Select</u>
      <u>Collection</u> <u>of</u> <u>Old</u> <u>English</u> <u>Plays</u>. Edited by Robert Dodsley.
      Vol. 12. London, pp. 349-437.
           Cited in <u>The</u> <u>National</u> <u>Union</u> <u>Catalogue</u>.

1715

*1   BULLOCK, CHRISTOPHER. <u>A</u> <u>Woman's</u> <u>Revenge,</u> <u>Or,</u> <u>A</u> <u>Match</u> <u>in</u>
      <u>Newgate</u>. London: Printed for E. Curll and J. Pemberton.
           An adaptation of <u>The</u> <u>Revenge</u>. Cited in <u>The</u> <u>National</u> <u>Union</u>
      <u>Catalogue</u>.

<u>Eastward</u> <u>Hoe</u>

1605

*1   Eastward Hoe. Made by Geo: Chapman, Ben: Ionson, and Iohn
      Marston. London: Printed for William Aspley, [64] pp.
      (Pollard and Redgrave 4971)
           Cited in Tannenbaum, 1940.5. Facsimile: <u>Eastward</u> <u>Hoe</u>
      1914.1. Discussion: 1928.1.

1744

*1   Eastward Hoe. In <u>A</u> <u>Select</u> <u>Collection</u> <u>of</u> <u>Old</u> <u>English</u> <u>Plays</u>.
      Edited by Robert Dodsley. Vol. 4. London, pp. 147-228.
           Cited in <u>The</u> <u>National</u> <u>Union</u> <u>Catalogue</u>.

<u>1756</u>

*1   Eastward <u>Hoe</u>. In <u>Memoirs</u> <u>of</u> <u>the</u> <u>Life</u> <u>and</u> <u>Writings</u> <u>of</u> <u>Ben.</u>
      <u>Jonson</u> . . . <u>To</u> <u>Which</u> <u>Are</u> <u>Added,</u> <u>Two</u> <u>Comedies</u> <u>(Wrote</u> <u>by</u> <u>Ben.</u>
      <u>Jonson</u> <u>&</u> <u>c.</u> <u>And</u> <u>Not</u> <u>Printed</u> <u>in</u> <u>His</u> <u>Works)</u> <u>Called</u> <u>The</u> <u>Widow,</u>
      <u>and Eastward Hoe</u>. Dublin, pp. 65–126.
             Cited in <u>The</u> <u>National</u> <u>Union</u> <u>Catalogue</u>.

<u>1780</u>

*1   Eastward <u>Hoe</u>. In <u>A</u> <u>Select</u> <u>Collection</u> <u>of</u> <u>Old</u> <u>English</u> <u>Plays</u>.
      <u>Edited</u> by Robert Dodsley. 2d ed. Vol. 4. London,
      pp. 199–302.
             Cited in <u>The</u> <u>National</u> <u>Union</u> <u>Catalogue</u>.

<u>1810</u>

1   Eastward <u>Hoe</u>. In <u>The</u> <u>Ancient</u> <u>British</u> <u>Drama</u>. [Edited by
     <u>Sir Walter</u> Scott.] Vol. 2. London: Printed for W. Miller,
     pp. 65–99.
             Prints a modernized version with some textual and explana-
      tory notes.

<u>1826</u>

*1   Eastward <u>Hoe</u>. In <u>A</u> <u>Select</u> <u>Collection</u> <u>of</u> <u>Old</u> <u>English</u> <u>Plays</u>.
      <u>Edited</u> by J. Payne <u>Collier</u> et al. 3d ed. Vol. 4. London:
      S. Prowett, pp. 183–280.
             A Victorian revision of Dodsley's earlier collection.
      Cited in <u>The</u> <u>National</u> <u>Union</u> <u>Catalogue</u>.

<u>1874</u>

1   Eastward <u>Hoe</u>. In <u>The</u> <u>Works</u> <u>of</u> <u>George</u> <u>Chapman</u>. [Edited by
     <u>R.H.</u> Shepherd.] London: J. Pearson, pp. 451–85.
             Presents an old spelling edition.

<u>1903</u>

1   Eastward <u>Hoe</u>. In <u>Eastward</u> <u>Hoe</u> <u>&</u> <u>The</u> <u>Alchemist</u>. Edited by
     Felix Schelling. Belles–lettres Series. Boston: Heath,
     pp. ix–xvi, 1–142, 143–58.
             Discusses the play, the controversy it occasioned, its
      merits and defects. Furnishes a modern spelling edition, with
      textual and explanatory notes in an appendix.

1913

1   Eastward <u>Hoe</u>. Edited by John W. Cunliffe. In <u>Representative</u>
<u>English</u> <u>Com</u>edies. Edited by Charles Mills Gayley. Vol. 2.
New York: Macmillan, pp. 395-502.

      Provides biographical sketches of Marston and Chapman and
discusses the authorship problem, offering suggestions as to the
assignment of scenes. Praises the play, seeing the collaboration
as effective, and commends the range of characters and their
individualism. Also discusses the controversy surrounding the
play and reproduces the letters of Chapman and Jonson concerning
their difficulties. Presents modern spelling edition with textual and explanatory notes.

1914

1   Eastward <u>Hoe</u>. Edited by J.S. Farmer. Tudor Facsimile Texts·.
Edinburgh: Issued for Subscribers by J.S. Farmer, [64] pp.
Reprint. New York: AMS Press, 1970.
     Facsimile of <u>Eastward</u> <u>Hoe</u> 1605.1.

2   _____. In <u>The</u> <u>Plays</u> <u>of</u> <u>George</u> <u>Chapman</u>. Edited by Thomas Marc
Parrott. Vol. 2. New York: Dutton, pp. 461-535, 835-67.
Reprint. New York: Russell & Russell, 1961.

      Provides much data: historical backgrounds, the con-
troversy over the insult to the king, the stage history, and
sources. Sees the play as a protest against the laxity and
confusion of morals in the citizen comedies of Middleton and
Dekker. Studies the authorship question, discussing each scene
individually, and offers reasons for assigning scenes to particular authors. Presents a modern spelling text with textual and
explanatory notes.

1926

*1   Eastward <u>Hoe</u>. Edited by J.H. Harris. New Haven: Yale
University Press, pp. lviii, 192.
     Cited in <u>The</u> <u>National</u> <u>Union</u> <u>Catalogue</u>.

1928

1   Eastward <u>Hoe</u>. In <u>Great</u> <u>English</u> <u>Plays</u>. Edited by Harold F.
Rubenstein. London: Gollancz, pp. 343-88.
     Presents a modern spelling edition.

1929

1 Eastward Hoe. In Shakespeare and His Fellow Dramatists.
   Edited by E.H.C. Oliphant. Vol. 1. New York: Scribner's,
   pp. 1005-50.
      Discusses the authorship and provides a chart, giving
   Oliphant's assignment of scenes. Presents a lukewarm apprecia-
   tion of the play, viewing it as flawed by didacticism and dull
   and inconsistent characterization. Sees it "nearly, but not
   quite, a great comedy." Provides a modern spelling edition with
   textual and explanatory notes. For a restatement of these views,
   see Eastward Hoe 1931.1.

1930

1 Eastward Hoe. In Early Seventeenth-Century Plays, 1600-1642.
   Edited by Harold R. Walley and John Harold Wilson. New York:
   Harcourt, Brace, pp. 221-91.
      Discusses Eastward Hoe's early and Restoration stage his-
   tory and comments upon the division of authorship. Praises the
   work for its portrayal of London life and the variety and realism
   of its satirical portraits. Views Touchstone as representing the
   idealization of middle-class attitudes and values. Presents a
   modern spelling text with textual and explanatory notes.

1931

1 Eastward Hoe. In Elizabethan Dramatists Other Than
   Shakespeare. Edited by E.H.C. Oliphant. New York:
   Prentice-Hall, pp. 543-90.
      Expresses the same views of the play as in Eastward Hoe
   1929.1. Also uses the same text.

1932

1 Eastward Hoe. In Ben Jonson. Edited by C.H. Herford and
   Percy Simpson. Vol. 4. Oxford: Clarendon Press, pp, 487-619.
      Provides old spelling text with textual notes. Introduc-
   tion is found on pp. 31-46 of vol. 2 of this set. Discusses the
   play's characters, then turns to the authorship problem, suggesting that textual studies can do little to elucidate the enigma,
   but speculates that Marston outlined the plot and that Jonson's
   contribution was marginal.

1933

1 Eastward Hoe. In English Drama, 1580-1642. Edited by C.F.
   Tucker Brooke and Nathaniel Burton Paradise. Boston: Heath,
   pp. 397-434.

Provides bibliographical data on early editions, discusses the date and the controversy surrounding the original perform- ances, sheds light on sources, and tackles the authorship problem, suggesting that the widespread use of prose makes determining the shares of the authorship difficult. Modern spelling.

2 _____. In Elizabethan Plays. Edited by Hazelton Spencer. Boston: Heath, pp. 473-516.
    Discusses the dating, sources, backgrounds, and controversy surrounding original performances. Modern spelling.

1968

1 Eastward Hoe. In The City and the Court: Five Seventeenth Century Comedies of London Life. Edited by Robin Chapman and Allan Grant. San Francisco: Chandler, pp. 1-82.
    Comments upon the authors' careers and touches upon contro- versy produced by the play. Presents a modern spelling edition with explanatory notes.

1973

1 Eastward Hoe. Edited by C.G. Petter. NMS. London: Benn, pp. xiii-xlvii.
    Discusses the authorship and assigns most of the first and third acts and portions of the rest of the play to Marston. Gives attention to the dating of the play. Discusses the satir- ical treatment of the characters and their follies. Gives con- siderable attention to alchemical symbolism permeating the play. Holds that the drama's satirical blade cuts two ways: the tar- gets of satire are not only pretenders and wastrels like Sir Petronel Flash and Quicksilver, but also the "virtuous" charac- ters such as Touchstone and Golding. Also takes up the play's stage history and the work's text. Appendices provide a map of the Jacobean Thames, the text of a ballad mocking King James's creation of knights, and the texts of the letters written by Jonson and Chapman during their imprisonment. Presents a modern spelling edition with textual and explanatory notes.

Adaptations of Eastward Hoe

1685

*1 TATE, NAHUM. Cuckolds-Haven; Or, An Alderman no Conjurer. London: Printed for J.H. (Wing T 180)
    Cited in The National Union Catalogue. A combined adapta- tion of Eastward Hoe and Jonson's The Devil Is an Ass.

<u>1775</u>

*1   LENNOX, Mrs. C. <u>Old City Manners</u>. <u>A Comedy</u>. London:
     T. Becket, pp. iv, 66.
        Cited in <u>The National Union Catalogue</u>.

<u>The History of Antonio and Mellida</u>

<u>1602</u>

*1   <u>The History of Antonio and Mellida</u>. <u>The First Part</u>. Written
     by I.M. London: Printed for Matthewe Lownes and Thomas
     Fisher, [72] pp. (Pollard and Redgrave 17473)
        Cited in Tannenbaum, 1940.5. Facsimile reprint: <u>Antonio
     and Mellida</u> 1921.1.

<u>1814</u>

*1   <u>The History of Antonio and Mellida</u>. In <u>Old English Plays</u>.
     [Edited by C.W. Dilke.] Vol. 2. London: Rodwell & Martin,
     pp. 99-193.
        Cited in Tannenbaum, 1940.5.

<u>1872</u>

1   <u>The History of Antonio and Mellida</u>. In <u>The Works of the
     British Dramatists</u>. Edited by J.S. Keltie. Edinburgh:
     W.P. Nimmo, pp. 347-64.
        Provides a general discussion of the play and presents a
     modern spelling text with textual and explanatory notes.

<u>1921</u>

1   <u>The History of Antonio and Mellida</u>. In <u>Antonio and Mellida
     and Antonio's Revenge</u>. Edited by by W.W. Greg. Malone
     Society Reprints. London: Malone Society, pp. xii, [152].
        Facsimile of <u>Antonio and Mellida</u> 1602.1. Introduction
     provides bibliographical information.

<u>1963</u>

1   <u>The History of Antonio and Mellida</u>. "A Critical Acting Edi-
     tion of <u>Antonio and Mellida</u>." Edited by Conrad Stolzenbach.
     Ph.D. diss., University of Michigan.
        Consists of three parts: (1) a discussion of the play's
     historical background, (2) an analysis of the play, and (3) the

acting version of the play itself. Presents the play in modern spelling with textual notes at the end.

1965

1 The History of Antonio and Mellida. Edited by G.K. Hunter. RRDS. London: Edward Arnold, pp. ix–xxi, 1–80.
   Discusses the play as a prime example of Marston's artistic techniques, suggesting that Marston wrote the play to parody the tragical style. Sees Marston making use of the boy actors to mock and satirize the adults whom they portray. Sees the play's love story as secondary to the satirization of such characters as court beauties, fops, would-be gentlemen, and tyrants and their viewpoints. Suggests that the center of the play's thematic concerns and of Marston's view of life is the conviction that none of the views of the characters (and indeed no points of view) can remain consistent or meaningful amid the complexities and fluxing turbulence of life. Relates Marston's techniques and outlook to those of the theater of the absurd. Presents a modern spelling edition with textual and explanatory notes.

1976

1 The History of Antonio and Mellida. "An Edition of John Marston's Antonio and Mellida." Edited by Katherine Louise Schoonover. Ph.D. diss., University of Toronto.
   Presents basically modern spelling. Includes numerous notes and annotations.

Histriomastix

1610

*1 Histrio-Mastix, Or, The Player Whipt. [Anonymous]. London: For Thomas Thorp, [58] pp. (Pollard and Redgrave 13529)
   Cited in Tannenbaum, 1940.5. Facsimile reprint: Histriomastix 1912.1.

1878

1 Histrio-Mastix, Or, The Player Whipt. In The School of Shakespeare. Edited by Richard Simpson. Vol. 2. London: Chatto & Windus, pp. 1–89. Reprint. New York: AMS Press, 1973.
   Suggests that Marston partly authored this play by revising an older text. Relates the play to the stage war with Jonson. Presents an old spelling edition with textual and explanatory notes.

1912

1   Histrio-Mastix, Or, The Player Whipt. Edited by J.S. Farmer.
     Tudor Facsimile Texts. Edinburgh: Printed for Subscribers by
     J.S. Farmer, pp. vi, 1-58. Reprint. New York: AMS Press,
     1970.
         Facsimile of Histriomastix 1610.1.

The Insatiate Countess

1613

*1   The Insatiate Countess. A Tragedy. Written by Iohn Marston.
     London: Printed by T.S. for Thomas Archer, [74] pp. (Pollard
     and Redgrave 17476)
         Some copies of this edition reveal that the ascription of
     the play to Marston was cut from the title page. In one instance
     the omission was replaced with blank paper. Brettle (1927.2)
     conjectures that after copies of the play became available to the
     public, Marston pressured the publisher to omit the ascription
     from the remaining books, either because Marston had little or
     nothing to do with the play or because Marston, having taken holy
     orders, did not wish his name associated with the work. The
     seventeenth-century ascription of the play to William Barksted
     (The Insatiate Countess 1631.2) has led some scholars to con-
     clude that Marston plotted and began the play, but abandoned it
     when be became a minister. Barksted, according to this view,
     finished the drama.

1616

*1   The Insatiate Countess. [Anonymous.] London: Printed by
     N.O. for Thomas Archer, [72] pp. (Pollard and Redgrave 17477)
         Cited in Tannenbaum, 1940.5. A second edition of The
     Insatiate Countess 1613.1. Authorial ascription omitted.
     Discussion: 1927.2; 1958.19.

1631

*1   The Insatiate Countess. Written by Iohn Marston. London:
     Printed by I.N. for Hugh Perrie, [74] pp. (Pollard and
     Redgrave 17478)
         Cited in Tannenbaum, 1940.5. Prints Marston's name as that
     of the author. Discussion: 1927.2.

*2   _____ . Written by William Barksted. London: Printed for
     Hugh Perrie, [74] pp. (Pollard and Redgrave 17478a)
         Cited in Tannenbaum, 1940.5. Barksted's name substituted
     for Marston's. Discussion: 1927.2.

1820

*1   The Insatiate Countess. London: Printed by F. Marshall,
      pp. xi–xiii, 1–89.
          Cited in Tannenbaum, 1940.5. Bound with a copy of Nicholas
      Udall's Ralph Royster Doyster and with The Princely Pleasures at
      Kenilworth.

Jack Drum's Entertainment

1601

*1   Iacke Drums Entertainement, or The Comedie of Pasquil and
      Katherine. [Anonymous.] London: Printed for Richard Olive,
      [68] pp. (Pollard and Redgrave 7243). Reprint. New York:
      AMS Press, 1970.
          Cited in Tannenbaum, 1940.5.

1616

*1   Iacke Drums Entertainement, or The Comedie of Pasquil and
      Katherine. Anonymous. London: Printed by W. Stansby for
      Philip Knight. (Pollard and Redgrave 7244)
          Cited in Tannenbaum, 1940.5.

1878

1   Iacke Drums Entertainment, or The Comedie of Pasquil and
      Katherine. In The School of Shakspere. Edited by Richard
      Simpson. Vol. 2. London: Chatto & Windus, pp. 125–208.
      Reprint. New York: AMS Press, 1973.
          Identifies Marston as the author and relates the play to
      the stage war with Jonson. Sees Brabant Senior as only partially
      representing Jonson. Points out contemporary allusions. Pre-
      sents an old spelling edition with textual and explanatory notes.

The Malcontent

1604

*1   The Malcontent. by Iohn Marston. London: Printed by V.S.
      for William Aspley, [62] pp. (Pollard and Redgrave 17479)
          Cited in Tannenbaum, 1940.5. Discussion: 1921.2; 1927.2.

*2   _____. By Iohn Marston. London: Printed by V.S. for William
      Aspley, [74] pp. (Pollard and Redgrave 17480)

Cited in Tannenbaum, 1940.5. The second edition.
Discussion: 1921.2; 1927.2.

*3 _____. Augmented by Marston With the Additions Played by the
   Kings Majesties Servants. Written Iohn Webster. London:
   Printed by V.S. for William Aspley, [72] pp. (Pollard and
   Redgrave 17481)
       Cited in Tannenbaum, 1940.5. The third edition, containing
   Webster's induction and additions to the text by Marston (and
   possibly by Webster). Discussion: 1921.2; 1927.2.

1744

*1 The Malcontent. In A Select Collection of Old English Plays.
   Edited by Robert Dodsley. Vol. 4. London, pp. 1-81.
       Cited in Tannenbaum, 1940.5.

1780

*1 The Malcontent. In A Select Collection of Old English Plays.
   Edited by Robert Dodsley. Vol. 4. London.
       Cited in Tannenbaum, 1940.5.

1810

1 The Malcontent. In The Ancient British Drama. [Edited by
   Sir Walter Scott.] Vol. 2. London: Printed with W. Miller,
   pp. 1-36.
       Prints a modernized version with some textual and explana-
   tory notes.

1826

*1 The Malcontent. In A Select Collection of Old English Plays.
   Edited by J. Payne Collier et al. 3d ed. Vol. 4. London:
   S. Prowett, pp. 1-98.
       A Victorian revision of Dodsley's earlier collections.
   Cited in Tannenbaum, 1940.5.

1859

1 The Malcontent. In The Works of John Webster. Edited by
   Alexander Dyce. London: G. Routledge, pp. 322-62.
       Presents a modernized text with textual and explanatory
   notes.

16

1911

1   The Malcontent. In The Chief Elizabethan Dramatists,
    Excluding Shakespeare. Edited by William Allen Neilson.
    Boston: Houghton Mifflin, pp. 456-84.
        Presents a modernized text with textual and explanatory
    notes.

1933

1   The Malcontent. In English Drama, 1580-1642. Edited by C.F.
    Tucker Brooke and Nathaniel Burton Paradise. Boston: Heath,
    pp. 361-96.
        Provides bibliographical information on early editions,
    discusses the dating of the play, and makes brief comments upon
    its structure. Presents a modernized text with textual and
    explanatory notes.

2   _____. Edited by G.B. Harrison. Temple Dramatists. London:
    Dent, pp. xii, 1-130.
        Presents a general discussion of the play and a modernized
    edition with textual and explanatory notes. Review: 1934.2.

3   _____. In Elizabethan Plays. Edited by Hazelton Spencer.
    Boston: Heath, pp. 559-97.
        Presents a general discussion of the play and praises it as
    Marston's masterpiece. Presents a modernized edition with textual
    and explanatory notes.

1934

1   The Malcontent. In Elizabethan and Stuart Plays. Edited by
    Charles Reed Baskervill et al. New York: Henry Holt,
    pp. 679-721.
        Provides a general discussion of The Malcontent and data on
    the text. Presents a modernized text with textual and explana-
    tory notes. For a revision of the first part of this anthology,
    containing The Malcontent, with new information on Marston, see
    The Malcontent 1971.1.

1948

*1 The Malcontent. Il Malcontento. Translated by Giorgio
    Melchiori. In Teatro elisabettiano. Florence, pp. 521-616.
        Cited in Annual Bibliography of English Language and
    Literature, 1948.

1963

1   The Malcontent. In An Anthology of Jacobean Drama. Edited by
    Richard C. Harrier. Vol. 1. New York: New York University,
    pp. ix-x, 115-209, 474-80.
       Presents basic data about Marston and an old spelling text
with explanatory notes. Includes list of variant readings.

1964

1   The Malcontent. Edited by M.L. Wine. RRDS. Lincoln:
    University of Nebraska, pp. xi-xxv, 1-117.
       Discusses the text and dating of the play. Stresses the
play's value as entertainment. Sees Marston's center of interest
in depicting a world of fools and knaves, a portrayal that looks
forward to the theater of the absurd. Judges Malevole to be a
superb dramatic creation. Suggests that the play provides no
assurance that mankind can overcome its foolishness. Presents a
modern spelling edition with textual and explanatory notes.

1967

1   The Malcontent. Edited by Bernard Harris. NMS. London:
    Benn, pp. xi-xxxiii, 1-105.
       Provides a biographical sketch of Marston and discusses the
dating and early performances of the play. Then presents a
detailed discussion of The Malcontent, surveying much criticism
and concentrating upon such topics as the themes of deception and
usurpation, satirical elements, the tragicomic structure, and the
problems of denouement. Presents a modern spelling text with
textual and explanatory notes.

1969

1   The Malcontent. In Jacobean Tragedies. Edited by A.H. Gomme.
    Oxford: Oxford University, pp. viii-xvi, 1-75.
       Provides basic data on the play and views it as a moral
fable. Presents modern spelling edition with textual and explanatory notes.

1970

1   The Malcontent. Menston, England: Scolar Press, [72] pp.
    Facsimile of The Malcontent 1604.3.

1971

1   The Malcontent. In Elizabethan Plays. Edited by Arthur H.
     Nethercot et al. New York: Holt, Rinehart, & Winston,
     pp. 751-99.
       A revision of the first part of the anthology containing
    The Malcontent 1934.1. Offers a detailed discussion of Marston's
family background, his entry into the theatrical world, his
career as a satirist and dramatist, and his life as a clergyman.
Then turns to The Malcontent, commenting upon its nature, style,
and many of its characters. Concludes by summing up opposing
views of Marston's value as a dramatist. Includes quotations
from original documents in the discussion of Marston's life.
Also cites much criticism while discussing The Malcontent and
Marston's reputation. Presents a modern spelling edition with
textual and explanatory notes.

1975

1   The Malcontent. Edited by G.K. Hunter. RP. London:
     Methuen, pp. xix-lxxxiv, 1-171.
       Provides a commentary on Marston's life, discusses in
detail the early quartos, textual problems, and the later editions of the play. Then analyzes the play itself. Comments upon
its relationship to other plays of its period and their influences upon it. Considers The Malcontent's satiric nature and its
genre classification as tragicomedy. Places weight upon the
protagonist's dual nature as Altofronto and Malevole. Sees the
play's thematic framework based upon the opposition of Stoic-
Christian-ascetic and Epicurean-Machiavellian viewpoints.
Stresses that The Malcontent presents a view of a corrupt world,
which neither royal nor political action can improve, but a
world, nevertheless, watched over by an inscrutable providence.
Sees much of the play's success residing in Marston's style and
the balance the play achieves in controlling conflicting tendencies in Marston's aesthetic techniques. Concludes with a discussion of the play's stage history. Presents a modern spelling
edition with numerous textual and explanatory notes.

Separate Editions of the Induction to The Malcontent

1857

1   "Induction to The Malcontent." In The Dramatic Works of John
     Webster. Edited by W.C. Hazlitt. Vol. 4. London: J.R.
     Smith, pp. 103-12.
       Presents a modern spelling edition.

1927

1   "Induction to The Malcontent." In The Complete Works of John
     Webster. Edited by F.L. Lucas. Vol. 3. London: Chatto &
     Windus, pp. 293-310.
         Provides an old spelling edition with textual and explana-
     tory notes.

Parasitaster, or The Fawne

1606

*1   Parasitaster, or The Fawne. [Anonymous.] London: Printed by
     T.P. for W.C., [72] pp. (Pollard and Redgrave 17483)
         Cited in Tannenbaum, 1940.5. Discussion: 1927.2.

*2   _____. London: Printed by T.P. for W.C., [62] pp. (Pollard
     and Redgrave 17484)
         Cited in Tannenbaum, 1940.5. Contains textual corrections
     by Marston. Discussion: 1927.2.

1814

*1   Parasitaster, or The Fawne. In Old English Plays. Edited by
     by C.W. Dilke. Vol. 2. London: Rodwell and Martin,
     pp. 291-406.
         Cited in Tannenbaum, 1940.5.

1965

1   Parasitaster, or The Fawne. "John Marston's Parasitaster, or
     The Fawne: A Critical Edition." Edited by Philip Whitney
     London. Ph.D. diss., University of Michigan.
         Suggests that the play should be studied as comedy rather
     than satire. Presents old spelling edition with textual and
     explanatory notes.

2   _____. Edited by Gerald A. Smith. RRDS. Lincoln:
     University of Nebraska, pp. xi-xx, 1-115.
         Sees the play as essentially satire and observes that
     instead of railing, Marston creates his satire by having the Fawn
     pretend to endorse the follies that he wishes to expose. Ana-
     lyzes the satire directed at various characters, then concludes
     that the play, though not great, is a delightful, effective
     satire of the world of the court. Presents a modern spelling
     edition with textual and explanatory notes.

1968

*1   Parasitaster, or The Fawne. "The Comedy of John Marston, with
     a Critical Edition of The Fawn." Edited by D.A. Blostein.
     Ph.D. diss., University of Toronto.
        Cited in Lawrence McNamee, Dissertations in English and
     American Literature, Supplement 1, 1964-1968. Published edition:
     The Fawn 1978.1.

1978

1   Parasitaster, or The Fawne. Edited by David A. Blostein. RP.
     Baltimore: Johns Hopkins, 244 pp.
        Stresses that a hard satirical spirit does not permeate the
     play. Instead, a tolerant comic spirit does. Sees this as an
     evolution in Marston's thought from the strict moralism of the
     satires. Judges the play in part an attack upon the Stoical
     suppression of the passions, indicating Marston's increased sym-
     pathy for the body's weaknesses. Stresses that the play deals
     with Marston's major concerns such as sex, courtship, and lan-
     guage. Analyzes the characters' relationship to the thematic
     design. Sees Hercules as a curative agent, employing flattery as
     his means of correction. Judges the play "a minor gem, but a
     gem, in which the facets sparkle within a single comic design."
     Discusses the dating of the play, probable sources, and early
     quartos. Presents modern spelling edition with textual and ex-
     planatory notes.

What You Will

1607

*1   What You Will. Written by Iohn Marston. London: By G. Eld
     for Thomas Thorpe, [62] pp. (Pollard and Redgrave 17487)
        Cited in Tannenbaum, 1940.5.

1814

*1   What You Will. In Old English Plays. [Edited by C.W. Dilke.]
     Vol. 2. London: Rodwell & Martin, pp. 195-290.
        Cited in Tannenbaum, 1940.5.

1898

*1   What You Will. In English Plays. Edited by Henry Morley.
     London: Cassell, Petter, Galpin, pp. 197-211.
        Cited in Tannenbaum, 1940.5.

The Wonder of Women or The Tragedie of Sophonisba

1606

*1   The Wonder of Women or The Tragedie of Sophonisba.   Written by
     John Marston.   London: Printed by Iohn Windet, [54] pp.
     (Pollard and Redgrave 17488)
         Cited in Tannenbaum, 1940.5.

1971

1   The Wonder of Women or The Tragedie of Sophonisba.   "A
    Critical Edition of John Marston's The Wonder of Women or The
    Tragedie of Sophonisba."   Edited by William Kemp.   Ph.D.
    diss., University of South Carolina.
        Presents old spelling text with textual and explanatory
    notes.   Printed edition: Sophonisba 1979.1.

1979

1   The Wonder of Women or The Tragedie of Sophonisba.   Edited by
    William Kemp.   Renaissance Drama, A Collection of Critical
    Editions.   New York: Garland, 191 pp.
        Considers sources and verbal borrowings.   Judges that the
    play does not indicate Marston's reawakened faith in Stoicism.
    For Sophonisba is exceptional: her fortitude and courage are
    beyond the grasp of most humanity.   Gives considerable attention
    to such techniques as rhetoric, contrasting scenes, and staging.
    Presents an old spelling edition with textual notes.

EDITIONS OF MARSTON'S POETRY

The Metamorphosis of Pigmalion's Image and Certain Satires

1598

*1   The Metamorphosis of Pigmalions Image.   And Certain Satires.
     London: Printed for Edmond Matts, [82] pp.   (Pollard and
     Redgrave 17482)
         Cited in Tannenbaum, 1940.5.

1613

*1   The Metamorphosis of Pigmalions Image. And Certain Satires.
London: n.p.
      Cited in Tannenbaum, 1940.5. Not cited in Pollard and
Redgrave.

1619

*1   The Metamorphosis of Pigmalions Image. And Certain Satires.
London.
      Cited in Tannenbaum, 1940.5. Not cited in Pollard and
Redgrave.

1628

*1   The Metamorphosis of Pigmalions Image. And Certain Satires.
London: Printed for Richard Hawkins.
     Cited in Tannenbaum, 1940.5. Not cited in Pollard and
Redgrave.

1764

*1   The Metamorphosis of Pigmalions Image. And Certain Satires.
In Miscellaneous Pieces of Antient English Poesie. Edited by
John Bowles. London: Printed for Robert Horsefield.
      Cited in Tannenbaum, 1940.5.

Individual Editions of The Metamorphosis of Pigmalion's Image

1926

*1   The Metamorphosis of Pigmalion's Image. Waltham, St.
Lawrence, Berkshire: Golden Cockerel Press, 17 pp.
      Includes engravings by Rene Ben Sussan. Edition limited to
325 copies.

1968

1   The Metamorphosis of Pigmalion's Image. In Elizabethan Verse
Romances. Edited by M.M. Reese. London: Routledge & Kegan
Paul, pp. 22-23, 188-97, 268-71.
      Presents a general discussion and sees some merit in the
work. Provides modern spelling edition with textual and explanatory notes.

Poems from <u>Love's</u> <u>Martyr</u>

1601

*1   Love's <u>Martyr</u>: or <u>Rosalins</u> <u>Complaint</u>. London: Imprinted for
      E.B.   (Pollard and Redgrave 5119).
           Cited in Tannenbaum, 1940.5.

1878

*1   Love's <u>Martyr</u>: or <u>Rosalins</u> <u>Complaint</u>. In <u>Robert</u> <u>Chester's</u>
      <u>Loves</u> <u>Martyr</u>, <u>or</u> <u>Rosalins</u> <u>Complaint</u>. Edited by A.B. Grosart.
      London: Published for the New Shakspere Society by N.
      Trübner, pp. 177-80.
           Cited in Tannenbaum, 1940.5.

1937

*1   Love's <u>Martyr</u>: or <u>Rosalins</u> <u>Complaint</u>. In <u>The</u> <u>Phoenix</u> <u>and</u> <u>the</u>
      <u>Turtle</u>:   <u>By</u> <u>William</u> Shakespeare, <u>John</u> <u>Marston</u>, <u>George</u> <u>Chapman</u>,
      <u>Ben</u> <u>Jonson</u> <u>and</u> Others. Edited by Bernard H. Newdigate.
      Oxford: B. Blackwell, pp. 10-14.
           Cited in Tannenbaum, 1940.5.

<u>The</u> <u>Scourge</u> <u>of</u> <u>Villainy</u>

1598

*1   <u>The</u> <u>Scourge</u> <u>of</u> <u>Villainie</u>; <u>Three</u> <u>Books</u> <u>of</u> <u>Satyres</u>. London:
      Printed by I.R. and Sold by I. Buzbie, [124] pp. (Pollard and
      Redgrave 17485)
           Cited in Tannenbaum, 1940.5.

1599

*1   <u>The</u> <u>Scourge</u> <u>of</u> <u>Villainy</u>. <u>Corrected</u>, <u>With</u> <u>the</u> <u>Addition</u> <u>of</u> <u>New</u>
      <u>Satyres</u>. London: Printed by I.R., [122] pp. (Pollard and
      Redgrave 17486)
           Cited in Tannenbaum, 1940.5. Despite the title page
      announcement, includes only one new satire, "Satyra Nova,"
      placed between the ninth and tenth satires.

*2   _____. <u>Corrected</u> <u>With</u> <u>the</u> <u>Addition</u> <u>of</u> <u>New</u> <u>Satires</u>. London:
      Printed by I.R. (Pollard and Redgrave 17486.5)
           Cited in Tannenbaum, 1940.5. Third edition. Type com-
      pletely reset from the second edition.

1764

*1   The Scourge of Villainy. In Miscellaneous Pieces of Antient
      English Poesie. Edited by John Bowles. London: Printed for
      Robert Horsefield, pp. 163–234.

1925

1   The Scourge of Villainy. Edited by G.B. Harrison. Bodley
     Head Quartos. London: John Lane, pp. v–xiii, 1–122.
     Reprint. New York: Barnes & Noble, 1966.
         Facsimile of The Scourge of Villainy 1599.2. On pp. 124–26
     is a note relating Jaques of Shakespeare's As You Like It to
     Marston's satirical vision.

Lust's Dominion

1657

*1   Lusts Dominion; Or, The Lascivious Queen, A Tragedie. By
      Christopher Marlowe. London: Printed for F.K. and are to be
      sold by Robert Pollard, [150] pp. (Wing L3504a)
          Cited in The National Union Catalogue. Copies of this
      edition appeared in 1658, with a new title page pasted over the
      original. This alteration provided new and false bibliographical
      data: "Printed by J.J. and are to be sold by R.P. and William
      Wright [sic] . . ." Brereton (Lust's Dominion 1931.1) observes
      that R.P. and Wright were not adverse to indulging in a little
      chicanery to enhance their popularity. Gustave Cross (1958.6)
      suggests that Marston, along with Dekker, Day, and Haughton, had
      a hand in this play. J.L. Simmons (1972.21) supports this view.

1661

*1   Lusts Dominion; Or, The Lascivious Queen, A Tragedie. London:
      Printed for Fr. Kirkman, [150] pp. (Wing L3504b)
          Cited in The National Union Catalogue. Apparently a reis-
      sue of the remaining stock of Lust's Dominion 1657.1, with a new
      title page.

1814

*1   Lusts Dominion; Or, The Lascivious Queen, A Tragedie. [Edited
      by C.W. Dilke.] Vol. 1. London: Rodwell & Martin, pp. 89–
      195.
          Cited in The National Union Catalogue.

1818

*1   Lusts Dominion; Or, The Lascivious Queen, A Tragedie. Edited
      by William Oxberry. London: Published for the Proprietors;
      sold by W. and J. Lowdes, pp. iv, 83.
      Cited in The National Union Catalogue.

1826

*1   Lusts Dominion; Or, The Lascivious Queen, A Tragedie. In The
      Works of Christopher Marlowe. Edited by George Robinson.
      Vol. 3. London: W. Pickering, pp. 203-315.

1876

1   Lusts Dominion; Or, The Lascivious Queen, A Tragedie. In A
      Select Collection of Old English Plays. Edited by W.C.
      Hazlitt. 4th ed. Vol. 14. London: Reeves & Turner, pp. 93-
      192. Reprint. New York: Benjamin Blom, 1964.
          Summarizes earlier critical opinions of the play, but holds
      that the monstrosity of the characters falsifies human nature.
      Provides modern spelling edition.

1931

1   Lusts Dominion; Or, The Lascivious Queen, A Tragedie. Edited
      by J. Le Gay Brereton. Materials for the Study of the Old
      English Drama, ser. 2, vol. 5. Louvain: Uystpruyst, pp. xi-
      xlii, 1-146, 147-261. Reprint. Vaduz: Kraus Reprint, 1965.
          Presents a detailed consideration of the authorship problem
      and judges the play mainly Dekker's, with contributions by Day
      and Haughton. Provides old spelling edition with extensive
      textual notes.

1961

1   Lusts Dominion; Or, The Lascivious Queen, A Tragedie. In The
      Dramatic Works of Thomas Dekker. Edited by Fredson Bowers.
      Vol. 4. Cambridge: University Press, pp. 115-230.
          Contains a bibliographical introduction and textual notes.
      Presents old spelling edition.

Adaptations of Lust's Dominion

1677

*1   BEHN, APHRA. Abdelazer; or, The Moors Revenge, a Tragedy.
     London: Printed for J. Magnes & R. Bentley. (Wing B 1715)
     Cited in The National Union Catalogue.

1915

1   BEHN, APHRA. Abdelazer; or, The Moor's Revenge, a Tragedy.
     In The Works of Aphra Behn. Edited by Montague Summers.
     Vol. 2. London: W. Heineman, pp. 1-98, 415-16. Reprint.
     New York: Benjamin Blom, 1967.
          Provides a plot summary, discusses sources, and sketches
     the theatrical history. Presents an old spelling text with
     textual notes.

Satiromastix, Or the Untrussing of the Humorous Poet.

1602

*1   Satiro-mastix, Or the Untrussing of the Humorous Poet.
     London: Printed for Edward White, [93] pp. (Pollard and
     Redgrave 6521)
          Generally this play is ascribed wholly to Dekker, but some
     scholars suggest that Marston had a hand in the planning, the
     composition, or both.

1773

*1   Satiro-mastix, Or the Untrussing of the Humorous Poet. In The
     Origin of the English Drama. Vol. 3. Oxford: Printed at the
     Clarendon Press for S. Leacroft, pp. 87-197.
     Cited in The National Union Catalogue.

1873

1   Satiro-mastix, Or the Untrussing of the Humorous Poet. In The
     Dramatic Works of Thomas Dekker. [Edited by R.H. Shepherd.]
     Vol. 1. London: J. Pearson, pp. 177-266, 332-36.
          Discusses the play's function in the stage war. Provides
     an old spelling edition with textual notes.

1907

1 Satiro-mastix, Or the Untrussing of the Humorous Poet. Edited
   by Hans Scherer. Materials for the Study of the Old English
   Drama, ser. 1, vol. 20. Louvain: Uystpruyst, pp. vi-xvi, 1-
   76, 77-136. Reprint. Vaduz: Kraus Reprint, 1963.
       Discusses the War of the Theaters, stressing identifica-
   tions of characters, considers sources, and treats the play's
   printing history. Provides old spelling text with textual and
   explanatory notes. Supplemental notes: 1909.10.

1913

1 Satiro-mastix, Or the Untrussing of the Humorous Poet. In
   Jonson's Poetaster and Dekker's Satiromastix. Edited by
   Josiah H. Penniman. Belles-Lettres Series. Boston: Heath,
   pp. xiii-lxx, 264-395, 397-446.
       Discusses the function of the play in the stage war. Pre-
   sents an old spelling text with textual and explanatory notes.

1961

1 Satiro-mastix, Or the Untrussing of the Humorous Poet. In The
   Dramatic Works of Thomas Dekker. Edited by Fredson Bowers.
   Vol. 1. Cambridge: University Press, pp. 299-385.
       Discusses the early edition of the play. Provides old
   spelling edition with textual notes.

Writings about Marston, 1598-1981

1598

1   GUILPIN, EVERARD. <u>Skialetheia, Or a Shadow of Truth in Cer-</u><u>tain Epigrams</u> <u>and</u> <u>Satyres</u>. London: Printed by I.R. for
Nicholas Ling, 56 pp. (Pollard and Redgrave 12504)
     Contains poems supporting Marston in the quarrel with Hall.
Facsimile edition: 1931.5. Other editions: 1878.2; 1974.4.

2   MERES, FRANCIS. <u>Palladis</u> <u>Tamia</u>: <u>Wits</u> <u>Treasury</u> <u>Being</u> <u>the</u>
<u>Second</u> <u>Part</u> <u>of</u> <u>Wits</u> <u>Common</u> <u>Wealth</u>. London: Printed by P.
Short for Cuthbert Burbie, FF 277^v and 283^v. (Pollard and
Redgrave 17834)
     Suggests that Marston is one of England's leading sati-
rists. Facsimile edition: 1938.8. Selection relating to
Marston: 1904.8.

1599

*1   WEEVER, JOHN. <u>Epigrammes</u> <u>in the</u> <u>Oldest</u> <u>Cut</u> <u>and</u> <u>Newest</u>
<u>Fashion</u>. London: n.p. (Pollard and Redgrave 25224)
     Contains the epigram "Ad Io. Marston & Ben Jonson." Modern
edition: 1911.9.

1600

*1   JONSON, BEN. <u>The</u> <u>Comicall</u> <u>Satyre</u> <u>of</u> <u>Every</u> <u>Man</u> <u>out</u> <u>of</u> <u>his</u>
<u>Humor</u>. London: Printed for William Holme, 133 pp. (Pollard
and Redgrave 14767)
     Satirizes Marston as Carlo Buffone and possibly as Clove.
Other editions: 1616.2: 1905.5; 1910.5; 1963.12; 1964.16.

*2   WEEVER, JOHN. <u>Faunus</u> <u>and</u> <u>Melliflora</u>. London: Printed by
Valentine Simmes. (Pollard and Redgrave 25225)
     Contains a criticism of the Elizabethan vogue of writing
satire and claims that Hall is a superior writer to Marston.
Reprinted: 1948.9.

1601

1   [BRETON, NICHOLAS.] <u>No Whippinge, Nor Trippinge: But a Kinde Friendly Snippinge</u>. London: For John Browne & John Deane, 64 pp. (Pollard and Redgrave 3672)
Replies to 1601.3, but agrees that too much energy is being devoted to the writing of satires and urges writers to turn their attention to religious subjects. Reprinted: 1951.3.

*2   [GUILPIN, EVERARD.] <u>The Whipper of the Satyre His Penance in a White Sheet; Or the Beadles Confutation</u>. London: Printed for Thomas Pauier. (Pollard and Redgrave 25351)
Replies to 1601.1 and defends the writings of satire. Reprinted: 1951.6.

*3   I[NGRAM], W[ILLIAM]. <u>The Whipping of the Satyre</u>. London: For John Flasket. (Pollard and Redgrave 25352)
Attacks Marston, Breton, and other satirical writers and charges that the writing of satire subverts the well being of society. Reprinted: 1951.8.

*4   JONSON, BEN. <u>The Fountayne of Selfe-Love, or Cynthias Revels</u>. London: Imprinted for Walter Burre. (Pollard and Redgrave 14773)
Possibly satirizes Marston as the character Hedon. Other editions or reprinted: 1616.1; 1905.4; 1910.4.

*5   _____. <u>The Poetaster; or the Arraignment</u>. London: Printed for M.L. (Pollard and Redgrave 14781)
Marston satirized as the poetaster Crispinus. Other editions or reprinted: 1616.3; 1905.6-7; 1910.6; 1913.5; 1934.5.

1606

*1   ANON. <u>The Return from Parnassus: or the Scourge of Simony. Publiquely Acted by the Students in Saint Iohns Colledge in Cambridge</u>. London: Printed by G. Eld for John Wright. (Pollard and Redgrave 19309)
Contains contemporary references to Marston and possibly satirizes him as the character Furor Poeticus. Other editions or reprinted: 1874.1; 1879.1; 1886.1; 1904.1 (selection); 1905.1; 1907.1; 1949.1.

*2   NIXON, ANTONY. <u>The Black Year</u>. London: E. Alde for W. Timme. (Pollard and Redgrave 18582)
Presents an early reference to <u>The Dutch Courtezan</u> and sees the play as morally corrupting. The passage is quoted on p. xxxvii (vol. 1) of Bullen's edition of Marston's plays.

1616

*1   JONSON, BEN. Cynthias Revels; or the Fountayne of Selfe-Love.
The Workes of Benjamin Jonson. London: Printed by W. Stansby
for I. Smithwicke. (Pollard and Redgrave 14751)
      Later edition of 1601.5. Other editions or reprinted:
1905.4; 1910.4.

*2   _____. Every Man Out of His Humour. A Comicall Satyr. The
Workes of Benjamin Jonson. London: Printed by W. Stansby for
I. Smithwicke, pp. 73-270. (Pollard and Redgrave 14751)
      Later edition of 1601.4. Other editions or reprinted:
1905.5; 1910.5.

*3   _____. The Poetaster; or His Arraignement. A Comicall Satyr.
The Workes of Benjamin Jonson. London: Printed by W. Stansby
for I. Smithwicke. (Pollard and Redgrave 14751)
      Later edition of 1602.1. Other editions or reprinted:
1905.6-7; 1910.6; 1913.5; 1934.5.

1675

*1   PHILLIPS, EDWARD. Theatrum Poetarum Anglicanorum, Containing
the Names & Characters of All the English Poets from the Reign
of Henry III to the Close of the Reign of Queen Elizabeth.
London: Printed for Charles Smith. Reprint. Canterbury: By
Simmons and Kirkby for J. White, 1800. (Wing P 2075)
      Cited in Tannenbaum, 1940.5.

1691

1   LANGBAINE, GERARD. An Account of the English Dramatic Poets:
or Some Observations and Remarks on the Lives and Writings of
All Those That Have Publish'd Either Comedies, Tragedies,
Tragi-Comedies, Pastorals, Masques, Interludes, Farces, or
Opera's in the English Tongue. Oxford: Printed by L.L. for
G. West and H. Clements, pp. 347-52. Reprint. New York:
Garland, 1970; Merrston, Eng.: Scolar Press, 1971. (Wing L
373)
      Provides a brief biographical sketch of Marston, lists his
plays and gives comments upon their sources, identifies the
theaters where they were first performed, and gives other pieces
of information.
      Antonio and Mellida, Antonio's Revenge, The Fawn, The
Insatiate Countess, The Malcontent, Sophonisba, What You Will

1719

1   JACOB, GILES. The Poetical Register: or the Lives and Characters of the English Dramatic Poets. With an Account of

Their Writings. London: E. Curll, pp. 173-74. Reprint.
London: A. Bettesworth, W. Taylor, and J. Batley, 1723; New
York: Garland, 1970.
      Lists Marston's eight solely authored plays and makes brief
comments upon them, such as dates of first performances and
possible sources.
      Antonio and Mellida, Antonio's Revenge, The Dutch
Courtezan, The Fawn, The Insatiate Countess, The Malcontent,
Sophonisba, What You Will

                                 1723

1   JACOB, GILES. The Poetical Register: or, the Lives and
      Characters of All the English Poets. Vol. 1. London:
      A. Bettesworth, W. Taylor, & J. Batley, pp. 173-74. Reprint.
      England: Westmead, Farnborough, Hants, 1969.
         Reprint of 1719.1. With an additional volume providing
      information on nondramatic poets.

                                 1738

*1   HAYWARD, THOMAS, ed. The British Muse: or, A Collection of
      Thoughts, Moral, Natural, and Sublime of Our English Poets:
      Who Flourished in the Sixteenth and Seventeenth Centuries.
      London: F. Cogan.
         Cited in Tannenbaum, 1940.5.

                                 1744

1   WHARTON, THOMAS. History of English Poetry. Vol. 4.
      London: J. Dodsley, pp. 55-68 and passim. Reprint.
      New York: Johnson Reprint, 1968.
         Discusses Marston as a nondramatic writer.
         Certain Satires, The Metamorphosis of Pigmalion's Image,
      The Scourge of Villainy

                                 1753

*1   CIBBER, THEOPHILUS. The Lives of the Poets of Great Britain
      and Ireland to the Time of Dean Swift. Vol. 1. London: R.
      Griffiths, pp. 120-23.
         Cited in Tannenbaum, 1940.5.

                                 1800

1   DIBDIN, CHARLES. A Complete History of the English Stage.
      Vol. 3. London: The Author, pp. 260-63. Reprint. New York:
      Garland, 1970.

Lists Marston's plays and makes brief comments upon them,
such as those dealing with first performances and possible sources.
Antonio and Mellida, Antonio's Revenge, The Dutch
Courtezan, The Fawn, The Insatiate Countess, The Malcontent,
Sophonisba, What You Will

1801

1   TODD, H.J., ed. The Poetical Works of John Milton. Vol. 5.
London: Printed for J. Johnson, etc. by Bye & Law,
pp. 149-54.
Contains selections from Marston's masque The Entertainment
of Alice, Dowager-Countess of Derby and general comments upon
them.

1812

1   BAKER, DAVID ERSKINE, and ISAAC REED. Biographia Dramatica;
or a Companion to the Playhouse. Vol. 1. London: Longman,
Hurst, Rees, Orm, & Browne, pp. 494-95. Reprint. New York:
AMS Press, 1966.
Lists Marston's plays and makes brief comments about them.
Antonio and Mellida, Antonio's Revenge, The Dutch
Courtezan, The Fawn, The Insatiate Countess, The Malcontent,
Sophonisba, What You Will

1817

1   DRAKE, NATHAN. Shakespeare and His Times. London: T. Cadell
& W. Davies, pp. 308, 309, 423, 608. Reprint. Paris:
Baudry's European Library, 1838; New York: Burt Franklin,
1969.
Provides general comments upon The Scourge of Villainy.

1820

1   COLLIER, JOHN PAYNE. The Poetical Decameron: or Ten Conversations on English Poets and Poetry, Particularly of the
Reigns of Elizabeth and James I. Edinburgh: A. Constable,
passim.
Provides passing comments on Marston.

2   LEFEBVRE-CAUCHY. "Marston, Jean." In Biographie Universelle,
ancienne et moderne. Vol. 27. Paris: L.G. Michaud, p. 265.
Provides a general article on Marston.

1821

1   C., J.   "Eastward Hoe--Jonson, Chapman, and Marston."
    Blackwood's Magazine 10:127-36.
        Introduces the play to readers as a fine example of Eliza-
    bethan comedy and provides a detailed plot summary. Includes
    lengthy excerpts from the dialogue and concludes by speculating
    that Jonson sketched out the plot, Chapman did most of the writ-
    ing, and Marston and Jonson added finishing touches.

1822

1   ANON.   "Article VII."   Retrospective Review 6:113-32.
        Presents a general discussion of Marston, provides detailed
    plot summaries of Antonio and Mellida and Antonio's Revenge, with
    generous quotations from the texts; then quotes passages from
    other plays and makes comments on these selections; concludes by
    assessing Marston's virtues and defects.
        The Dutch Courtezan, The Fawn, The Insatiate Countess, The
    Malcontent, Sophonisba, What You Will

*2 NARES, ROBERT. A Glossary: or Collection of Words, Phrases,
    Names, and Allusions to Customs, Proverbs, etc. Which Have
    Been Thought to Require Illustration in the Works of English
    Authors, Particularly Shakespeare and His Contemporaries.
    London: R. Triphook, p. 270.
        Cited in Tannenbaum, 1940.5.

1828

1   ANON.   Letter to the Editor.   Gentleman's Magazine 98:317-18.
        Presents a letter from a prospective editor of Marston,
    soliciting subscribers for an edition of Marston's plays. Gives
    a favorable view of Marston as a dramatist. This edition, how-
    ever, was not published.

1830

*1 K., T.H.,   "John Marston."   Dramatic Magazine 2:365-68.
        Cited in Tannenbaum, 1940.5.

1831

1   COLLIER, JOHN PAYNE. The History of English Dramatic Poetry
    to the Time of Shakespeare and Annals of the Stage to the
    Restoration. 3 vols. London: John Murray, passim.
        Provides passing comments upon Marston.

1832

1   GENEST, JOHN. Some Account of the English Stage from the
     Restoration in 1660 to 1830. Vol. 10. Bath: Thomas Rodd,
     pp. 9-10.
         Provides a plot summary of The Insatiate Countess.

1836

1   COLLIER, JOHN PAYNE. New Particulars Regarding the Works of
     William Shakespeare. In a Letter to the Rev. Alexander Dyce
     . . . from J. Payne Collier. London: T. Rodd, pp. 60-61.
         Discusses a pastoral allegedly written by Marston.

1837

*1   COLLIER, JOHN PAYNE. A Catalogue, Bibliographical and
     Critical, of Early English Literature. London: T. Rodd,
     pp. 191-94.
         Cited in Tannenbaum, 1940.5.

1840

*1   HAZLITT, WILLIAM. Lectures on the Dramatic Literature of the
     Age of Elizabeth. London: J. Templeman.
         Later edition: 1931.7.

1841

1   COLLIER, JOHN PAYNE, ed. Memoirs of Edward Alleyn, Founder of
     Dulwich College: Including Some New Particulars Respecting
     Shakespeare, Ben Jonson, Massinger, Marston, Dekker. London:
     Printed for the Shakespeare Society, p. 154.
         Contains a letter forged by Collier and ascribed to
     Marston.

1842

1   JONSON, BEN. Notes of Ben Jonson's Conversations with William
     Drummond of Hawthornden. Edited by D. Laing. London:
     Printed for the Shakespeare Society, passim.
         Contains Jonson's well-known remarks on Marston. Later
     editions: 1906.8; 1923.6. For comment on Jonson's remarks, see
     1899.3.

.

1847

1   S., L.   "Marston and Webster's The Malcontent."   Shakespeare
Society Papers of London 3:85-86.
        Illustrates the classical source of the phrase Ad
Parmenonis suem used in the induction to this play.

1851

*1   KNIGHT, CHARLES.   Studies of Shakspere.   London: Charles
Knight, pp. 267-69.
        Cited in Tannenbaum, 1940.5.

1853

1   I., B.R.   "Marlowe's Lust's Dominion."   NQ 7:253.
        Defends Marlowe's supposed authorship of the play.

1856

1   ANON.   "John Marston."   Gentleman's Magazine 201:306-13.
        Assesses Marston's stature as a playwright and provides
comments upon Halliwell's edition of Marston's plays (Collected
edition 1856.1).
        Antonio and Mellida, Antonio's Revenge, The Fawn, The
Malcontent, The Metamorphosis of Pigmalion's Image, The Scourge
of Villainy

2   HALLIWELL, JAMES ORCHARD.   "Notes on Marston's Malcontent."
NQ 13:71.
        Supplies additional notes to his edition of the play (Col-
lected edition 1856.1).

1858

1   C., W.B.   "John Marston's Works, By J. O. Halliwell."   NQ
6:368-69.
        Criticizes Halliwell for not eliminating typographical
errors found in early printings from his edition of the plays
(Collected edition 1856.1).   For a reply to this article, see
1858.2.

2   KEIGHTLY, THOMAS.   "Marston's Works."   NQ 6:435-36.
        Defends Halliwell's edition of Marston's plays (Collected
edition 1856.1) from the strictures of W.B.C. (see 1858.1), but
points out errors in the text.

1860

1   GIFFORD, WILLIAM. "Memoirs of Ben Jonson." In The Works of
    Ben Jonson. Vol. 1. Boston: Crosby, Nichols, Lee, & Co.,
    pp. 7-77, passim.
         Presents a strongly critical view of Marston as a dramatist.

2   HALLIWELL, JAMES ORCHARD. A Dictionary of Old English Plays.
    London: J.R. Smith, passim. Reprint. Naardon: Anton W.
    Berhoven, 1968.
         Lists each of Marston's plays, provides the name of the
    theatrical company that originally staged each play, dates early
    and modern editions of the text, and makes general comments about
    the play.
         Antonio and Mellida, Antonio's Revenge, The Dutch
    Courtezan, The Fawn, The Insatiate Countess, The Malcontent,
    Sophonisba, What You Will

3   HAMILTON, N.E.S.A. An Inquiry into the Genuineness of the
    Manuscript Corrections in Mr. J. Payne Collier's Annotated
    Shakspere, Folio 1623; and of Certain Shaksperian Documents
    Likewise Published by Mr. Collier. London: R. Bentley,
    pp. 120-21. Reprint. New York: AMS Press, 1972.
         Discusses an alleged letter by Marston (actually forged by
    John Payne Collier) in which a Marston play on Columbus is men-
    tioned. Casts doubt that Marston wrote such a play.

4   HARDY, Sir THOMAS DUFFUS. A Review of the Present State of
    the Shakespearean Controversy. London: Longman, Green,
    Longman, & Roberts, p. 67.
         Discusses the forged Marston letter in which a play on
    Columbus is mentioned.

5   WALKER, WILLIAM SIDNEY. A Critical Examination of the Text of
    Shakespeare, with Remarks on His Language and That of His
    Contemporaries. London: J.R. Smith, passim.
         Provides passing comments on Marston.

1861

1   INGLEBY, C.M. A Complete View of the Shakspere Controversy.
    London: Nattali & Bond, pp. 272-74.
         Provides a facsimile of Collier's forged Marston letter, in
    which a Marston play on the subject of Columbus is mentioned, and
    a printed reproduction and a facsimile of a letter written by
    Marston. Does so to discredit Collier's "discovery."

*2 LOWNDES, WILLIAM THOMAS. The Bibliographer's Manual of
    English Literature. Revised by Henry G. Bohn. Vol. 2.
    London: George Bell & Sons, pp. 1486-87.
         Cited in Tannenbaum, 1940.5.

1862

1   [CARTWRIGHT, ROBERT.] The Footsteps of Shakspere: Or, a
     Ramble with the Early Dramatists, Containing New and Interest-
     ing Information Respecting Shakspere, Lyly, Marlowe, Greene,
     and Others. London: J.R. Smith, pp. 33-34.
          Presents an emendation to Halliwell's edition of Antonio
     and Mellida (Collected edition 1856.1).

1863

*1   GRÄSSE, JOHANN GEORGE THEODOR. Trésor de livres rares et
     précieux. Vol. 4. Dresden: R. Kuntze, p. 418.
          Cited in Tannenbaum, 1940.5.

1864

1   [CARTWRIGHT, ROBERT.] Shakspere and Jonson. Dramatic Versus
     Wit-Combats. Auxilary Forces: Beaumont and Fletcher,
     Marston, Decker, Chapman, and Webster. London: J.R. Smith,
     pp. 34-42.
          Discusses Ben Jonson's attack upon the diction employed in
     Marston's plays.
          Antonio and Mellida, The Dutch Courtezan, Histriomastix,
     The Malcontent

1865

1   ANON. "The English Drama During the Reigns of Elizabeth and
     James." Cornhill Magazine 11:604-18, 706-16.
          Presents a detailed discussion of Elizabethan-Jacobean
     drama, its social background, techniques, themes, genres,
     authors, and actors, and provides comments upon and quotations
     from Marston.

*2   COLLIER, JOHN PAYNE. A Bibliographical and Critical Account
     of the Rarest Books in the English Language. 4 vols. London:
     J. Lilly.
          Cited in The National Union Catalogue. American edition:
     1886.1.

3   NICHOLSON, B. "James I and Marston." NQ 31:38-39.
          Suggests that Marston mocked King James in What You Will
     and suggests that the original version of Eastward Hoe contained
     passages criticizing James, which were excised from printed
     texts.

1866

1   COLLIER, JOHN PAYNE. A <u>Bibliographical</u> <u>and</u> <u>Critical</u> <u>Account</u>
     <u>of</u> <u>the</u> <u>Rarest</u> <u>Books</u> <u>in</u> <u>the</u> <u>English</u> <u>Language</u>. Vol. 2. New
     York: D.G. Francis, pp. 319-22. Reprint. New York: AMS
     Press, 1966.
          Remarks upon early editions of <u>The</u> <u>Metamorphosis</u> <u>of</u>
     <u>Pigmalion's</u> <u>Image</u> and <u>The</u> <u>Scourge</u> <u>of</u> <u>Villainy</u>. American
     edition of 1865.2.

1867

1   EDMONDS, CHARLES. "Destruction of Books at Stationers' Hall
     in the Year 1599." <u>NQ</u> 36:436-37.
          Reprints a copy of the Order for Conflagration, which
     called for the burning of <u>The</u> <u>Metamorphosis</u> <u>of</u> <u>Pigmalion's</u> <u>Image</u>,
     <u>Certain</u> <u>Satires</u>, <u>The</u> <u>Scourge</u> <u>of</u> <u>Villainy</u>.

1868

1   MANNINGHAM, JOHN. <u>The</u> <u>Diary</u> <u>of</u> <u>John</u> <u>Manningham</u>. Edited by
     John Bruce. London: Camden Society Publications, p. 86.
          Contains the anecdote of Marston's insult to Alderman
     More's wife's daughter. Discussions as to authenticity of story:
     1954.15; 1956.5; 1957.15, 20. Modern edition: 1976.10.

1869

1   WHIPPLE, EDWIN PERCY. <u>The</u> <u>Literature</u> <u>of</u> <u>the</u> <u>Age</u> <u>of</u> <u>Elizabeth</u>.
     Boston: Fields, Osgood, pp. 125-31.
          Provides a general discussion of Marston.

1871

1   SWINBURNE, ALGERNON CHARLES. "John Ford." <u>Fortnightly</u> <u>Review</u>
     10:42-63.
          Compares Marston and Ford and suggests that if Marston had
     been able to maintain the high level of writing he occasionally
     reached, he would have excelled Ford as a dramatist.

1873

1   KINGSLEY, CHARLES. <u>Plays</u> <u>and</u> <u>Puritans</u> <u>and</u> <u>Other</u> <u>Historical</u>
     <u>Essays</u>. London: Macmillan, passim.
          Provides passing comments on Marston.

1874

1   ANON. The Return from Parnassus. In A Select Collection of
     Old English Plays. Edited by W.C. Hazlitt. Vol. 9. London:
     Reeves & Turner, pp. 97-217. Reprint. New York: Benjamin
     Blom, 1964.
          Later edition of 1606.1. Other editions: 1879.1; 1886.1;
     1904.1 (selection); 1905.1; 1907.1; 1949.1.

1875

*1   ARBER, EDWARD, ed. A Transcript of the Registers of the
     Company of Stationers of London, 1554-1640. 5 vols. London:
     Privately Printed, passim. Reprint. Gloucester, Mass.:
     Peter Smith, 1967.
          Cited in Tannenbaum, 1940.5.

*2   WARD, ADOLPHUS WILLIAM. A History of English Dramatic Litera-
     ture to the Death of Queen Anne. London: Macmillan.
          Cited in The National Union Catalogue. Revised and
     enlarged edition: 1899.5.

1876

1   GROSART, A.B., ed. Introduction to The Poems of William
     Barksted. Unique or Very Rare Books, no. 3. Manchester:
     Printed for Subscribers by C.E. Simms, pp. xxi-xxii.
          Suggests that The Insatiate Countess is mainly Marston's
     work and that Barksted made additions to Marston's manuscript.

1877

1   PHILLIPS, W. "Marlowe's Faustus." NQ 42:493.
          Suggests that the prologue to Dr. Faustus refers to Lust's
     Dominion and thus by implication reveals that the latter play is
     by Marlowe.

1878

*1   DAVIES, JOHN. The Complete Works of John Davies of Hereford.
     Edited by Alexander B. Grosart. Edinburgh: T. & A.
     Constable, passim.
          Cited in Tannenbaum, 1940.5.

2   GUILPIN, EVERARD. Skialetheia of Edward [sic] Guilpin.
     Edited by Alexander B. Grosart. Unique or Very Rare Books,
     no. 21. Blackburn, Eng.: Printed for Subscribers by C.E.
     Simms, Manchester, 88 pp. Reprint. London: Oxford University.
          Later edition of 1598.1. For another edition, see 1974.4.

1879

1 ANON. The Return from Parnassus. In The English Scholar's
  Library of Old and Modern Works. Edited by Edward Arber.
  Vol. 1. London: The Author, pp. 1-72. Reprint. New York:
  AMS Press, 1967.
      Later edition of 1606.1. Other editions: 1874.1; 1886.1;
  1904.1 (selection); 1905.1; 1907.1; 1949.1.

2 CORSER, THOMAS. Collectanea Anglo-Poetica: Or a Bibliograph-
  ical and Descriptive Catalogue of a Portion of a Collection of
  Early English Poetry. Part 9. Manchester: Printed for the
  Chetham Society.
      Cited in Tannenbaum, 1940.5.

3 NICHOLSON, B. "The Insatiate Countess: The White Devil."
  NQ 61:226.
      Suggests that the character of Vittoria in Webster's The
  White Devil and that of Marston's lascivious heroine in The
  Insatiate Countess are based upon the notorious Countess of
  Essex. For additional support for this theory, see 1881.2.

4 _____. "Marston and Shakespeare." NQ 59:363.
      Points out a word Shakespeare might have borrowed from
  Marston, then discusses the meanings of various words in Marston
  and Shakespeare.

5 TEGG, WILLIAM. Shakespeare and his Contemporaries. London:
  William Tegg, pp. 92-93.
      Provides a general discussion of Marston.

1881

1 MEZIÈRES, ALFRED JEAN FRANÇOIS. Contemporains et successeurs
  de Shakespeare. 3d ed. Paris: Hachette et cie, pp. 203-15.
      Discusses Marston's relationship with Ben Jonson and the
  War of the Theaters.

2 NICHOLSON, B. "The Insatiate Countess: The White Devil." NQ
  63:106.
      Submits additional data to support the theory expressed in
  1879.3.

1882

*1 PROLSS, ROBERT. Geschichte des neueren Dramas. Vol. 2.
  Leipzig: B. Schlicke, pp. 173-74.
      Cited in Tannenbaum, 1940.5.

1884

*1   ANON., ed. Catalogue of Books in the Library of the British
     Museum Printed in England, Scotland, and Ireland and of Books
     in English Printed Abroad to the Year 1640. Vol. 2. London:
     British Museum, pp. 1066-67.
          Cited in Tannenbaum, 1940.5.

2   ELZE, KARL. Notes on Elizabethan Dramatists. With
     Conjectural Emendations of the Text. Halle: Max Niemeyer,
     pp. 113-17.
          Presents a general discussion of The Insatiate Countess.

3   FEIS, JACOB. Shakespeare and Montaigne: An Endeavor to Ex-
     plain the Tendency of Hamlet from Allusions in Contemporary
     Works. London: K. Paul, Trench, pp. 199-208. Reprint. New
     York: AMS Press, 1970.
          Suggests that in The Malcontent Marston represents
     Shakespeare as Malevole and thereby criticizes Shakespeare as
     a freethinker.

4   FLEAY, FREDERICK GARD. "Shakespeare and Marston."
     Shakespeariana 1:103-6, 136-40.
          Investigates supposed references to Shakespeare in
     Marston's plays and references to Marston in Shakespeare's plays.
          Antonio's Revenge, The Fawn, Eastward Hoe, The Insatiate
     Countess, Sophonisba

5   GIBBS, HENRY. "Quaint Phrases Employed by Marston." NQ
     69:51-52.
          Replies to Marshall's request in 1884.7 for information
     about unusual words and phrases employed by Marston. For other
     replies, see 1884.8-9, 11.

6   LEE, VERNON. Pseudonym of Violet Paget. See 1884.10.

7   MARSHALL, F.A. "Quaint Phrases Employed by John Marston." NQ
     69:7-8.
          Lists a number of unusual words and expressions found in
     Marston's plays and asks readers if they know the meanings of
     them. For answers to this request, see 1884.5, 8-9, 11.

8   NICHOLSON, B. "Quaint Phrases Employed by Marston." NQ
     69:93-94.
          Replies to Marshall's request in 1884.7 for information
     about unusual words and phrases employed by Marston. For other
     replies, see 1884.5, 9, 11.

9   _____. "Quaint Phrases Employed by Marston." NQ 69:236.
          Replies to Marshall's request in 1884.7 for information
     about unusual words and phrases employed by Marston. For other
     replies, see 1884.5, 8, 11.

10 PAGET, VIOLET [Vernon Lee]. "The Italy of the Elizabethan
   Dramatists." In Euphorion: Being Studies of the Antique and
   the Medieval in the Renaissance. London: T. Fisher Unwin,
   pp. 55-108.
      Cited in Tannenbaum, 1940.5.

11 R., R. "Quaint Phrases Employed by Marston." NQ 69:315.
      Replies to Marshall's request in 1884.7 for information
   about unusual words and phrases employed by Marston. For other
   replies, see 1884.5, 8-9.

1885

1 LAMB, CHARLES. The Art of the Stage as Set out in Lamb's
   Dramatic Essays. Edited by Percy Fitzgerald. London:
   Remington, pp. 108-9.
      Praises the portrayal of Andrugio's adversity in Antonio
   and Mellida and stresses the skillfulness of the prologue to
   Antonio's Revenge. Also uses a line in What You Will to comment
   upon the symbolic value that the variety of Elizabethan clothing
   styles presented the dramatists. Reprinted: 1923.7.

1886

1 ANON. The Return from Parnassus. Edited by William Dunn
   Macray. Oxford: Clarendon Press, passim.
      An edition of 1606.1. Other editions: 1874.1; 1879.1;
   1904.1 (selection); 1905.1; 1907.1; 1949.1.

2 FURNIVALL, F.J., ed. Some 300 Fresh Allusions to Shakspere
   from 1594 to 1694 A.D. Gathered by Members of the New
   Shakspere Society. London: Published for the New Shakspere
   Society by N. Trübner, passim.
      Presents supposed Marston allusions to Shakespeare.

*3 LOCKER-LAMPSON, FREDERICK. The Rowfant Library. London:
   B. Quaritch, pp. 73-75.
      Cited in Tannenbaum, 1940.5.

*4 Von SCHOLTEN, WILHELM. Metrische Untersuchungen zu John
   Marstons Trauerspielen. Halle: n.p.
      Cited in Tannenbaum, 1940.5.

1887

1 ANON. Review of Bullen's Edition of Marston's Works.
   Athenaeum, 6 August, pp. 190-91.
      Praises Bullen's edition (Collected edition 1887.1) for
   correcting many textual faults in Halliwell's edition (Collected

edition 1856.1), but notes that some errors remain in Bullen's text and offers emendations for lines in Antonio and Mellida, The Fawn, and Sophonisba. Then attempts to assess Marston's dramatic stature. Seems to fault Marston for his prevalent use of obscenity and his portrayal of animalistic women, criticizes Marston's verbal style, gives some attention to Marston's dependence upon and borrowing from Shakespeare, but concludes this section with praise for Marston and places him in the first rank of Elizabethan dramatists. Closes with a note of strong regard for Bullen's work. For other emendations, see 1893.2; 1896.2; 1903.2; 1906.4; 1908.8; 1943.8, 10; 1948.6.

2   SWINBURNE, ALGERNON CHARLES. "Thomas Dekker." Nineteenth
     Century 20:81-103.
        On pp. 91-92 discusses Lust's Dominion as a tragedy and upholds Dekker's sole authorship of this play.

                                   1888

1   ANON. "Clifton Shakspere Society." Academy, 14 April,
     p. 261.
        Presents abstracts of papers on Marston given at a meeting of this society. H.P. Stokes's and S.E. Bengough's essays are critical of Marston's dramaturgy in Antonio and Mellida. L.M. Griffith's paper points out similarities between Marston and Shakespeare in Antonio and Mellida. For a published version of Griffith's paper, see 1890.3.

2   ANON. "Clifton Shakspere Society." Academy, 16 June,
     pp. 417-18.
        Presents abstracts of papers on Marston given at a meeting of this society. Emma Phipson's paper is a general study of Marston and a criticism of his dramatic skills. L.M. Griffith's essay defends Antonio's Revenge, and the paper of S.E. Bengough studies similes and metaphors in Antonio's Revenge. For a published version of Griffith's paper, see 1890.2.
        Antonio and Mellida, The Dutch Courtezan, Eastward Hoe, The Fawn, The Malcontent, Sophonisba

3   NICHOLSON, B. "Jack Drum's Entertainment." NQ 78:285.
        Argues for Marston's part authorship of this play.

4   SWINBURNE, ALGERNON CHARLES. "John Marston." Nineteenth
     Century 24:531-47.
        Begins by acknowledging Marston's faults in diction and characterization, but defends Marston by stressing that his virtues outweigh his weaknesses. Praises Marston's capacity for portraying virtuous characters and points out that at times Marston writes passages of exceptional beauty and pathos. Then proceeds to make various comments about the plays. For instance, sees The Dutch Courtezan as one of Marston's best works and

doubts that Histriomastix is Marston's. Concludes by stating
that Marston is closer in spirit to Jonson than to other Elizabethan dramatists, by valuing Marston's basically moral outlook,
and by viewing Marston's attempts at writing tragedy as his
greatest achievements. Reprinted in 1908.9.
    Antonio and Mellida, Antonio's Revenge, Eastward Hoe, The
Fawn, The Insatiate Countess, Jack Drum's Entertainment,
Sophonisba

1889

1   HUYSHE, WENTWORTH. "The Word 'Corbed' in Marston." Academy,
     14 December, p. 388.
         Defines this word, which appears in Antonio and Mellida.

2   NICHOLSON, B. "Marston and Histriomastix." NQ 79:66-67.
         Argues for Marston's authorship of a great part of this play.

1890

*1   FLEAY, FREDERICK GARD. A Chronicle History of the London
     Stage, 1559-1642. London: Reeves & Turner, passim. Reprint.
     New York: G.E. Stechert, 1909.
         Cited in Tannenbaum, 1940.5.

2   GRIFFITHS, L.M. "Antonio's Revenge and Hamlet." Poet-Lore
     2:414-21.
         Provides a detailed plot summary of Antonio's Revenge in
     which parallels with Hamlet are pointed out and comments upon and
     analyzes much of the dramatic action of Antonio's Revenge.
     Concludes that although Shakespeare is the superior dramatist,
     Marston is an interesting, rewarding author in his own right. A
     printed version of the paper in 1888.2.

3   _____. "Marston's Shakespeareanisms." Poet-Lore 2:289-99,
     360-67.
         Provides a detailed plot summary of Antonio and Mellida in
     which parallels with Shakespeare's plays are observed. Also
     comments upon and analyzes Marston's verse and the play's
     dramatic action. A printed version of the paper in 1888.1.

1891

1   FLEAY, FREDERICK GARD. A Biographical Chronicle of the
     English Drama, 1559-1642. Vol. 2. London: Reeves & Turner,
     pp.68-82. Reprint. New York: Burt Franklin, 1962.
         Provides a biographical sketch of Marston and information
     about the first performances of his plays and about hstorical and
     personal allusions in them. Also presents data on the publica-
     tion of Marston's plays. Offers linguistic analyses of his

poetry and gives numerous bits of factual and theoretical infor-
mation. Does not offer thematic interpretations of the plays.
Antonio and Mellida, Antonio's Revenge, The Dutch
Courtezan, Eastward Hoe, The Fawn, Histriomastix, The Insatiate
Countess, Jack Drum's Entertainment, The Malcontent, Sophonisba,
What You Will

2 MINTO, WILLIAM. Characteristics of English Poets from Chaucer
   to Shirley. Boston: Ginn, pp. 332-36.
   Provides a general discussion of Marston.

1892

1 HAZLITT, W.C. A Manual for the Collector and Amateur of Old
   English Plays. London: Pickering & Chatto, passim. Reprint.
   New York: Johnson Reprint, 1967.
   Lists Marston's plays and provides bibliographical data on
the early editions. Also includes brief biographical, critical,
and other kinds of remarks.

1893

1 CUNLIFFE, JOHN W. The Influence of Seneca on Elizabethan
   Tragedy. London: Macmillan, pp. 98-107. Reprint. Hamden,
   Conn.: Archon Books, 1965.
   Discusses Marston's use of Senecan dramatic techniques and
points out numerous verbal borrowings from the Roman philosopher
and poet.
   Antonio and Mellida, Antonio's Revenge, The Insatiate
Countess, The Malcontent

2 DEIGHTON, KENNETH. Marston's Works: Conjectural Readings.
   London: George Bell & Sons, 16 pp.
   Provides emendations to Bullen's edition (Collected edition
1887.1) of Marston's works. For additional emendations to Bullen's
text by this author, see 1896.2. For other emendations by other
authors, see 1887.1; 1903.2; 1906.4; 1908.8; 1943.8, 10; 1948.6.
   Antonio and Mellida, Eastward Hoe, The Fawn, The Insatiate
Countess, The Malcontent, The Scourge of Villainy, Sophonisba
What You Will,

3 MORLEY, HENRY. English Writers: An Attempt Towards a History
   of English Literature. Vol. 10. London: Cassell, pp. 403-4.
   Provides a general discussion of Marston.

1894

1 GOSSE, EDMUND. The Jacobean Poets. London: John Murray,
   passim.
   Provides passing comments upon Marston.

1895

1   ANON. "Clifton Shakspere Society." Academy, 14 December, pp. 527-28.

Provides abstracts of papers on Marston given at a meeting of this society. A paper by Arthur S. Way points out characteristics of Marston's satires and discusses the poet's early career. A paper by Louisa S. Davies faults the dramatic structure of Antonio and Mellida. Julia Gillard's essay concerns the use of music in Antonio and Mellida.

2   ARONSTEIN, PHILIPP. "John Marston als Dramatiker." Englische Studien 20:377-96; 21:28-79.

Provides a detailed discussion of Marston's plays and Marston's dramatic career.

Antonio and Mellida, Antonio's Revenge, The Dutch Courtezan, The Fawn, Histriomastix, The Insatiate Countess, Jack Drum's Entertainment, The Malcontent, Sophonisba, What You Will

3   FLETCHER, ROBERT. Medical Lore of the Older English Dramatists and Poets (Exclusive of Shakespeare). Baltimore: Friedenwald Co., pp. 19-20.

Refers to The Dutch Courtezan to illustrate Elizabethan knowledge of syphilis.

4   WOOD, HENRY. "Shakespeare Burlesqued by Two Fellow Dramatists." American Journal of Philology 16:273-99.

Suggests that Marston in Histriomastix burlesqued Shakespeare and the Falstaff plays. Also offers the view that Jonson parodied Shakespeare.

1896

1   ANON. "Clifton Shakspere Society." Academy, 21 March, pp. 244-45.

Provides an abstract of a paper by Arthur S. Way on Marston given at a meeting of this society. The paper stresses Marston's fitful, but genuine, lyric power.

Antonio and Mellida

2   DEIGHTON, KENNETH. The Old Dramatists: Conjectural Readings on the Texts of Marston, Beaumont & Fletcher, Peele, Marlowe, Chapman, Heywood, Greene, Middleton, Dekker, Webster. Westminster: Archibald Constable, pp. 1-30.

Provides emendations to Bullen's edition of Marston's plays (Collected edition 1887.1). For other emendations to Bullen's edition by this author, see 1893.2. For other emendations by other authors, see 1887.1; 1903.2; 1908.8; 1943.8, 10; 1948.6.

Antonio and Mellida, The Dutch Courtezan, The Fawn, The
Insatiate Countess, The Malcontent, The Scourge of Villainy,
Sophonisba, What You Will

3   KÖPPEL, EMIL. Quellen-Studien zu den Dramen Ben Jonson's,
     John Marston's und Beaumont's und Fletcher's. Erlangen: A.
     Deichert, pp. 21-32.
          Attempts to locate sources for Marston's plays.
          Antonio and Mellida, Antonio's Revenge, The Dutch
     Courtezan, Eastward Hoe, The Fawn, The Insatiate Countess, The
     Malcontent, Sophonisba, What You Will

*4   SARRAZIN, G. Review of Köppel's Quellen-Studien zu den Dramen
     Ben Jonson's, John Marston's, und Beaumont's und Fletcher's.
     Archiv für das Studium der neueren Sprachen und Literaturen
     97:412-16.
          Cited in Tannenbaum, 1940.5.

5   SMALL, ROSCOE ADDISON. "The Authorship and Date of The
     Insatiate Countess." Harvard Studies and Notes in Philology
     and Literature 5:277-82.
          Suggests that The Insatiate Countess is completely, or
     almost entirely, the work of William Barksted and that if Marston
     had anything to do with the drama, he simply sketched the plot.
     Also conjectures that the play was produced between 1610 and
     1613.

                                   1897

1   CRAIK, GEORGE L. A Compendious History of English Literature
     and of the English Language from the Norman Conquest. Vol. 1.
     New York: Scribner's, p. 597.
          Praises Marston's poetic skills to the detriment of his
     dramatic abilities.

2   FOARD, JAMES T. "The Dramatic Dissensions of Jonson, Marston,
     and Dekker." Papers of the Manchester Literary Club 23:1-18,
     175-92.
          Provides a detailed analysis of the War of the Theaters and
     sees it in a larger perspective of a native English literature
     attempting to free itself from classical models and regulations
     with Jonson upholding the classical stand and Marston and Dekker
     the English.
          Histriomastix, Jack Drum's Entertainment, Satiromastix, The
     Scourge of Villainy, What You Will

3   MEYER, EDWARD STOCKTON. Machiavelli and the Elizabethan
     Drama. Weimar: E. Felber, passim.
          Provides passing comments on Marston.

4   PENNIMAN, JOSIAH H. The War of the Theatres. Boston: Ginn,
    passim. Reprint. New York: AMS Press, 1970.
       Discusses the War of the Theaters involving Marston,
    Jonson, and Dekker and focuses attention upon the various plays
    used as artillery in this literary battle.
       Histriomastix, Jack Drum's Entertainment, Satiromastix, The
    Scourge of Villainy

5   SARGENT, ARTHUR JOHN. English Satirical Writers in Prose and
    Poetry Since 1500. Oxford; B.H. Blackwell, passim.
       Provides passing comments on Marston.

6   Von WURZBACH, WOLFGANG. "John Marston." SJ 33:85-119.
       Provides a detailed discussion of Marston, his career,
    works, merits, and defects.
       Antonio and Mellida, Antonio's Revenge, The Dutch
    Courtezan, Eastward Hoe, The Fawn, The Insatiate Countess, The
    Malcontent, The Metamorphosis of Pigmalion's Image, The Scourge
    of Villainy, Sophonisba, What You Will

                                1898

1   ALLIBONE, S. AUSTIN. A Critical Dictionary of English
    Literature and British and American Authors. Vol. 2.
    Philadelphia: Lippincott, pp. 1229-30.
       Presents a general article on Marston and includes quota-
    tions from Langbaine, Gifford, William Hazlitt, and others on
    Marston and his works.

2   AULD, THOMAS. "Marston and Shakespeare." NQ 98:294.
       Suggests that the first satire of The Scourge of Villainy
    supports the view that Bacon wrote Shakespeare's plays. A response
    to 1898.4.

3   DEWISCHEIT, CURT. "Shakespeare und die Stenographie." SJ
    34:170-220.
       On pp. 173-74, quotes Marston's comments on writing from
    the prefaces to The Fawn and The Malcontent.

4   HARRIS, C.S. "Marston and Shakespeare." NQ 98:183.
       Suggests that Castilio in the first satire of The Scourge
    of Villainy is a caricature of Shakespeare. For a response to
    this article, see 1898.2. For a correction to this article, see
    1898.5.

5   _____. "Marston and Shakespeare." NQ 98:378.
       Makes a minor correction to 1898.4.

*6 WOODBRIDGE, ELIZABETH. Studies in Jonson's Comedy.
       Provides a plot summary of Poetaster. Reprinted: 1966.23.

1899

1   ALDEN, RAYMOND MacDONALD. The Rise of Formal Satire in
     England Under Classical Influence. Philadelphia: University
     of Pennsylvania, pp. 129-48, 164-65. Reprint. Hamden, Conn.:
     Archon Books, 1962.
         Provides a basic discussion of Marston's nondramatic sat-
     ires and considers such topics as Marston's views of the nature
     of satire, his satiric style, his borrowings from classical
     sources, and the substance of his satires.
         Certain Satires, The Metamorphosis of Pigmalion's Image,
     The Scourge of Villainy

2   LEE, SIDNEY. A Life of William Shakespeare. London: Smith,
     Elder, pp. 109, 145, 171-76.
         Provides a general discussion of Marston's quarrel with
     Jonson. Abridgement: 1900.2.

3   LITTLEDALE, HAROLD. "Two Notes on John Marston's Satires."
     Athenaeum, 1 April, p. 400.
         Suggests that the "browne Ruscus" of The Scourge of
     Villainy is not Jonson, but Sir John Davies, and that Jonson's
     remark that he took Marston's pistol from him does not refer to
     physical conflict but simply means that Jonson silenced Marston
     as a satirist. For the source of this remark, see 1842.1.

4   SMALL, ROSCOE ADDISON. The Stage Quarrel Between Ben Jonson
     and the So-Called Poetasters. Breslow: M. & H. Marcus,
     pp. 62-132. Reprint. New York: AMS Press, 1966.
         Provides detailed basic discussion of the War of the
     Theaters involving Marston and Jonson.
         Antonio and Mellida, Antonio's Revenge, The Dutch
     Courtezan, The Fawn, Histriomastix, Jack Drum's Entertainment,
     The Malcontent, Satiromastix, What You Will

5   WARD, ADOLPHUS, WILLIAM. A History of English Dramatic Lit-
     erature to the Death of Queen Anne. 2d ed. Vol. 2. London:
     Macmillan, pp. 472-93. Reprint. New York: Frederick
     Ungar, 1970.
         Presents a biographical sketch of Marston, then analyzes
     the plays, giving information about sources and plots, discussing
     characters, and highlighting strengths and weaknesses. Concludes
     by judging Marston an inferior dramatist and reproves Marston for
     his stylistic eccentricities, his absorbing interest in grossly
     immoral characters, and the numerous weaknesses in the dramatic
     structure of his plays. Revised and enlarged edition of 1875.2.
         Antonio and Mellida, Antonio's Revenge, The Dutch
     Courtezan, Eastward Hoe, The Fawn, Histriomastix, The Insatiate
     Countess, Jack Drum's Entertainment, The Malcontent, Sophonisba,
     What You Will

1900

1   GREG, W.W. A List of English Plays Written before 1643 and
     Printed before 1700. London: Blades, East, & Blades, pp. 70-
     71. Reprint. St. Claire Shores, Mich.: Scholarly Press,
     1972.
           Lists Marston's plays and provides bibliographical informa-
     tion about early collected and single editions of his dramas.

2   LEE, SIDNEY. Shakespeare's Life and Work. London:
     Macmillan, passim.
           Provides passing comments on Marston and condenses material
     on Marston. Abridgement of 1899.2.

*3   NAUMANN, JULIUS. Die Beschmacksrichtungen im englischen Drama
     bis zur Schliessung der Theatre durch die Puritaner nach
     Theorie und Praxis der dichter Charackterisiert. Rostock:
     n.p.
           Cited in Tannenbaum, 1940.5.

*4   SAINTSBURY, GEORGE. A Short History of English Literature.
     New York: Macmillan.
           Cited in The National Union Catalogue. Revised edition:
     1966.13.

5   SYMONDS, JOHN ADDINGTON. Shakspere's Predecessors in the
     English Drama. London: Smith, Elder, passim. Reprint.
     London: John Murray, 1924.
           Provides passing comments on Marston.

1901

*1   ARONSTEIN, PHILIPP. Review of R.A. Small's The Stage-Quarrel
     Between Jonson and the So-Called Poetasters. Beiblatt
     12:294-304.
           Cited in Tannenbaum, 1940.5.

2   LOUNSBURY, THOMAS R. Shakespeare as a Dramatic Artist, with
     an Account of His Reputation at Various Periods. New York:
     Scribner's, p. 38. Reprint. New York: Frederick Ungar,
     1965.
           Suggests that Jonson had only a slight hand in Eastward
     Hoe.

1902

1   ANON. "Marston, John," In Chamber's Cyclopaedia of English
     Literature. Edited by David Patrick. Vol. 1. Philadelphia:
     Lippincott, pp. 462-64. Reprint. 1938.

Provides a sketch of Marston's literary career and discusses Marston's poetic style, presenting generous excerpts from
Antonio's Revenge, The Insatiate Countess, What You Will.

2   BALLMAN, OTTO. "Chaucers Enfluss auf das englische Drama im
    Zeitalter der königin Elisabeth und der beiden ersten Stuart-
    könige." Anglia 25:1-85.
        On pp. 77-78, discusses Chaucer's influences upon Marston.

3   BOYLE, ROBERT. "Troilus and Cressida." Englische Studien
    3:21-59.
        Suggests that Marston wrote a large portion of Troilus and
    Cressida.

4   THORNDIKE, ASHLEY H. "The Relations of Hamlet to Contemporary
    Revenge Plays." PMLA 17:125-220.
        Discusses Antonio and Mellida and Antonio's Revenge and
    compares them to other plays of the revenge tradition, such as
    Kyd's The Spanish Tragedy and the anonymous Fratricide Punished.
    Concludes that Marston made advances in the development of the
    revenge play and that Antonio is a superior character to Kyd's
    Hieronimo.

                                    1903

1   [BEGLEY, WALTER.] Is It Shakespeare? The Great Question of
    Elizabethan Literature Answered in the Light of New Revela-
    tions and Important Contemporary Evidence. London: John
    Murray, p. 29-31 and passim.
        Suggests that The Scourge of Villainy provides evidence
    that Bacon wrote Shakespeare's narrative poems and the sonnets.

2   BRERETON, JOHN Le GAY. "Notes on the Text of John Marston."
    Englische Studien 33:224-38.
        Provides textual emendations to Bullen's edition of
    Marston's works (Collected edition 1887.1). For other emenda-
    tions to Bullen's edition of Marston's plays, see 1887.1; 1893.2;
    1896.2; 1906.4; 1908.8; 1943.8, 10; 1948.6.
        Antonio and Mellida, Antonio's Revenge, Certain Satires,
    The Dutch Courtezan, Eastward Hoe, The Fawn, The Insatiate
    Countess, The Malcontent, The Metamorphosis of Pigmalion's Image,
    Sophonisba, The Scourge of Villainy, What You Will

3   GARNETT, RICHARD, and EDMUND GOSSE. English Literature, an
    Illustrated Record. Vol. 2. New York: Macmillan, pp. 336-
    38. Reprint. 1923.
        Provides a sketch of Marston's literary career and presents
    quotations from Antonio's Revenge and What You Will.

4   HART, H.C. "Gabriel Harvey, John Marston, and Ben Jonson."
    NQ 107:202-3, 281-82, 343-45, 501-2.

Suggests that the Torquatus attacked by Marston in The
Scourge of Villainy is Gabriel Harvey rather than Ben Jonson.

*5   WINCKLER, CARL. John Marstons literarische Anfange. Breslau:
      n.p.
      Cited in Tannenbaum, 1940.5.

6   ____. "Marstons Erstlingswerke und ihre Beziehungen zu
      Shakespeare." Englische Studien 33:216-24.
      Concludes that a number of similarities exist between The
Scourge of Villainy and Shakespeare's plays and suggests that
Marston influenced Shakespeare.

                              1904

1   ANON. Selection from The Return to Parnassus. In Elizabethan
      Critical Essays. Edited by George Gregory Smith. Vol. 2.
      Oxford: Clarendon Press, pp. 398-403. Reprint. London:
      Oxford University, 1964.
      Selection from 1606.1. On p. 402, comments on Marston are
given. Other editions: 1874.1; 1879.1; 1886.1; 1905.1; 1907.1;
1949.1.

*2   BECKER, PAUL. Das Verhältnis von John Marstons What You Will
      zu Plautus' Amphitruo und Sforza d' Oddi's I Morti Viri.
      Cited in Tannenbaum, 1940.5.

3   BRADLEY, A.C. Shakespearean Tragedy: Lectures on Hamlet,
      Othello, King Lear, Macbeth. New York: Macmillan, pp. 471-
      72. Reprint. Greenwich, Conn.: Fawcett, 1964.
      Discusses echoes of Shakespeare in Marston's plays, partic-
ularly in Sophonisba.

4   BRERETON, JOHN Le GAY. Elizabethan Drama. Sydney: W.
      Brooks, pp. 92-123.
      Provides a detailed general discussion of Marston and his
works. Section on Marston reprinted: 1948.2.
      Antonio and Mellida, Antonio's Revenge, The Dutch
Courtezan, Eastward Hoe, The Fawn, Histriomastix, The Insatiate
Countess, Jack Drum's Entertainment, The Malcontent, The
Metamorphosis of Pigmalion's Image, Sophonisba, The Scourge of
Villainy, What You Will

5   ELTON, CHARLES ISAAC. William Shakespeare, His Family and
      Friends. London: John Murray, passim.
      Provides passing comments on Marston.

6   FRIES, CARL. "Zu Marston's Pygmalion." Englische Studien
      34:445-46.
      Suggests that The Metamorphosis of Pigmalion's Image
influenced Shakespeare in composing the final act of The Winter's
Tale, in which Hermione's "statue" comes to life.

7　HENSLOWE, PHILIP. Henslowe's Diary. Edited by W.W. Greg.
　　Vol. 1. London: A.H. Bullen, p. 112.
　　　　Includes Henslowe's reference to a payment given to a Mr.
　　Maxton "in earneste of a Boocke." Maxton has been identified
　　with Marston. For a more recent edition of Henslowe's Diary, see
　　1961.12.

8　MERES, FRANCIS. Selection from Palladis Tamia. In
　　Elizabethan Critical Essays. Edited by George Gregory Smith.
　　Vol. 2. Oxford: Clarendon Press, pp. 308-24. Reprint. 1964.
　　　　Selection from 1598.2. On p. 312, comment on Marston is
　　given. Facsimile: 1938.9.

9　OTT, ADÈLE. Die italienische Novelle in englischen Drama von
　　1600 bis zur Restauration. Zürich: Zürcher & Furrer,
　　passim.
　　　　Provides passing comments on Marston.

10　SWINBURNE, ALGERNON CHARLES. "John Marston." In The Poems of
　　Algernon Charles Swinburne. Vol. 5. London: Chatto &
　　Windus, p. 308.
　　　　A sonnet on Marston. Cited in Tannenbaum, 1940.5.

11　WENDELL, BARRETT. The Temper of the Seventeenth Century in
　　English Literature. New York: Scribner's, pp. 57, 75, 93,
　　106.
　　　　Provides passing comments on Marston.

1905

1　ANON. The Return from Parnassus. Edited by Oliphant Smeaton.
　　Temple Dramatists. London: Dent, passim.
　　　　Modern edition of 1606.1. Other editions: 1874.1; 1879.1;
　　1886.1; 1904.1 (selection); 1907.1; 1949.1.

2　CRAWFORD, CHARLES. "Montaigne, Webster, and Marston:
　　Dr. Donne and Webster." NQ 112:41-43, 121-23, 202-3.
　　　　Traces the influence of Montaigne's writings (particularly
　　through the medium of John Florio's translation of the essays)
　　upon Webster and Marston and concludes that both dramatists were
　　independently influenced by Montaigne and that both independently
　　borrowed concepts and phrasings from him. Also judges that
　　Webster more skillfully worked Montaigne's ideas into his plays
　　than Marston did into his. Gives some attention to Webster's
　　borrowings from Donne. Article continued: 1906.3. Full article
　　reprinted: 1907.3.
　　　　The Dutch Courtezan, The Fawn

3　GRAY, JOSEPH WILLIAM. Shakespeare's Marriage, His Departure
　　from Stratford and Other Incidents in His Life. London:
　　Chapman & Hall, p. 175.

Reprints the dedicatory poem signed I.M. from the First
Folio of Shakespeare's plays and suggests that the lines are
Marston's.

4   JONSON, BEN. Cynthia's Revels; or the Fountayne of Selfe-
     Love. In Ben Jonson's Dramen. Edited by W. Bang. Materials
     for the study of the Old English Drama, ser. 1, vol. 7.
     Louvain: Uystpruyst, pp. 177-269. Reprint. Vaduz: Kraus
     Reprint, 1963.
         Modern edition of 1616.1. Originally printed: 1601.5.
     Other edition: 1910.4.

5   _____ . Every Man Out of His Humour. In Ben Jonson's Dramen.
     Edited by W. Bang. Materials for the study of the Old English
     Drama, ser. 1, vol. 7. Louvain: Uystpruyst, pp. 73-175.
     Reprint. Vaduz: Kraus Reprint, 1963.
         Modern edition of 1616.2. Originally printed: 1601.4.
     Other edition: 1910.5.

6   _____ . The Poetaster; or His Arraignement. In Ben Jonson's
     Dramen. Edited by W. Bang. Materials for the study of the
     Old English Drama, ser. 1, vol. 7. Louvain: Uystpruyst,
     pp. 271-354. Reprint. Vaduz: Kraus Reprint, 1963.
         Modern edition of 1616.3. Originally printed: 1602.1.
     Other editions: 1905.7; 1910.6; 1913.5; 1934.5.

7   _____ . The Poetaster; or the Arraignment. Edited by Herbert
     S. Mallory. Yale Studies in English, no. 27. New York:
     Holt, passim.
         Modern edition of 1616.3. Originally printed: 1602.1.
     Other editions: 1905.6; 1910.6; 1913.5; 1934.5.

*8   REYNOLDS, GEORGE FULLMER. Some Principles of Elizabethan
     Staging. Chicago: University of Chicago Press.
         Cited in Tannenbaum, 1940.5.

9   ROBERTSON, J.M. Did Shakespeare Write Titus Andronicus?
     London: Watts, p. 179.
         Raises the possibility that Marston wrote additions to The
     Spanish Tragedy.

10   STOLL, ELMER EDGAR. John Webster: The Periods of His Work as
     Determined in His Relations to the Drama of His Day. Boston:
     Mudge, pp. 55-62, 98-103, 211-12. Reprint. New York:
     Gordian Press, 1967.
         Suggests that Marston, instead of Webster, wrote the addi-
     tions to The Malcontent when it was performed by the King's Men
     and discusses Marston's position in the history of the drama.
         Antonio and Mellida, Antonio's Revenge, Lust's Dominion

1906

1   ANKENBRAND, HANS. Die Figur des Geistes im Drama der englischen Renaissance. Leipzig: A. Deichert, pp. 53-58, 72-74.

     Discusses the appearance of ghosts in Antonio's Revenge and Sophonisba.

2   BAYLEY, HAROLD. The Shakespeare Symphony: An Introduction to the Ethics of the Elizabethan Drama. London: Chapman & Hall, passim.

     Presents numerous comments upon and discussions of Marston, his career, and his plays.

     Antonio and Mellida, Certain Satires, The Dutch Courtezan, Eastward Hoe, The Fawn, The Insatiate Countess, The Malcontent, The Scourge of Villainy, Sophonisba, What You Will

3   CRAWFORD, CHARLES. "Montaigne, Webster, and Marston. Dr. Donne and Webster." NQ 113:301-3, 382-83; 114:22-24, 122-24, 242-44.

     Continuation of 1905.2. Full article reprinted: 1907.3.
     The Dutch Courtezan, The Fawn

4   D., K. "What You Will, V. i. 241-42." NQ 114:386.

     Recommends an emendation to Bullen's edition of the play (Collected edition 1887.1). For other emendations to this edition, see 1887.1; 1893.2; 1896.2; 1903.2; 1908.8; 1943.8, 10; 1948.6.

5   GRIEBEN, ERNST. Das Pagenmotiv im englischen Drama. Rostock: Alders Erben, pp. 35-36.

     Provides a plot summary of Antonio and Mellida and briefly comments upon the conventionality of Mellida's disguising herself as a page.

6   GRIERSON, HERBERT J.C. The First Half of the Seventeenth Century. Edinburgh: W. Blackwood, pp. 104-6. Reprint. Folcroft, Penn.: Folcroft Press, 1969.

     Provides a general discussion of Marston.

7   HENRY, AURELIA, ed. Epicoene: or The Silent Woman by Ben Jonson. Yale Studies in English, no. 31. New York: Holt, passim.

     Presents comments on Marston in the notes to this edition of the play.

8   JONSON, BEN. Conversations of Ben Jonson with William Drummond. Edited by Philip Sidney. London: Gay & Bird, passim.

     Modern edition of 1842.1. Another edition: 1923.6.

9　KÖPPEL, EMIL. <u>Ben</u> <u>Jonson's</u> <u>Wirkung</u> <u>auf</u> <u>zeitgenössische</u>
　　<u>Dramatiker</u>. Heidelberg: Carl Winter, passim.
　　　　Provides passing comments on Marston.

10　SMITH, K.F. "A Note on Marston's <u>Malcontent</u>." <u>American</u>
　　<u>Journal</u> <u>of</u> <u>Philology</u> 27:318-24.
　　　　Discusses the meaning of the name "Dipsas," applied to
　　Maquerelle.

11　STOLL, ELMER EDGAR. "Shakspere, Marston, and the Malcontent
　　Type." <u>MP</u> 3:281-303.
　　　　Suggests that the stage malcontent was a creation of
　　Marston's and that Shakespeare, in fashioning Hamlet and Jaques
　　of <u>As</u> <u>You</u> <u>Like</u> <u>It</u>, drew upon Marston's portrayals of melancholy
　　intellectuals in <u>Antonio</u> <u>and</u> <u>Mellida</u> and <u>The</u> <u>Malcontent</u>. For
　　criticism and defense of this article, see 1935.4; 1939.4;
　　1944.8.

1907

1　ANON. <u>The</u> <u>Return</u> <u>from</u> <u>Parnassus</u>. Edited by J.S. Farmer.
　　Tudor Facsimile Texts. Edinburgh: Issued for Subscribers by
　　J.S. Farmer, passim. Reprint. New York: AMS Press, 1970.
　　　　Facsimile of 1606.1. Other editions: 1874.1; 1879.1;
　　1886.1; 1904.1 (selection); 1905.1; 1949.1.

2　CHANDLER, FRANK WADLEIGH. <u>The</u> <u>Literature</u> <u>of</u> <u>Roguery</u>. Vol. 1.
　　Boston: Houghton Mifflin Co., pp. 242-43.
　　　　Points out elements of roguery in <u>The</u> <u>Dutch</u> <u>Courtezan</u> and
　　<u>Eastward</u> <u>Hoe</u>.

3　CRAWFORD, CHARLES, "Montaigne, Webster, and Marston: Dr.
　　Donne and Webster." In <u>Collectanea,</u> <u>Second</u> <u>Series</u>.
　　Stratford-on-Avon: Shakespeare Head Press, pp. 1-63.
　　　　Combined reprint of 1905.2; 1906.3.

4　CURTIS, H.D. "Source of the Petronel-Winifred Plot in
　　<u>Eastward</u> <u>Hoe</u>." <u>MP</u> 5:101-8.
　　　　Traces the sources of this portion of the play's plot to the
　　thirty-fourth and fortieth novels of Masuccio.

5　GREG, W.W. <u>Henslowe</u> <u>Papers:</u> <u>Being</u> <u>Documents</u> <u>Supplementary</u> <u>to</u>
　　<u>Henslowe's</u> <u>Diary</u>. London: A.H. Bullen, p. 71.
　　　　Prints a letter from Robert Daborne to Henslowe in which
　　<u>Eastward</u> <u>Hoe</u> is mentioned.

*6　HELMECKE, FRANZ. <u>Die</u> <u>Technik</u> <u>der</u> <u>Sprache</u> <u>in</u> <u>den</u> <u>Tragödien</u>
　　<u>John</u> <u>Marstons</u>. Halle: C.A. Kaemmerer.
　　　　Cited in Tannenbaum, 1940.5.

7 WEGENER, RICHARD. Die Bühneneinrichtung des Shakespeareschen
   Theaters nach den zeitgenössischen Dramen. Halle:
   M. Niemeyer, passim.
   Provides passing comments on Marston.

                              1908

1 BAETKE, WALTER. Kindergestalten bei den Zeitgenossen und
   Nachfolgern Shakespeares. Halle: C.A. Kaemmerer, pp. 23-27,
   84.
       Discusses Antonio's murder of the child Julio in Antonio's
   Revenge and views the scene as inept. Suggests that, in con-
   structing this episode, Marston drew upon the murder of Arthur in
   Shakespeare's King John.

2 BROOKE, C.F. TUCKER, ed. Introduction to The Shakespeare
   Apocrypha: Being a Collection of Fourteen Plays Which Have
   Been Ascribed to Shakespeare. Oxford: Clarendon Press,
   pp. xxx-xxxi. Reprint. 1918.
       Suggests that Marston had a hand in The Puritan Widow, one
   of the plays ascribed to Shakespeare. For a criticism of this
   theory, see 1930.3.

3 BROWN, CARLTON F. "Additional Note on 'bicched bones.'" MLN
   23:159-60.
       Discusses the use of this phrase in Eastward Hoe. For
   additional commentary on the use of the phrase in Eastward Hoe,
   see 1911.7.

4 HAZLITT, W.C. Shakespeare, Himself and His Work. London:
   Bernard Quaritch, passim.
       Provides passing comments on Marston.

5 ROBERTSON, J.M. Montaigne and Shakespeare and Other Essays on
   Cognate Questions. London: Adam & Charles Black, passim.
       Provides passing comments on Marston.

6 SCHELLING, FELIX. Elizabethan Drama, 1558-1642. 2 vols.
   Boston: Houghton Mifflin Co., passim.
       Provides numerous comments upon Marston, his life, career,
   plays, and relationship to the drama of his age.
       Antonio and Mellida, Antonio's Revenge, The Dutch
   Courtezan, Eastward Hoe, Histriomastix, Lust's Dominion, The
   Malcontent, Sophonisba

7 SCHÜCKING, LEVIN LUDWIG. Shakespeare im literarischen Urteil
   seiner Zeit. Heidelburg: Carl Winter, passim.
       Provides passing comments on Marston.

8 SMITH, G.C. "Old English Dramatists." NQ 117:301-2.
       Offers emendations to standard editions of Marston,
   Chapman, Heywood, Middleton, and Greene. On p. 301 emendations

to the Bullen texts (Collected edition 1887.1) of The Dutch
Courtezan and Sophonisba are given. For other emendations, see
1887.1; 1893.2; 1896.2; 1903.2; 1906.4; 1943.8, 10; 1948.6.

9   SWINBURNE, ALGERNON CHARLES. "John Marston." In The Age of
     Shakespeare. London: Chatto & Windus, pp. 140-46. Reprint.
     Folcroft, Penn.: Folcroft Press, 1973.
        Reprint of 1884.4.

*10   THOMANN, WILLY. Der eifersüchtige Ehemann im Drama der
     elisabethanische Zeit. Halle: n.p.
        Cited in Tannenbaum, 1940.5.

11   THORNDIKE, ASHLEY H. Tragedy. Boston: Houghton Mifflin Co.,
     pp. 146-49.
        Provides a general discussion of Antonio's Revenge as an
example of Senecan tragedy.

12   UPHAM, ALFRED HORATIO. The French Influence in English Lit-
     erature from the Accession of Elizabeth to the Restoration.
     New York: Columbia University Press, pp. 176, 289. Reprint.
     New York: Octagon Books, 1965.
        Provides brief comments upon Marston's use of Du Bartas and
Montaigne.
        The Fawn, The Scourge of Villainy

13   WALLACE, C.W. The Children of the Chapel at Blackfriars 1597-
     1603. Lincoln: University of Nebraska Press, passim.
     Reprint. New York: AMS Press, 1970.
        Discusses The Dutch Courtezan, The Malcontent, What You
Will in light of the conventions of the children's theaters.

14   WATT, LAUCHLAN MACLEAN. Attic and Elizabethan Tragedy. New
     York: Dutton, p. 331. Reprint. Port Washington, N.Y.:
     Kennikat Press, 1968.
        Sees Antonio's Revenge as a terribly exaggerated play, an
unconscious travesty of what a revenge play should be.

15   WESTCOTT, ALLAN F. "Traces of the Classical Style in Poetry
     of the Early Seventeenth Century." SR 16:257-76.
        Provides passing comments on Marston's poetry.

16   WOLFF, MAX JOSEF. Shakespeare: der Dichter und sein Werk.
     Munich: C.H. Beck, passim.
        Provides passing comments on Marston.

1909

1   ALBRIGHT, VICTOR E. The Shakespearean Stage. New York:
     Columbia University, pp. 3, 169, 172, 178, 180, 181. Reprint.
     New York: AMS Press, 1965.
        Provides passing comments on Marston.

2   CALISCH, EDWARD, ed. The Jew in English Literature as Author
    and as Subject. Richmond, Va.: Bell Book & Stationery Co.,
    p. 91. Reprint. Port Washington, N.Y.: Kennikat Press,
    1969.
        Points out a reference to the Lopez affair in The
    Malcontent and discusses the treatment of Jews in The
    Insatiate Countess.

3   DIESTEL, HEINRICH. Die schuldlos verdächtigte Frau im
    elisabethanischen Drama. Rostock: C. Hinstorff, passim.
        Provides passing comments on Marston.

4   KETTLER, FRANZ. Lateinische Zitate in den Dramen namhaster
    Zeitgenossen Shakespeares. Bremen: H.M. Hauschild,
    pp. 78-93.
        Lists quotations from Latin authors that Marston uses in
    his works and suggests that Marston employed these quotations as
    a means of heightening the grandeur of a scene.

5   MUNRO, JOHN, et al., eds. The Shakspere Allusion-Book: A
    Collection of Allusions to Shakspere from 1591-1700. New
    York: Duffield, passim. Reprint. London: H. Milford,
    Oxford University, 1932.
        Presents references to Marston scattered amidst those to
    Shakespeare.

6   REYHER, PAUL Les Masques anglais: Étude sur les ballets et
    la vie de cour en Angleterre (1512-1640). Paris: Librairie
    Hachette, passim.
        Provides passing comments on Marston.

7   SHEAVYN, PHOEBE. The Literary Profession in the Elizabethan
    Age. Manchester: Manchester University Press, passim.
        Cited in Tannenbaum, 1940.5. Revised edition: 1967.19.

8   THOMPSON, ELBERT N.S. "Elizabethan Dramatic Collaboration."
    Englische Studien 40:30-46.
        Eastward Hoe is briefly discussed.

9   WILLIAMS, W.H. "Notes on Dekker's Satiro-Mastix." Englische
    Studien 40:312-15.
        Supplies supplementary notes to Scherer's edition of the
    play (Satiromastix 1907.1; Satiromastix 1963.1).

                                    1910

1   BOOTH, WILLIAM STONE. The Hidden Signatures of Francesco
    Colonna and Francis Bacon: A Comparison of Their Methods,
    with the Evidence of Marston and Hall That Bacon Was the
    Author of Venus and Adonis. Boston: W.A. Butterfield,
    pp. 29-37.

Suggests that Marston believed that Bacon wrote <u>Venus</u> <u>and</u>
<u>Adonis</u>.

2 ECKHARDT, EDUARD. <u>Die</u> <u>Dialekt</u> und <u>Ausländertypen</u> <u>des</u> <u>älteren</u>
   <u>englischen</u> Dramas: <u>Teil</u> <u>1</u> <u>Die</u> <u>Dialekttypen</u>. Materials for
   the Study of the Old English Drama, ser. 1, vol. 27. Louvain:
   Uystpruyst, passim.
        Provides passsing comments on the use of dialects and
   foreign accents in Marston's plays. For the second part of this
   work, see 1911.4. For a reprint of both volumes, see 1963.7.
   <u>The</u> <u>Dutch</u> <u>Courtezan</u>, <u>The</u> <u>Fawn</u>, <u>The</u> <u>Insatiate</u> <u>Countess</u>, <u>The</u>
   <u>Malcontent</u>

3 HARRIS, FRANK. <u>Shakespeare</u> <u>and</u> <u>His</u> <u>Love</u>: <u>A</u> <u>Play</u> <u>in</u> <u>Four</u> <u>Acts</u>
   <u>and</u> <u>an</u> <u>Epilogue</u>. London: F. Palmer, 194 pp.
        Presents Marston as one of the characters.

4 JONSON, BEN. <u>Cynthia's</u> <u>Revels</u>: <u>or</u> <u>the</u> <u>Fountain</u> <u>of</u> <u>Self-Love</u>.
   In <u>The</u> <u>Complete</u> <u>Plays</u> <u>of</u> <u>Ben</u> <u>Jonson</u>. Edited by Felix
   Schelling. Everyman's Library, no. 489. Vol. 1. London:
   Dent, pp. 149-232. Reprint. 1964.
        Modern edition of 1601.5. Other editions: 1616.1; 1905.4.

5 _____. <u>Every</u> <u>Man</u> <u>Out</u> <u>of</u> <u>His</u> <u>Humour</u>. In <u>The</u> <u>Complete</u> <u>Plays</u> <u>of</u>
   <u>Ben</u> <u>Jonson</u>. Edited by Felix Schelling. Everyman's Library,
   no. 489. Vol. 1. London: Dent, pp. 59-148. Reprint. 1964.
        Modern edition of 1601.4. Other editions: 1616.2;
   1905.5.

6 _____. <u>The</u> <u>Poetaster</u>; <u>or</u> <u>His</u> <u>Arraignment</u>. In <u>The</u> <u>Complete</u>
   <u>Plays</u> <u>of</u> <u>Ben</u> <u>Jonson</u>. Edited by Felix Schelling. Everyman's
   Library, no. 489. Vol. 1. London: Dent, pp. 233-307.
   Reprint. 1964.
        Modern edition of 1602.1. Other editions: 1616.3; 1905.6,
   7; 1913.5; 1934.5.

7 MURRAY, JOHN TUCKER. <u>English</u> <u>Dramatic</u> <u>Companies</u>, <u>1558-1642</u>.
   Vol. 1. Boston: Houghton Mifflin Co., p. 355. Reprint. New
   York: Russell & Russell, 1963.
        Briefly discusses the controversy surrounding <u>Eastward</u> <u>Hoe</u>.

8 RISTINE, FRANK H. <u>English</u> <u>Tragicomedy</u>: <u>Its</u> <u>Origin</u> <u>and</u>
   <u>History</u>. New York: Columbia University Press, pp. 99, 100,
   108.
        Provides general comments on <u>The</u> <u>Malcontent</u>.

9 SAINTSBURY, GEORGE. <u>A</u> <u>History</u> <u>of</u> <u>Elizabethan</u> <u>Literature</u>. New
   York: Macmillan, pp. 153-55, 195-99.
        Provides a general discussion of Marston's nondramatic and
   dramatic verse.

10   WALLACE, C.W. "Shakespeare and His London Associates as
     Revealed by Recently Discovered Documents. Nebraska
     University Studies 10:336-60.
         Sheds light on the lawsuit of 1610 involving Blackfriars
     and mentions Marston as one involved in the suit.

                                    1911

1   ARNOLD, MORRIS LeROY. The Soliloquies of Shakespeare: A
     Study in Technic. New York: Columbia University Press,
     pp. 11-12, 60, 142. Reprint. New York: AMS Press, 1965.
         Speaks favorably of Antonio's opening soliloquy in Antonio
     and Mellida.

2   BASKERVILL, CHARLES REED. English Elements in Jonson's Early
     Comedy. Austin: University of Texas Press, passim. Reprint.
     New York: Gordian Press, 1967.
         Provides comments on Marston and the War of the Theaters.

3   BROOKE, C.F. TUCKER. The Tudor Drama: A History of English
     National Drama to the Retirement of Shakespeare. Boston:
     Houghton Mifflin Co., pp. 378-80 and passim.
         Discusses the War of the Theaters and provides passing
     comments on Lust's Dominion.

4   ECKHARDT, EDUARD. Die Dialekt und Ausländertypen des älteren
     englischen Dramas: Teil 2, Die Ausländertypen. Materials for
     the Study of the Old English Drama, ser. 1, vol. 32. Louvain:
     Uystpruyst, passim.
         Provides passsing comments on the use of foreign characters
     in Marston's plays. For the first part of this work, see 1910.2.
     For a reprint of both volumes, see 1963.7.
         The Dutch Courtezan, The Fawn, The Insatiate Countess, The
     Malcontent

5   FRIEDLAND, LOUIS SIGMUND. "The Dramatic Unities in England."
     JEGP 10:56-87.
         Discusses Marston as a rebel against the belief in the
     validity of "rules" of classical drama.

6   HUNT, MARY LELAND. Thomas Dekker: A Study. New York:
     Columbia University Press, pp. 66-67 and passim. Reprint.
     New York: Russell & Russell, 1964.
         Discusses the War of the Theaters and suggests neither
     Dekker, Day, nor Houghton had a hand in Lust's Dominion.

7   JONAS, J.B.E. "Eastward Hoe and 'bicched bones.'" MLN
     26:198.
         Discusses the use of this phrase in Eastward Hoe. A reply
     to 1908.3.

8   OLIPHANT, E.H.C. "Problems of Authorship in Elizabethan
    Dramatic Literature." MP 8:411-59.
       Makes passing comments upon authorship problems concerning
    Histriomastix, The Insatiate Countess, Jack Drum's Entertainment.

9   WEEVER, JOHN. Epigrammes in the Oldest Cut and Newest
    Fashion. Edited by R.B. McKerrow. London: Sedgwick &
    Jackson.
       Cited in The National Union Catalogue. Modern edition of
    1599.1.

                              1912

1   BULAND, MABLE. The Presentation of Time in Elizabethan Drama.
    New York: Holt, pp. 150-53, 298-303 and passim.
       Points out that Marston painstakingly worked out time se-
    quences in his plays and that his presentations of time are
    realistic and in accord with the "rules" of the neoclassical
    critics.
       Antonio and Mellida, Antonio's Revenge, The Fawn, The
    Insatiate Countess, The Malcontent, Sophonisba, What You Will

2   FOSTER, FRANCES A. "Dumb Show in Elizabethan Drama before
    1620." Englische Studien 44:8-17.
       Discusss the dumb shows in Antonio's Revenge, Sophonisba,
    What You Will and points out Marston's fondness for dumb shows
    that merge with dialogue.

3   LAWRENCE, W.J. "Light and Darkness in the Elizabethan
    Theatre." Englische Studien 45:182-200.
       Uses the induction to What You Will to suggest that the
    private theaters were not lighted until the play was ready to
    begin.

4   NIBBE, HUNOLD, ed. Introduction to The Fleire by Edward
    Sharpham. Materials for the Study of the Old English Drama,
    ser. 1, vol. 36. Louvain: Uystpruyst, pp. 10-21. Reprint.
    Vaduz: Kraus Reprint, 1963.
       Discusses the influence of Marston and The Fawn upon
    Sharpham's play.

5   WALLACE, C.W. The Evolution of the English Drama up to
    Shakespeare. Berlin: G. Reimer, pp. 129, 185, 196. Reprint:
    Port Washington, N.Y.: Kennikat Press, 1968.
       Provides passing comments on Marston.

                              1913

1   ACHESON, ARTHUR. Mistress Davenant: The Dark Lady of
    Shakespeare's Sonnets. London: B. Quaritch, passim.
       Provides passing comments on Marston.

2   COWLING, G.H. <u>Music</u> <u>on</u> <u>the</u> <u>Shakespearean</u> <u>Stage</u>. Cambridge: Cambridge University Press, passim.
        Provides passing comments on Marston.

*3   FRIEDRICH, ERNST. John <u>Marstons</u> <u>Tragödie</u> <u>The</u> <u>Insatiate</u> <u>Countess</u>: <u>Verhältnis</u> <u>zu</u> <u>den</u> <u>Quellen,</u> <u>Charakterzeichung</u> <u>und</u> <u>Stil</u>. Königsburg: Karg & Manneck.
        Cited in Tannenbaum, 1940.5.

4   GÖTZ, HERMANN JOSEF. <u>Die</u> <u>komischen</u> <u>Bestandteile</u> <u>von</u> <u>Shakespeares</u> <u>Tragödien</u> <u>in</u> <u>der</u> <u>literarischen</u> <u>Kritik</u> <u>Englands</u>. Worms: Eugen Kranzbühler, pp. 12-13.
        Compares Marston's attitude toward the mixing of comedy and tragedy with those of his contemporaries.

5   JONSON, BEN. <u>The</u> <u>Poetaster;</u> <u>or</u> <u>His</u> <u>Arraignment</u>. <u>Jonson's</u> <u>Poetaster</u> <u>and</u> <u>Dekker's</u> <u>Satiromastix</u>. Edited by Josiah H. Penniman. Belles-Lettres Series. Boston: Heath, pp. 1-178.
        Modern edition of 1602.1. Other editions: 1616.3; 1905.6, 7; 1910.6; 1934.5.

6   LAWRENCE, W.J. "Music and Song in the Elizabethan Theatre." In <u>The</u> <u>Elizabethan</u> <u>Playhouse</u> <u>and</u> <u>Other</u> <u>Studies</u>. Philadelphia: Lippincott, pp. 73-96. Reprint. New York: Russell & Russell, 1963.
        Discusses the music in Marston's plays.

7   MATTHEWS, BRANDER. <u>Shakspere</u> <u>as</u> <u>a</u> <u>Playwright</u>. New York: Scribner's, p. 222.
        Suggests that Marston's concern with portraying the grosser aspects of sex influenced Shakespeare to do the same.

8   POEL, WILLIAM. <u>Shakespeare</u> <u>in</u> <u>the</u> <u>Theatre</u>. London: Sedgwick & Jackson, p. 103. Reprint. New York: Benjamin Blom, 1968.
        Briefly discusses Marston and <u>The</u> <u>Poetaster</u>.

<u>1914</u>

1   BERGHÄUSER, WILHELM. <u>Die</u> <u>Darstellung</u> <u>des</u> <u>Wahnsinns</u> <u>im</u> <u>englischen</u> <u>Drama</u> <u>bis</u> <u>zum</u> <u>Ende</u> <u>des</u> <u>18</u> <u>Jahrhunderts</u>. Mainz: Oscar Schneider, pp. 34-37.
        Discusses the portrayal of madness in <u>Antonio's</u> <u>Revenge</u> and finds it worthwhile. Draws parallels between <u>Hamlet's</u> and Antonio's madness.

2   BOAS, FREDERICK S. <u>University</u> <u>Drama</u> <u>in</u> <u>the</u> <u>Tudor</u> <u>Age</u>. Oxford: Oxford University Press, passim. Reprint. New York: Benjamin Blom, 1966.
        Provides passing comments on Marston.

3   BOYER, CLARENCE VALENTINE. The Villain as Hero in Elizabethan
    Tragedy. New York: Dutton, pp. 141, 145. Reprint. New
    York: Russell & Russell, 1964.
        Discusses Marston's influence on Webster and Tourneur.

4   FORSYTHE, ROBERT STANLEY. The Relations of Shirley's Plays to
    the Elizabethan Drama. New York: Columbia University Press,
    passim. Reprint. New York: Benjamin Blom, 1965.
        Provides general comments on Marston's plays and lists
    similarities between the works of Marston and Shirley.

5   SCHELLING, FELIX. English Drama. London: Dent, pp. 126-29
    and passim.
        Provides a general discussion of Antonio's Revenge.

6   STOPES, Mrs. C.C. Shakespeare's Environment. London: G.
    Bell & Sons, pp. 290-91.
        Refers to a comment by Marston on Shakespeare.

7   WILSON, F.P. "Marston, Lodge, and Constable." MLR 9:99-100.
        Provides evidence from the British Museum's Additional MS.
    11, 402, that Marston was imprisoned in Newgate in 1608.

                                1915

1   FREEBURG, VICTOR OSCAR. Disguise Plots in Elizabethan Drama:
    A Study in Stage Traditions. New York: Columbia University
    Press, pp. 162-69. Reprint. New York: Benjamin Blom, 1965.
        Discusses the use of the device of a disguised duke spying
    upon the vices and crimes at court in The Fawn and The Malcontent
    and in Shakespeare's Measure for Measure, and suggests that
    Shakespeare was influenced by Marston in choosing this dramatic
    technique.

2   WHITMORE, CHARLES EDWARD. The Supernatural in Tragedy.
    Cambridge, Mass.: Harvard University Press, pp. 236-40 and
    passim. Reprint. Mamaroneck, N.Y.: Paul P. Appel, 1971.
        Sees Marston's use of supernatural devices such as ghosts
    and eerie dreams as masterful.
        Antonio's Revenge, Sophonisba

                                1916

1   BROOKE, RUPERT. John Webster and the Elizabethan Drama.
    London: Sidgwick & Jackson, pp. 229-31, 256, and passim.
    Reprint. New York: Russell & Russell, 1967.
        Discusses the possibility that John Webster wrote part of
    The Malcontent but decides that he wrote only the induction.
    Points out and discusses plot similarities between The Dutch
    Courtezan and Webster's A Cure for a Cuckold.

                                 65

2   GREIZENACH, WILHELM. The English Drama in the Age of
     Shakespeare. Philadelphia: Lippincott, passim.
          Provides passing comments on Marston.

3   SPENS, JANET. An Essay on Shakespeare's Relation to
     Tradition. Oxford: Blackwell, passim.
          Provides passing comments on Antonio's Revenge.

4   SYKES, H. DUGDALE. "The Spanish Moor's Tragedy, or Lust's
     Dominion." NQ 133:81-84.
          Suggests that the two titles given above are alternate ones
     for the same play.

                                    1917

1   ADAMS, JOSEPH QUINCY. Shakespearean Playhouses: A History of
     English Theatres from the Beginnings to the Restoration.
     Boston: Houghton Mifflin Co., pp. 217-18 and passim.
          Discusses the controversy surrounding Eastward Hoe and its
     effect upon the children's theaters.

2   DIXON, W. MACNEILE. "Chapman, Marston, Dekker." In The
     Cambridge History of English Literature. Edited by A.W. Ward
     and A.R. Waller. Vol. 6, The Drama to 1642, Part 2.
     Cambridge: Cambridge University Press, pp. 33-65. Reprint.
     1933.
          Discusses Marston. Provides a detailed general article on
     him, gives biographical information, outlines his career, dis-
     cusses most of his plays in some depth, pointing out merits and
     defects, and concludes that Marston was an unequal writer, but
     one who had flashes of genius and achieved success only in comedy.

                                    1918

1   EAGLE, R.L. "Shakespeare in Contemporary Satire." TLS, 24
     January, pp. 81-82.
          Suggests that Marston in The Metamorphosis of Pigmalion's
     Image mocks Shakespeare's Venus and Adonis and that the Labeo
     referred to in the poem is Shakespeare. For responses to this
     article, see 1918.2, 4.

2   L., H. "Shakespeare in Contemporary Satire." TLS,
     7 February, p. 70.
          Quotes a passage from Sonnet 13 of Samuel Daniel's Delia,
     lines that Marston might have referred to in The Metamorphosis of
     Pigmalion's Image. A response to 1918.1. For another response
     to 1918.1, see 1918.4.

*3   RADEBRECHT, FRIEDRICH BERTHOLD. Shakespeares Abhängigkeit von
     John Marston. Halle: E. Karras.
          Cited in Tannenbaum, 1940.5.

4   ROBERTS, FREDERIC. "Shakespeare in Contemporary Satire."
     TLS, 14 February, pp. 81-82.
         Disagrees with Eagle's assertion in 1918.1 that the Labeo
     Marston refers to is Shakespeare. For another response to
     Eagle's article, see 1918.2.

*5   WENZEL, PAUL Cyril Tourneur's Stellung in der Geschichte des
     englischen Drama. Breslau: n.p.
         Cited in Tannenbaum, 1940.5.

                                   1919

1   LOCKERT, LACY. "Marston, Webster, and the Decline of the
     Elizabethan Drama." SR 27:62-81.
         Defines the decadence of Elizabethan drama as an interest
     in and preference for theatricality over the portrayal of charac-
     ter and disagrees with the common assertion that Fletcher was
     responsible for this development in dramatic writing. Instead
     sees the emphasis in theatricality at the expense of literary
     qualities as a danger latent in the very nature of Elizabethan
     drama itself and sees Marston as the dramatist who first brought
     this danger to the surface, thus adversely influencing later
     playwrights, among them Webster.
         Antonio and Mellida, Antonio's Revenge, The Dutch
     Courtezan, The Insatiate Countess, The Malcontent

2   LYON, JOHN HENRY HOBART. A Study of the Newe Metamorphosis
     Written by J.M., Gent. 1600. New York: Columbia University
     Press, pp. 110-21 and passim.
         Considers the possibility that Marston wrote The Newe
     Metamorphosis and rejects the theory.

3   SMTIH, G. GREGORY. Ben Jonson. English Men of Letters.
     London: Macmillan, passim. Reprint. St. Clair Shores,
     Mich.: Scholarly Press, 1972.
         Provides passing comments on Marston.

                                   1920

1   ACHESON, ARTHUR. Shakespeare's Lost Years in London, 1586-
     1592. London; B. Quaritch, passim.
         Provides passing comments on Marston.

2   ALLEN, MORSE S. The Satire of John Marston. Columbus, Ohio:
     F.H. Heer, 187 pp. Reprint. New York: Haskell House, 1965.
         Provides biographical information on Marston, discusses his
     quarrels with Hall and Jonson, comments upon his style, and
     analyzes and criticizes his works. Sees a conflict in Marston
     between the satirist and dramatist, which was never resolved and
     which flawed most of his plays. Suggests that at the beginning

of his literary career Marston upheld an idealistic belief that
satire could reform society, but as he continued writing, he
became disillusioned with this theory and became intensely more
bitter against humanity in general and women in particular, whom
he increasingly tended to portray as lustful monsters. Judges
Marston an interesting, but flawed writer, one whose gifts for
satire, characterization, and realistic portrayal of life would
possibly have found a more congenial form of expression in the
novel rather than in verse drama. Review: 1922.8.

 Antonio and Mellida, Antonio's Revenge, Certain Satires,
The Dutch Courtezan, Eastward Hoe, The Fawn, Histriomastix, The
Insatiate Countess, The Malcontent, The Scourge of Villainy,
Satiromastix, Sophonisba, What You Will

3 GROSSMAN, RUDOLF. Spanien und das elisabethanische Drama.
  Hamburg: L. Friederichsen, passim.
   Provides passing comments on Marston.

4 THOMAS, HENRY. Spanish and Portuguese Romances of Chivalry.
  Cambridge: Cambridge University Press, pp. 270, 271, 273,
  290, 292.
   Provides passing comments on Marston.

1921

1 BRAWLEY, BENJAMIN. A Short History of the English Drama. New
  York: Harcourt, Brace, pp. 92, 101-2.
   Provides a general discussion of Marston.

2 GREG, W.W. "John Marston: The Malcontent." Library, 4th
  ser. 2:49-57.
   Discusses the three 1604 editions of The Malcontent, desig-
  nated A, B, and C, and notes variations among them. Concludes
  that A was printed from a poor manuscript, that B was hurriedly
  produced, with last-minute corrections probably by Marston, and
  that C, including augmentations, was not printed with care because of discrepancies among copies of this edition. See The
  Malcontent 1604.1; The Malcontent 1604.2; The Malcontent 1604.3.

3 LANG, ANDREW. A History of English Literature from Beowulf to
  Swinburne. London: Longmans, Green, pp. 250-51.
   Provides a general discussion of Marston.

4 PATMORE, COVENTRY. "John Marston." In Courage in Politics
  and Other Essays. New York: Oxford University Press, pp. 51-
  54. Reprint. London: Nether Press, 1968.
   Sees Marston as providing only antiquarian interest and
  faults his use of meter and his poetic diction. Comments upon
  Bullen's edition (Collected edition 1887.1).

1922

1   ACHESON, ARTHUR. Shakespeare's Sonnet Story, 1592-1598.
    London: B. Quaritch, pp. 488-92, 544-52. Reprint. New York:
    Haskell House, 1971.
        Outlines the War of the Theaters. Suggests that Brabant
    Senior and Master Puffe of Jack Drum's Entertainment represent
    Shakespeare and the Earl of Southampton.

2   BRADLEY, JESSE FRANKLIN, and JOSEPH QUINCY ADAMS. The Jonson
    Allusion Book: A Collection of Allusions to Ben Jonson
    from 1597 to 1700. New Haven: Yale University Press, passim.
        Includes references to Marston scattered amidst those to
    Jonson.

3   BROOKE, C.F. TUCKER. "The Marlowe Canon." PMLA 37:367-417.
        On pp. 406-12, discusses Lust's Dominion and suggests that
    this play may be by Kyd, who was possibly influenced by Marlowe.

4   COURTHOPE, W.J. A History of English Poetry. Vol. 3.
    London: Macmillan, 68-73.
        Discusses Marston's nondramatic satires, outlines his quar-
    rel with Hall, comments on the characteristics of and themes in
    his satires, judges that he had an extremely Calvinistic outlook,
    discusses his diction, and concludes that his satires fail to
    uphold moral truths and to provide a convincing portrait of the
    manners of his age.
        Certain Satires, The Metamorphosis of Pigmalion's Image,
    The Scourge of Villainy

5   _____. A History of English Poetry. Vol. 4. London:
    Macmillan, pp. 246-52.
        Judges Marston an uninspired, incompetent dramatist and
    provides a plot summary of Antonio's Revenge to point up
    Marston's faults.
        Antonio and Mellida

6   GRAVES, T.S. "Some Aspects of Extemporal Acting." SP 19:
    429-56.
        Cites an instance of extemporal acting in The Insatiate
    Countess and comments upon it.

7   GREG, W.W. "Notes on Old Books: A Study of Wormholes."
    Library, 4th ser. 3:53-54.
        Examines wormholes in a copy of the 1602 quarto of
    Antonio's Revenge (Antonio's Revenge 1602.1) and uses this
    information to discover how the pages were bound.

8   HILLEBRAND, HAROLD N. Review of Morse S. Allen's The Satire
    of John Marston. JEGP 71:703-4.
        Provides an outline of Allen's study (1920.2), underscoring
    some of his main points. Praises it as cautious, avoiding flam-
    boyant theories and attempting to stick closely to facts.

9   LUCAS, F.L. Seneca and Elizabethan Tragedy. Cambridge:
     Cambridge University Press, pp. 123-25 and passim.
          Stresses Marston's interest in Seneca and highlights
     Senecan dramatic elements in Antonio and Mellida and Antonio's
     Revenge. Also points out paraphrases of and parallels with
     passages from Seneca's works in these two plays.

10   MATHEW, FRANK. An Image of Shakespeare. London: Jonathan
     Cape, pp. 335-37.
          Suggests that Thersites in Shakespeare's Troilus and
     Cressida is a caricature of Marston.

*11 SAUPE, GERHARD. Die Sophonisbe-tragödien der englischen
     Literatur des 17 und 18 Jahrhunderts. Halle: n.p.
          Cited in Tannenbaum, 1940.5.

12   SCHÜCKING, LEVIN LUDWIG. Character Problems in Shakespeare's
     Plays. New York: Holt, passim.
          Provides general comments on Marston.

13   THALER, ALVIN. Shakspere to Sheridan: A Book about the
     Theater of Yesterday and To-Day. Cambridge, Mass.: Harvard
     University Press, pp. 28, 143, 189. 298. Reprint. New York:
     Benjamin Blom, 1963.
          Provides passing comments on Marston.

                              1923

1   ARCHER, WILLIAM. The Old Drama and the New: An Essay in Re-
     Valuation. Boston: Small, Maynard, pp. 46, 92-95, 128.
     Reprint. New York: Benjamin Blom, 1972.
          Presents a withering attack on Marston and accuses him of
     being an inept writer, dedicated to portraying unseemly violence
     and depraved characters.
          Antonio and Mellida, Antonio's Revenge, The Malcontent

2   CHAMBERS, Sir E.K. The Elizabethan Stage. Oxford: Clarendon
     Press, vol. 3, pp. 427-35; vols. 1, 2, 4, passim.
          Provides a biographical sketch of Marston, lists collected
     editions and single editions of each play from Elizabethan times
     until the time of Chambers's writing; gives information concern-
     ing the dating of each play. For criticism of Chambers's dating
     of The Malcontent, see 1935.16.
          Antonio and Mellida, Antonio's Revenge, The Dutch
     Courtezan, Eastward Hoe, The Fawn, The Insatiate Countess, The
     Malcontent, Sophonisba, What You Will. Also provides information
     on the The Entertainment of Alice, Dowager-Countess of Derby.

3   HARRISON, G.B. Shakespeare's Fellows: Being a Brief
     Chronicle of the Shakespearean Age. London: John Lane,

pp. 140-43 and passim. Reprint. Norwood, Penn.: Norwood
Edition, 1980.
    Presents a general article on Marston.
    Antonio and Mellida, Histriomastix, Satiromastix, What You
Will

4   HOLZKNECHT, KARL J. Literary Patronage in the Middle Ages.
    Philadelphia: University of Pennsylvania Press, p. 22.
        Discusss Marston's dedication "To the World's Mighty
Monarch, Good Opinion" from The Metamorphosis of Pigmalion's
Image.

5   JONSON, BEN. Ben Jonson's Conversations with William Drummond
    of Hawthornden. Edited by R.F. Patterson. London: Blackie &
    Son, passim.
        Modern edition of 1842.1. Other editions: 1906.8;
1966.16.

6   LAMB, CHARLES. Lamb's Criticism: A Selection from the
    Literary Criticism of Charles Lamb. Edited by E.M.W.
    Tillyard. Cambridge: Cambridge University Press, pp. 18-19.
    Reprint. Folcroft, Penn.: Folcroft Press, 1970.
        For an earlier edition, see 1885.1.

7   ROBERTSON, J.M. The Baconian Heresy: A Confutation. London:
    Herbert Jenkins, pp. 64, 391, 560, 561.
        Suggests that Shakespeare in Macbeth echoes lines from The
    Insatiate Countess.

8   SAINTSBURY, GEORGE. A History of English Prosody from the
    Twelfth Century to the Present Day. Vol. 2. London:
    Macmillan, pp. 74-75.
        Discusses Marston's verse, points out its roughness,
Marston's dislike of redundant syllables, and other qualities of
his poetry.

9   SCHELLING, FELIX. Foreign Influences in Elizabethan Plays.
    New York: Harper, passim.
        Provides passing comments on Marston.

                                  1924

1   BUNDY, MURRAY W. "Shakespeare and Elizabethan Psychology."
    JEGP 23:516-49.
        Quotes a passage from The Scourge of Villainy to illustrate
conventional Elizabethan views of the psychology of sin.

2   CAMP, CHARLES W. The Artisan in Elizabethan Literature. New
    York: Columbia University Press, pp. 101-7.
        Analyzes the satire implied by the social aspirations and
greed of Gertrude, Quicksilver, and Sir Petronel Flash of
Eastward Hoe.

3   DOBRÉE, BONAMY. Restoration Comedy, 1660-1720. Oxford:
    Clarendon Presss, pp. 40, 41, 93.
        Compares repartee in The Dutch Courtezan to that in
    Congreve's The Way of the World.

4   HARRISON, G.B. The Story of Elizabethan Drama. Cambridge:
    Cambridge University Press, pp. 95-96.
        Provides a general discussion of Antonio's Revenge as a
    revenge play.

5   ROBERTSON, J.M. An Introduction to the Study of the
    Shakespeare Canon. London: George Routledge, pp. 250, 251,
    392-400.
        Considers whether Marston wrote A 'Larum for London, but
    rejects the idea.

                                   1925

1   ADAMS, JOSEPH QUINCY. A Life of William Shakespeare. Boston:
    Houghton Mifflin Co., pp. 290-91, 320-30, 340-42.
        Provides general comments on Marston and outlines the War
    of the Theaters.
        Satiromastix

2   DUNN, ESTHER CLOUDMAN. Ben Jonson's Art: Elizabethan Life
    and Literature as Reflected Therein. Northampton, Mass.:
    Smith College Press, pp. 52-57.
        Discusses the War of the Theaters and analyzes in detail
    the charges that Jonson and Marston made against each other in
    their satirical plays.
        What You Will

3   GRAVES, ROBERT. Poetic Unreason and Other Studies. London:
    C. Palmer, p. 214.
        Identifies the drunken sailors of Shakespeare's The Tempest
    with Jonson, Chapman, and Marston. For a more detailed treatment
    by Graves of this theory, see 1949.3.

4   HERFORD, C.H., and PERCY SIMPSON, eds. Ben Jonson. Vol. 1.
    Oxford: Clarendon Press, pp. 24-27, 406-10, 414-41, and
    passim.
        Discusses Marston's relationship with Jonson and the War of
    the Theaters.

5   LAWRENCE, BASIL E. Notes on the Authorship of the Shakespeare
    Plays and Poems. London: Gay & Handcock, pp. 84-86, 88-90.
        Suggessts that Certain Satires and The Scourge of Villainy
    furnish information that Bacon wrote Shakespeare's Venus and
    Adonis and The Rape of Lucrece.

6   REBORA, PIERO. L'Italia nel dramma inglese. Milan:
    Modernissima, passim.
        Provides passing comments on Marston.

7   SCHELLING, FELIX. Elizabethan Playwrights: A Short History
    of the English Drama from Mediaeval Times to the Closing of
    the Theaters in 1642. New York: Harper, passim.
        Provides passing comments on Marston.

8   SUGDEN, EDWARD H. A Topographical Dictionary to the Works of
    Shakespeare and His Fellow Dramatists. Manchester:
    Manchester University Press, passim.
        Discusses places referred to and employed in plays by
    Elizabethan dramatists.

9   WALKER, HUGH. English Satire and Satirists. London: Dent,
    pp. 80-82, 114-17.
        Provides a general disscussion of Marston, his satirical
    style of writing, and the War of the Theaters.
        Certain Satires, The Metamorphosis of Pigmalion's Image,
    The Scourge of Villainy

                              1926

1   BECKWITH, E.A. "On the Hall-Marston Controversy." JEGP
    25:84-89.
        Suggests that Hall knew Marston's writings in manuscript
    and did indeed paste an insulting epigram in copies of The
    Metamorphosis of Pigmalion's Image at Cambridge; thus claims that
    Hall was quarreling with Marston before The Scourge of Villainy
    saw print. Also suggests that the Labeo satirized by Hall in
    Book VI of Virgidemiarum is Marston.

2   HILLEBRAND, HAROLD N. The Child Actors: A Chapter in
    Elizabethan Stage History. Urbana: University of Illinois
    Press, passim. Reprint. New York: Russell & Russell, 1964.
        Discusses Antonio and Mellida, Antonio's Revenge, Eastward
    Hoe, Jack Drum's Entertainment, The Malcontent, What You Will,
    and their relationship to the child actors and the theaters in
    which they performed.

3   JUSSERAND, J.J. A Literary History of the English People.
    Vols. 2, 3. New York: Putnam's, passim.
        Provides passing comments on Antonio and Mellida, Antonio's
    Revenge, Eastward Hoe, The Insatiate Countess, Sophonisba.

4   LAWRENCE, W. J. "The Date of Hamlet." TLS, 8 April, p. 263.
        Uses topical references to date the first performance of
    Hamlet in 1600 and claims that Antonio and Mellida and Antonio's
    Revenge have been falsely dated 1599. Also suggests that these

                               73

plays were written after <u>Hamlet</u> and drew upon Shakespeare's masterpiece.

5   LEGOUIS, ÉMILE. <u>A History of English Literature</u>. Vol. 1, <u>The Middle Ages and Renaissance</u>. New York: Macmillan, pp. 206-7, 456-64.
     Presents a general discussion of Marston. For a revised edition combined with Cazamian's second volume, see 1964.20.

*6   PASSMAN, HANS. <u>Der Typus der Kurtisane im elisabethanischen Drama</u>. Munich: n.p.
     Cited in Tannenbaum, 1940.5.

7   POLLARD, A.W., and R.G. Redgrave, eds. <u>A Short-Title Catalogue of Books Printed in England, Scotland, and Ireland and of English Books Printed Abroad</u>. <u>1475-1640</u>. London: Bibliographical Society, pp. 394-95.
     Lists early editions of Marston's plays.

8   STEELE, MARY SUSAN. <u>Plays and Masques at Court during the Reigns of Elizabeth, James and Charles</u>. New Haven: Yale University Press, pp. 179, 183, 186, 201-2.
     Cites performances of <u>The Dutch Courtezan</u> at court and a performance of <u>Eastward Hoe</u> before the king. Reprints a Jacobean discussion of a performance of <u>The Mountebank's Masque</u>.

9   WINSLOW, OLA ELIZABETH. <u>Low Comedy as a Structural Element in English Drama from the Beginnings to 1642</u>. Menasha, Wis.: Private Edition Distributed by the University of Chicago Libraries, passim. Reprint. Folcroft, Penn.: Folcroft Press, 1969.
     Provides passing comments on Marston.

<u>1927</u>

1   ALBRIGHT, EVELYN MAY. <u>Dramatic Publication in England, 1580-1640: A Study of Conditions Affecting Content and Form of Drama</u>. New York: Heath, passim.
     Provides numerous comments upon Marston, his life as a writer and the literary world of his time.
     <u>Eastward Hoe</u>, <u>The Malcontent</u>

2   BRETTLE, R.E. "Bibliographical Notes on Some Marston Quartos and Early Collected Editions." <u>Library</u> 4th ser. 8:336-48.
     Discusses peculiarities of and discrepancies among the Jacobean editions of <u>The Fawn</u>, <u>The Insatiate Countess</u>, and <u>The Malcontent</u> (<u>The Fawn</u> 1601.1; <u>The Fawn</u> 1601.2; <u>The Insatiate Countess</u> 1613.1; <u>The Insatiate Countess</u> 1631.1; <u>The Insatiate Countess</u> 1631.2; <u>The Malcontent</u> 1604.1; <u>The Malcontent</u> 1604.2; <u>The Malcontent</u> 1604.3). Also sheds light on the printing and nature of the early collected editions of Marston's works

(Collected edition 1633.1; Collected edition 1633.2; Collected edition 1652.1).

*3   ____. "John Marston." Ph.D. diss., Oxford University.
        Cited in Tannenbaum, 1940.5.

4   ____. "John Marston, Dramatist, at Oxford." RES 3:398-405.
        Provides information on Marston's stay at Oxford in the
early 1590s and in the years before 1609. Also speculates upon
the direction of Marston's education.

5   ____. "John Marston, Dramatist: Some New Facts about His
        Life." MLR 22:7-14.
        Provides information on Marston's life at the Middle
Temple, his joining the ministry, his possibly being the victim
of a robbery, and the death of his infant son.

6   ____. "Marston Born in Oxfordshire." MLR 22:317-19.
        Provides evidence to show that Marston was born not in
Coventry but at Wardington in Oxfordshire.

7   LAWRENCE, W.J. Pre-Restoration Stage Studies. Cambridge,
        Mass.: Harvard University Press, passim.
        Provides general and basic observations upon Marston's
plays.
        Antonio and Mellida, Antonio's Revenge, The Dutch
Courtezan, The Insatiate Countess, Sophonisba

8   LUCAS, F.L., ed. The Complete Works of John Webster. London:
        Chatto & Windus, 2:180; 4:55.
        In the commentary upon The Duchess of Malfi and the
Overburian characters, points out Websterian borrowings from The
Malcontent.

9   OLIPHANT, E.H.C. The Plays of Beaumont and Fletcher. New
        Haven: Yale University Press, pp. 20, 21, 123, 496.
        Provides passing comments on Marston.

10   SCHELLING, FELIX. English Literature during the Lifetime of
        Shakespeare. New York: Holt, passim.
        Provides passing comments on Lust's Dominion.

11   STOLL, ELMER EDGAR. Shakespeare Studies, Historical and
        Comparative in Method. New York: Macmillan, passim.
        Provides passing comments on Marston.

12   SUMMERS, MONTAGUE. "John Marston (?1575-1634)." In A History
        of English Literature. Edited by John Buchan. New York:
        Thomas Nelson, pp. 130-31.
        Provides a general discussion of Marston.

13   WELSFORD, ENID. <u>The Court Masque: A Study in the Relation-
      ship between Poetry and the Revels</u>. Cambridge: Cambridge
      University Press, p. 182. Reprint. New York: Russell &
      Russell, 1962.
          Discusses the <u>Entertainment of Alice, Dowager-Countess of
      Derby</u>.

14   WRIGHT, LOUIS B. "Extraneous Song in Elizabethan Drama after
      the Advent of Shakespeare." <u>SP</u> 24:261-74.
          Suggests that the songs in <u>Antonio and Mellida</u> and
      <u>Antonio's Revenge</u> were inserted simply to divert the audience and
      allow the boy players to sing; the songs have little bearing on
      the plot.

                                   <u>1928</u>

1   BRETTLE, R.E. "<u>Eastward Hoe</u>, 1605. By Chapman, Jonson, and
      Marston. Bibliography and Circumstances of Production."
      <u>Library</u>, 4th ser. 9:287-304.
          Discusses and analyzes the text of <u>Eastward Hoe</u> (1605.1)
      and concludes that the performance of the play, not its publica-
      tion, occasioned the controversy.

2   _____. "The 'Poet Marston' Letter to Sir Gervase Clifton,
      1607." <u>RES</u> 4:212-14.
          Disagrees with W.H. Flood's dating of this letter in
      1928.4. and suggests that the letter was written between 1603 and
      1607, the later date being highly probable. Suggests that the
      book mentioned was a copy of <u>Entertainment of Alice, Dowager-
      Countess of Derby</u>; attempts to identify persons mentioned in the
      letter and provides additional information about Clifton. For
      support of Brettle's identification, see 1977.17.

3   ECKHARDT, EDUARD. <u>Das englische Drama im Zeitalter der
      Reformation und der Hochrenaissance</u>. Berlin: Walter de
      Gruyter, pp. 168, 237, 240.
          Provides passing comments on Marston.

4   FLOOD, W.H. "A John Marston Letter." <u>RES</u> 4:86-87.
          Reprints a letter by Marston to Sir Gervase Clifton in
      which Marston apologizes for not having sent the latter a copy of
      a book. Also dates the letter between 1614 and 1615 and provides
      biographical information about Clifton. For a response to this
      article, see 1928.2.

5   GERRARD, ERNEST A. <u>Elizabethan Drama and Dramatists</u>. Oxford:
      Oxford University Press, p. 284. Reprint. New York: Cooper
      Square Publishers, 1972.
          Holds that <u>Lust's Dominion</u> does not resemble the known
      works of Day, Haughton, and Dekker, a trio to whom the authorship
      of the play is often ascribed.

6   GOLDING, S.R. "The Authorship of Lust's Dominion." NQ
     155:399-402.
         Suggests that no theory of the play's authorship is
     irrefutable.

7   GREG, W.W. Review of Evelyn May Albright's Dramatic Publica-
     tion in England, 1580-1640. RES 4:91-100.
         Discusses the publication of the 1633 collected edition of
     Marston's plays (Collected edition 1633.1; Collected edition
     1633.2).

8   SECCOMBE, THOMAS, and J.W. ALLEN. The Age of Shakespeare.
     Vol. 2. London: G. Bell & Sons, pp. 191-92.
         Provides a general discussion of Marston.

9   SISSON, CHARLES J. The Elizabethan Dramatists Except
     Shakespeare. London: E. Benn, pp. 54-56. Reprint.
     Folcroft, Penn.: Folcroft Press, 1969.
         Provides a general discussion of Marston.

10   SOLVE, NORMA DOBIE. Stuart Politics in Chapman's Tragedy of
     Chabot. Language and Literature, no. 4. Ann Arbor: Univer-
     sity of Michigan, pp. 18-19.
         Discusses the satire upon the Scots in Eastward Hoe and
     lists grievances of the time that gave birth to such satirical
     writings.

11   SYMONDS, E.M. "The Diary of John Greene, (1635-57)." English
     Historical Review 63:385-94.
         Points out a reference in Greene's diary to a 1635 perform-
     ance of The Malcontent.

                              1929

1   ARONSTEIN, PHILIPP. Das englische Renaissancedrama. Leipzig:
     B.G. Teubner, pp. 202-6.
         Provides a general discussion of Marston.
         Antonio and Mellida, Antonio's Revenge, The Dutch
     Courtezan, The Fawn, The Malcontent, Sophonisba, What You Will

2   BASKERVILL, CHARLES REED. The Elizabethan Jig and Related
     Song Drama. Chicago: University of Chicago Press, passim.
         Provides comments on Marston, some pointing out and
     discussing references to music, dances, and musical plot devices
     in Marston's plays.

3   ECKHARDT, EDUARD. Das englische Drama der Spätrenaissance,
     Shakespeares Nachfolgern. Berlin: Walter de Gruyter,
     pp. 131-39.

Provides a general discussion of Marston.
Antonio and Mellida, Antonio's Revenge, The Dutch
Courtezan, The Fawn, The Insatiate Countess, Jack Drum's
Entertainment, The Malcontent, Sophonisba, What You Will

4   HOLMES, ELIZABETH. Aspects of Elizabethan Imagery. Oxford:
    Blackwell, pp. 102-9.
        Points out that Marston's imagery is limited in comparison
    with the imagery of many Elizabethan writers and that he seldom
    employs images of beauty or color. Stresses that his imagery
    tends to be bleak, gloomy, emphasizing violence and human wretch-
    edness, and that it often expresses a sense of confinement in a
    small dark place or a sense of constriction or suffocation.
    Suggests that on the whole Marston's imagery implies that man is
    a suffering, unhappy creature and that life is indeed dark. Also
    suggests that Marston was a gifted writer whose talents but
    fitfully bore fruit as excellent drama.
        Antonio and Mellida, Antonio's Revenge, Sophonisba

5   MARKWARDT, ALBERT H. "A Fashionable Expression: Its Status
    in Poetaster and Satiromastix." MLN 44:93-96.
        Discusses the satirical treatments in both plays of the
    phrase "in (or out) of one's element."

6   MOORE, JOHN ROBERT. "The Songs of the Public Theaters in the
    Time of Shakespeare." JEGP 28:166-202.
        Provides a general discussion of the function of songs in
    The Malcontent and points out that the words of most of these
    have not come down to us. Also suggests that the King's Men in
    performing The Malcontent did not hesitate to use the music and
    song associated with the children's theaters.

7   MOTTER, T.H. VAIL. The School Drama in England. New York:
    Longmans, Green, p. 148. Reprint. Port Washington, N.Y.:
    Kennikat Press, 1968.
        Quotes from Jack Drum's Entertainment to suggest that
    Lyly's plays were out of favor when Marston began to write.

8   NICOLL, ALLARDYCE. Introduction to The Works of Cyril
    Tourneur. London: Fanfrolico Press, pp. 6-9.
        Presents a general discussion of Marston's influence upon
    Tourneur.

9   THORNDIKE, ASHLEY H. English Comedy. New York: Macmillan,
    pp. 147-49. Reprint. New York: Cooper Square, 1965.
        Provides a general discussion of Marston.

10 UPTON, ALBERT W. "Allusions to James I and His Court in
    Marston's Fawn and Beaumont's Woman Hater." PMLA 44:1048-65.
        Suggests that Gonzago, the foolish, pompous duke in The
    Fawn, is a satirical portrait of King James I.

11   WOLFE, HUMBERT. <u>Notes</u> <u>on</u> <u>English</u> <u>Verse</u> <u>Satire</u>. New York:
      Harcourt, Brace, pp. 53-54.
          Provides a general discussion of Marston.

                              1930

1   BASTIAENEN, JOHANNES ADAM. <u>The</u> <u>Moral</u> <u>Tone</u> <u>of</u> <u>Jacobean</u> <u>and</u>
     <u>Caroline</u> <u>Drama</u>. Amsterdam: H.J. Paris, pp. 82-83 and passim.
     Reprint. New York: Haskell House, 1966.
         Holds that Marston and his fellow dramatists were inexcus-
     ably obsessed with dramatizing the obscene and morally grotesque
     and condemns <u>The</u> <u>Insatiate</u> <u>Countess</u> for illustrating and wal-
     lowing in decadence.

2   CHAMBERS, Sir E.K. <u>William</u> Shakespeare: <u>A</u> <u>Study</u> <u>of</u> <u>the</u> <u>Facts</u>
     <u>and</u> <u>Problems</u>. Vols. 1, 2. Oxford: Clarendon Press, passim.
         Provides passing comments on Marston.

3   DUNKEL, WILBUR. "The Authorship of <u>The</u> <u>Puritan</u>." <u>PMLA</u>
     45:804-8.
         Attacks C.F. Tucker Brooke's theory (1908.2) that Marston
     wrote this play.

4   FENTON, DORIS. <u>The</u> <u>Extra-Dramatic</u> <u>Moment</u> <u>in</u> <u>Elizabethan</u> <u>Plays</u>
     <u>before</u> <u>1616</u>. Philadelphia: University of Pennsylvania Press,
     passim.
         Provides passing comments on Marston.

5   HARBAGE, ALFRED. <u>Thomas</u> <u>Killigrew</u>: <u>Cavalier</u> <u>Dramatist,</u> <u>1612-</u>
     <u>83</u>. Philadelphia: University of Pennsylvania Press, p. 230.
     Reprint. New York: Benjamin Blom, 1967.
         Doubts that Killigrew had a hand in <u>The</u> <u>Revenge</u> (<u>The</u> <u>Dutch</u>
     <u>Courtezan</u> 1680.1), a Restoration adaptation of <u>The</u> <u>Dutch</u> <u>Courtezan</u>.

6   HÖHNA, HEINRICH. <u>Der</u> <u>Physiologus</u> <u>in</u> <u>der</u> <u>elisabethanischen</u>
     <u>Literatur</u>. Erlangen: Höfer & Limmert, pp. 52-53.
         Quotes from Marston's works to illustrate and comment upon
     Elizabethan animal lore.

7   JONES, F.L. "Echoes of Shakespeare in Later Elizabethan
     Drama." <u>PMLA</u> 45:791-803.
         Suggests that Marston drew upon Shakespeare's <u>The</u> <u>Merchant</u>
     <u>of</u> <u>Venice</u> in creating Mamon of <u>Jack</u> <u>Drum's</u> <u>Entertainment</u>.

8   LINDABURY, RICHARD VLIET. <u>A</u> <u>Study</u> <u>of</u> <u>Patriotism</u> <u>in</u> <u>the</u>
     <u>Elizabethan</u> <u>Drama</u>. Princeton: Princeton University Press,
     passim.
         Provides passing comments upon <u>Satiromastix</u>.

1931

1   ACHESON, ARTHUR. Shakespeare, Chapman, and Sir Thomas More.
    New York: Edmond Byrne Hackett, passim.
        Provides passing comments on Marston.

2   ADAMS, JOSEPH QUINCY. "Eastward Hoe and Its Satire against
    the Scots." SP 28:689-701.
        Argues that the performance of Eastward Hoe, not its publi-
    cation, occasioned the king's anger. Also suggests that Marston
    authored the offensive passages and that these were removed from
    the first edition (Eastward Hoe 1605.1).

3   BRETTLE, R.E. "More Bibliographical Notes on Marston."
    Library, 4th ser. 12:235-42.
        Discusses the early editions of The Scourge of Villainy
    (The Scourge of Villainy 1598.1; The Scourge of Villainy 1599.1;
    The Scourge of Villainy 1599.2) and points out and accounts for
    variations among them. Also discusses the setting of type for
    printings of the first edition of Eastward Hoe (Eastward Hoe
    1605.1).

4   GREEN, A. WIGFALL. The Inns of Court and Early English Drama.
    New Haven: Yale University Press, p. 117. Reprint. New
    York: Benjamin Blom, 1965.
        Discusses the possibility that Marston wrote The
    Mountebank's Masque.

5   GUILPIN, EVERARD. Skialetheia of Edward [sic] Guilpin.
    London: Published for the Shakespeare Association by H.
    Milford, Oxford University, 78 pp.
        Facsimile of 1598.1. Other editions: 1878.2; 1974.4.

6   HARRISON, G.B. A Second Elizabethan Journal. New York:
    Macmillan, pp. 306-7.
        Written as though the author were an Elizabethan recording
    events of prominence and interest. The goal is to give the
    student of literature a sense of what living in the time of
    Shakespeare was like. Discusses the appearance in print of The
    Scourge of Villainy.

7   HAZLITT, WILLIAM. Lectures on the Dramatic Literature of the
    Age of Elizabeth. In The Complete Works of William Hazlitt.
    Edited by P.P. Howe et al. Vol. 6. London: Dent, pp. 223-
    30. Reprint. New York: AMS Press, 1967.
        Modern edition of 1840.1. Praises Marston as "a writer of
    great merit," presents general observations on his satirical
    style, and judges The Fawn and The Malcontent to be Marston's
    best plays. For commentary on one of Hazlett's theories, see
    1972.1.
        Antonio and Mellida, Antonio's Revenge

8   LAWRENCE, WILLIAM WITHERLE. <u>Shakespeare's Problem Comedies</u>.
     New York: Macmillan, pp. 215-16.
        Points out similarities in character types, use of lan-
     guage, and themes between <u>The Malcontent</u> and Shakespeare's
     <u>Measure for Measure</u>. Does not, however, speculate on which
     writer influenced the other. Instead suggests that tracing the
     influence of one writer upon another is difficult, if not
     impossible.

9   LEA, KATHLEEN M. "An Emendation for Satire X of <u>The Scourge
     of Villanie</u>." <u>RES</u> 7:334-36.
        Suggests that an emendation in Satire X clarifies a
     hitherto obscure passage and compares Curio, a gallant in
     the satire, to Italian comic dancers of the Renaissance.

10   TIMBERLAKE, PHILIP WOLCOTT. <u>The Feminine Ending in English
     Blank Verse: A Study of Its Use by Early Writers in the
     Measure and Its Development in the Drama up to the Year 1595</u>.
     Menasha, Wis.: n.p.
        Cited in Tannenbaum, 1940.5.

11   WATSON, HAROLD FRANCIS. <u>The Sailor in English Fiction and
     Drama, 1550-1800</u>. New York: Columbia University Press,
     pp. 59-61, 90, 93.
        Points out comments upon and references to sailors in
     Marston's works.
        <u>Eastward Hoe</u>

                              <u>1932</u>

1   ATKINS, SIDNEY. "John Marston and Everard Guilpin." <u>TLS</u>,
     9 June, p. 427.
        Suggests that Marston and Guilpin were close friends.

2   BUSH, DOUGLAS. <u>Mythology and the Renaissance Tradition in
     English Poetry</u>. Minneapolis: University of Minnesota Press,
     pp. 180-84 and passim. Reprint. New York: Norton, 1963.
        Sees <u>The Metamorphosis of Pigmalion's Image</u> as a weak poem,
     but believes that Marston intended it not as an amatory poem but
     as a satire upon erotic verse.

3   GREG, W.W. <u>English Literary Autographs, 1550-1650</u>. Oxford:
     Clarendon Press, plate 18. Reprint. Nendeln, Liechtenstein:
     Kraus Reprint, 1968.
        Reproduces autograph portions of the manuscript of
     Marston's pageant presented to James I and King Christian IV of
     Denmark.

4   HART, A. "The Length of Elizabethan and Jacobean Plays." <u>RES</u>
     8:139-54.
        Provides passing comments on Marston's plays.

*5   HARVEY, Sir PAUL. The Oxford Companion to English Literature.
      Oxford: Oxford University Press.
      Cited in revised edition: 1967.17.

6   SCHERER, BERNHARD. Vers und Prosa beiden Jüngeren
      dramatischen Zeitgenossen Shakespeares: Ein Beitrag zum
      Studium der Formtechnik im Englischen Renaissance Drama.
      Bottrop: n.p.
      Cited in Tannenbaum 1940.5.

                              1933

1   BOAS, FREDERICK S. An Introduction to Tudor Drama. Oxford:
      Clarendon Press, p. 56.
      Discusses Jonson's satirizing Marston in Poetaster.

2   CLOUGH, WILSON O. "The Broken English of Foreign Characters
      of the Elizabethan Stage." PQ 12:255-68.
          Points out that Cocledemoy's use of various dialects in The
      Dutch Courtezan is a standard device in disguise plots.

3   CUNLIFFE, JOHN W. Pictured Story of English Literature from
      Its Beginnings to the Present Day. New York: D. Appleton-
      Century, p. 99.
          Provides a general discussion of Marston.

4   DAVENPORT, ARNOLD. "Some Notes on References to Joseph Hall
      in Marston's Satires." RES 9:192-96.
          Discusses various charges Marston made in The Scourge of
      Villainy against Hall and points out that Marston often misunder-
      stood or misrepresented Hall. Also points out verbal borrowings
      in The Scourge of Villainy from Hall's Virgidemiarum.

5   d'EXIDEUIL, PIERRE. "Vengeance." Cahiers du Sud 10:67-74,
      passim.
          Discusses the tradition of the Elizabethan revenge play and
      points out aspects of the treatment of revenge. Provides passing
      comments on Marston and his use of the theme of revenge.

6   HARRISON, G.B. A Last Elizabethan Journal, 1599-1603. New
      York: Macmillan, pp. 55, 225-26, 250, 253.
          Written as though the author were an Elizabethan recording
      events of prominence and interest. The goal is to give the
      student of literature a sense of what living in the time of
      Shakespeare was like. Discusses the original productions of
      Antonio's Revenge and What You Will.

7   _____. "Note sur John Marston." Translated by F.W. Crosse.
      Cahiers du Sud 10:186-88.
          Presents a general discussion of Marston, highlighting his
      cynicism.

Antonio and Mellida, Antonio's Revenge, Eastward Hoe, What
You Will

8   . Shakespeare under Elizabeth. New York: Holt,
pp. 192-96, 241-56. Reprinted as Shakespeare at Work, 1592-
1603. Ann Arbor: University of Michigan Press, 1958.
Discusses the theatrical world and climate in which
Shakespeare wrote and treats Marston as one of Shakespeare's
contemporaries. Also provides plot summaries and critical comments upon the following Marston plays: Antonio and Mellida,
Antonio's Revenge, Jack Drum's Entertainment, What You Will.
Reprinted: 1958.13.

9   LATHROP, HENRY BURROWES. Translations from the Classics into
English from Caxton to Chapman, 1477-1620. Madison: University of Wisconsin Press, p. 139.
Briefly comments upon the Senecan influence upon Marston
and others.

10   PRÉVOST, JEAN. "L'insatiable Comtesse." Cahiers du Sud 10:
189-91.
Emphasizes Marston's treatment of sex in The Insatiate
Countess, the play's relationship to Juvenalian satire, and con-
nections between the play and Marston's personality and outlook
upon life.

11   SIBLEY, GERTRUDE MARIAN. The Lost Plays and Masques 1500-
1642. Ithaca: Cornell University Press, pp. 29, 104, 135.
Reprint. New York: Russell & Russell, 1971.
Provides known data on the lost plays Columbus and Robert
II, which have been ascribed to Marston.

12   SMITH, LOGAN PEARSALL. On Reading Shakespeare. New York:
Harcourt Brace, p. 14.
Quotes from the prologue to Antonio's Revenge to describe
Elizabethan theatrical conditions.

13   STOLL, ELMER EDGAR. Art and Artifice in Shakespeare.
Cambridge: Cambridge University Press, passim. Reprint. New
York: Barnes & Noble, 1951.
Provides passing comments upon Marston and the tradition of
the revenge play.

14   WALLEY, HAROLD R. "The Dates of Hamlet and Marston's
Malcontent." RES 9:397-409.
Because of similarities in the action of the two plays, in
the use of satire, and in the personalities of the protagonists,
believes that the question of which play was written first is
important and suggests that The Malcontent is the later play, ca.
1604, and that Marston drew upon Hamlet in writing The
Malcontent.

15   WILLIAMS, CHARLES, and Sir E.K. CHAMBERS. A Short Life of
     Shakespeare with the Sources. Oxford: Clarendon Press,
     pp. 49-50, 193, 208, 214.
         Discusses Shakespeare's possible role in the War of the
     Theaters.

                                1934

1   BRETTLE, R.E. "Marston Bibliography: A Correction."
     Library, 4th ser. 15:241-42.
         Provides a correction to his earlier commentary upon early
     editions of The Fawn (1927.2).

2   [ELIOT, T.S.] "John Marston." TLS, 26 July, pp. 517-18.
         Reviews vol. 1. of H. Harvey Wood's edition of Marston's
     plays (Collected edition 1934.1) and G.B. Harrison's edition (The
     Malcontent 1933.2). Praises the efforts of both editors, but
     criticizes them for including only factual annotations and not
     including speculative notes. Then considers Marston's value and
     significance as a writer. Finds him an erratic author whose
     plays were mostly failures, yet a writer of genius. Suggests
     that his dramatic talents did not lend themselves to vital ex-
     pression through the medium of Elizabethan dramatic conventions.
     Nevertheless, sees Marston's genius residing in an ability to
     suggest a significance beyond the literal action of the play, "a
     pattern behind the pattern into which the characters deliberately
     involve themselves; the kind of pattern which we perceive in our
     own lives only at rare moments of inattention and detachment,
     drowsing in sunlight." Believes that Marston but imperfectly
     expressed this pattern in most of his plays. Only in Sophonisba
     did this special gift of his find complete and powerful achieve-
     ment. Concludes by suggesting that Marston's dramatic talents
     were more congenial to French classicism than to Elizabethan
     dramaturgy; had he followed in the footsteps of Racine and
     Corneille rather than Shakespeare, his name would probably be
     more significant in the history of English letters. Reprinted:
     1934.3; 1951.5; 1956.11.
         Antonio and Mellida, Antonio's Revenge, The Dutch
     Courtezan, The Malcontent, The Scourge of Villainy, Sophonisba

3   ELIOT, T.S. "John Marston." In Elizabethan Essays. London:
     Faber & Faber, pp. 177-95.
         Reprint of 1934.2. Other reprints: 1951.5; 1956.11.

4   HART, ALFRED. Shakespeare and the Homilies and Other Pieces
     of Research into the Elizabethan Drama. Melbourne: Melbourne
     University Press, pp. 91, 130-31. Reprint. New York:
     Octagon Books, 1970.
         Quotes from the induction to The Malcontent to provide a
     basis for speculation as to the different lengths of plays per-
     formed respectively by the children's and the adult companies.

5   JONSON, BEN. <u>The Poetaster or the Arraignment</u>. Edited by
    Henry De Vocht. Materials for the Study of the Old English
    Drama, ser. 2, vol. 9. Louvain: Uystpruyst, pp. 1-98, 99-
    142. Reprint. Vaduz: Kraus Reprint, 1965.
        An old spelling edition of 1602.1. Other editions:
    1905.7; 1910.6; 1913.5; 1916.3.

6   NEILSON, WILLIAM ALLAN, and ASHLEY H. THORNDIKE. <u>The Facts
    about Shakespeare</u>. New York: Macmillan, pp. 103, 104, 106,
    107, 134-35.
        Provides passing comments on Marston. Quotes from preface
    to <u>The Malcontent</u> to illustrate printing practices of Eliza-
    bethan England.

7   PALMER, JOHN. <u>Ben Jonson</u>. New York: Viking, pp. 40, 45-64,
    85-86, 94-95, 191.
        Provides a basic discussion of Marston's relationship with
    Jonson and the War of the Theaters.
        <u>Eastward Hoe</u>, <u>Histriomastix</u>, <u>Satiromastix</u>, <u>What You Will</u>

8   SPENCER, THEODORE. "John Marston." <u>Criterion</u> 13:581-99.
        Provides a thoughtful, detailed discussion of Marston and
    his relationship to the tormenting intellectual and spiritual
    problems of his age. Comments upon the style of his verse and
    finds his poetic abilities half developed; censures Marston's
    experiments with diction and rhythm; believes that these are
    failures as far as his own writings are concerned, but that they
    prepared the way for other poetic developments, such as the
    metaphysical style. Discusses Marston's intense satirical strain
    and sees him at the forefront in grappling with the intellectual
    problems of his age, particularly that of reason versus emotion.
    Sees him as fertilizing the soil in which Shakespeare's tragedies
    grew. Pronounces <u>The Dutch Courtezan</u> Marston's best play.
    Speculates upon and discusses Marston's psychological problems as
    betrayed by and evidenced in his works. Sees him as a writer who
    never perfected his aesthetic skills, a writer who, nevertheless,
    struggled to come to terms with the central problems of his age,
    a writer whose personality with its intricacies and painful
    conflicts interests us more than his plays and poems. Reprinted:
    1966.31.

9   SUMMERS, MONTAGUE. <u>The Restoration Theatre</u>. London: Kegan
    Paul, Trench, Trübner, pp. 102, 107, 178, 233, 266.
        Provides passing comments upon Aphra Behn's <u>Abdelazar; or
    The Moor's Revenge</u>, a Restoration adaptation of <u>Lust's Dominion</u>.

1935

1   BRADBROOK, M.C. <u>Themes and Conventions in Elizabethan
    Tragedy</u>. Cambridge: Cambridge University Press, passim.
    Reprint. 1957.

Provides passing comments on Marston's plays and their relationship to dramatic traditions and upon the appearance of dramatic conventions in them.
Antonio and Mellida, Antonio's Revenge, The Malcontent

2   BRANDES, GEORGE. William Shakespeare. New York: Macmillan, passim.
    Provides passing comments on Marston.

3   BRETTLE, R.E. Review of vol. 1 of Wood's edition of Marston's Plays. RES 11:221-28.
    Chastises Wood (Collected edition 1934) for inaccuracies in and omissions of data in his discussion of Marston's life, for faults in the bibliographical data provided, and for other lapses. Disagrees with some of Wood's aesthetic judgments of Marston. Faults Wood's choice of texts and his editing, particularly criticizes him for eccentricities in punctuating Marston's plays. Remarks that his annotations are too sparse and inadequate and complains that they frequently refer the reader to outside sources rather than provide the information themselves.

4   CAMPBELL, OSCAR JAMES. "Jaques." Huntington Library Bulletin 8:71-102.
    Attempts to discover the nature of the melancholy of Jaques in Shakespeare's As You Like It and disagrees with E.E. Stoll's assertion (1906.11) that Jaques should be considered a malcontent. Stresses that he should be seen as one suffering from an excess of melancholy humors and, therefore, prone to dark and unhappy moods. In making this point, contrasts Jaques and Malevole in The Malcontent, who represents the true malcontent type, one who feels himself ostracized from society and who, therefore, is embittered. For Stoll's reply, see 1939.4.

5   CRAIG, HARDIN. The Enchanted Glass. New York: Oxford University Press, pp. 177-79. Reprint. 1950.
    Discusses the use of physiological imagery to express grief in Antonio and Mellida.

6   DAVENPORT, ARNOLD. "John Weever's Epigrammes and the Hall-Marston Quarrel." RES 11:66-68.
    Suggests that Weever entered the Marston-Hall quarrel on the side of Marston.

7   DAVID, RICHARD. The Janus of Poets: Being an Essay on the Dramatic Value of Shakespeare's Poetry Both Good and Bad. Cambridge: Cambridge University Press, pp. 77-79.
    Compares Marston's poetic style with Shakespeare's.

8   FINK, Z.S. "Jaques and the Malcontent Traveller." PQ 14: 237-52.
    Suggests that Jaques in Shakespeare's As You Like It is to be understood as a portrait of the traveler made unhappy by his

travels and contact with unhappiness and suggests that
Shakespeare's treatment of this character was influenced
by the view of the melancholy traveler expressed by Marston.
Certain Satires

9   HASELDEN, REGINALD. Scientific Aids for the Study of
    Manuscripts. Oxford: Oxford University Press for the
    Bibliographical Society, p. 97, plate 13.
        Discusses the manuscript of the Entertainment of Alice,
    Dowager-Countess of Derby.

10 KREIDER, PAUL V. Elizabethan Comic Character Conventions as
    Revealed in the Comedies of George Chapman. Language and
    Literature, no 17. Ann Arbor: University of Michigan Press,
    pp. 160-61. Reprint. New York: Octagon, 1975.
        Discusses the letter Chapman wrote during the controversy
    over Eastward Hoe.

11 LAWRENCE, W.J. Those Nut-Cracking Elizabethans: Studies of
    the Early Theatre and Drama. London: Argonaut Press,
    pp. 185-86. Reprint. New York: Haskell House, 1969.
        Discusses the similarity of the play titles of
    Shakespeare's As You Like It, or What You Will and Marston's What
    You Will.

12 MOULTON, CHARLES WELLS, ed. The Library of Literary Criticism
    of English and American Authors. Vol. 1. New York: Peter
    Smith, pp. 735-39.
        Contains excerpts of criticism of Marston. Revised edi-
    tion: 1966.21.

13 PEARN, B.R. "Dumb-Show in Elizabethan Drama." RES 44:
    385-405.
        Provides passing comments on Marston.

14 PRAZ, MARIO. Review of Vol. 1 of Wood's edition of Marston's
    plays. ES 17:149-54.
        Begins by judging Marston an inept writer whose poetic
    style was awkward and who simply manipulated dramatic conventions
    without skill or direction. Then considers Wood's edition of the
    plays (Collected edition 1934.1). Sees his introductory material
    as the most important portion of the work. Feels that Wood's
    notes are inadequate and that in editing the text, Wood should
    have offered more conjectural emendations.

15 SHARPE, ROBERT BOIES. The Real War of the Theaters:
    Shakespeare's Fellows in Rivalry with the Admiral's Men, 1594-
    1603. Boston: Heath, pp. 131-38, 159-63, and passim.
        Discusses Marston within the contexts of the rivalry be-
    tween the Lord Chamberlain's men and the Admiral's Men and of the
    fluctuation of Elizabethan dramatic styles and genres. Concen-
    trates upon Marston's earlier plays, sees him as a powerful

influence upon the drama, especially in his use of satire, and
credits him with revitalizing the revenge play.
    Antonio and Mellida, Antonio's Revenge, Histriomastix, Jack
Drum's Entertainment, What You Will

16   STOLL, ELMER EDGAR. "The Date of The Malcontent: A
      Rejoinder." RES 11:42-50.
          Criticizes E.K. Chamber's assertion in The Elizabethan
      Stage (1923.2) that The Malcontent was written in 1604 and sug-
      gests that the play appeared about 1600.

17   WHITE, HAROLD OGBURN. Plagiarism and Imitation during the
      Renaissance: A Study in Critical Distinctions. Cambridge,
      Mass.: Harvard University Press, pp. 124-26, 128-38.
      Reprint. New York: Octagon, 1965.
          Discusses Marston's dislike of paraphrasing classical
      authors and suggests that although Marston was inspired by
      classical satirists, the material and ideas of his satirical
      writings are his own. Also outlines and discusses the War of
      the Theaters.
          The Scourge of Villainy, What You Will

18   WILSON, JOHN DOVER. What Happens in Hamlet. Cambridge:
      Cambridge University Press, p. 55.
          Doubts that Antonio's Revenge preceded Hamlet. Revised
      edition: 1967.25.

19   WRIGHT, LOUIS B. Middle-Class Culture in Elizabethan England.
      Chapel Hill: University of North Carolina Press, pp. 112,
      383, 474, 630-31, 651. Reprint. New York: Octagon Books,
      1980.
          Suggests that Eastward Hoe upholds the orthodox values of
      the Elizabethan middle class.

                                1936

1   BRADFORD, GAMALIEL. Elizabethan Women. Boston: Houghton
      Mifflin Co., pp. 30, 58, 102, 103, 112, 176.
          Provides passing comments on the treatment of women in
      Marston's plays and stresses that some of the women he portrays
      are admirable.

2   CAMPBELL, OSCAR JAMES. "The Dramatic Construction of
      Poetaster." Huntington Library Bulletin 9:37-62.
          Provides passing comments on Marston satirized as
      Crispinus.

3   DUNN, ESTHER CLOUDMAN. The Literature of Shakespeare's
      England. New York: Scribner's, pp. 256-60.
          Provides a detailed discussion of The Malcontent, comment-
      ing upon its characters, theatricality, use of music, and so
      forth, and concludes that the play is a successful work. Sees

much of the play's force and meaning residing in the fact that
Marston allows his characters to see into the moral realities of
life.

4   ELLIS-FERMOR, UNA. The Jacobean Drama: An Interpretation.
     London: Methuen, pp. 223-35.
        Sees Marston as a skilled writer, a man of the theater, a
     tireless experimenter who had a pervasive influence upon Eliza-
     bethan drama in the creation of characters, in the use of imagery
     and stage devices, and in the spreading of a critical attitude
     toward life. Suggests, however, that although Marston had a
     talent for the writing of both comedy and tragedy, he was not
     able to fulfill his potentialities.
        Antonio and Mellida, Antonio's Revenge, The Fawn, The
     Malcontent, Sophonisba

5   LINTHICUM, MARIE CHANNING. Costume in the Drama of
     Shakespeare and His Contemporaries. Oxford: Clarendon
     Press, passim. Reprint. New York: Hacker, 1972.
        Provides passing comments on Marston.

6   RAVEN, ANTON ADOLPH, ed. A Hamlet Bibliography and Reference
     Guide. Chicago: University of Chicago Press, passim.
        Lists unannotated Marston entries in a bibliography relat-
     ing to Hamlet.

7   SISSON, CHARLES J. Lost Plays of Shakespeare's Age.
     Cambridge: Cambridge University Press, pp. 186-87. Reprint.
     Totowa, N.J.: Biblio Distribution Center, 1970.
        Discusses the satirical climate in which Marston wrote.

8   SPENCER, THEODORE. Death and Elizabethan Tragedy: A Study of
     Convention and Opinion in the Elizabethan Drama. Cambridge,
     Mass.: Harvard University Press, passim. Reprint. New York:
     Pageant Books, 1960.
        Provides comments on the ways in which Marston's plays
     treat such themes as death, courage in the face of death, and
     immortality.

1937

1   BECKINGHAM, C.F. "Seneca's Fatalism and Elizabethan Tragedy."
     MLR 32:434-38.
        Suggests that Marston was not a fatalist and notes the
     appearance of the view of freedom of the will in Sophonisba.

2   BOWERS, FREDSON. "Ben Jonson the Actor." SP 34:392-406.
        Presents passing comments on Marston and Satiromastix.

3   CHEW, SAMUEL C. The Crescent and the Rose, Islam and England
     during the Renaissance. New York: Oxford University Press,
     passim. Reprint. New York: Octagon Books, 1965.
         Provides passing comments on the treatment of the East, its
     customs, and peoples in the works of Marston.

4   CLARK, ELEANOR GRACE. Elizabethan Fustian: A Study in the
     Social and Political Backgrounds of the Drama, with Particular
     Reference to Christopher Marlowe. New York: Author, passim.
         Provides passing comments on Marston. Another edition:
     1941.2.

5   CRUNDELL, H.W. "Marston's 'Drusus.'" TLS, 30 October,
     p. 803.
         Suggests that the actor Drusus referred to in The Scourge
     of Villainy is Shakespeare.

6   EIDSON, J.O. "A Marston Note." MLN 52:198.
         Points out two quotations from The Aeneid in Antonio and
     Mellida.

7   _____. "Senecan Elements in Marston's Antonio and Mellida."
     MLN 52:196-97.
         Points out quotations from Seneca and from The Aeneid in
     Antonio and Mellida.

8   FARMER, A.J. "Une source de Eastward Hoe: Rabelais." EA
     1:325.
         Suggests that Touchstone's remarks on cuckoldry in Act V,
     scene v, 11. 212-27 of Eastward Hoe were derived from the third
     book of Gargantua and Pantagruel, Chapter 38. Suggests that
     Marston might well have authored this speech, since it recalls
     certain remarks of Crispinella in The Dutch Courtezan.

9   LAWRENCE, W.J. Speeding Up Shakespeare: Studies of the
     Bygone Theatre and Drama. London: Argonaut Press, pp. 107-8,
     123-24. Reprint. New York: Benjamin Blom, 1968.
         Provides basic discussion of Eastward Hoe and Jack Drum's
     Entertainment.

10   MILLS, LAURENS. One Soul in Bodies Twain: Friendship in
     Tudor Literature and Stuart Drama. Bloomington, Ind.:
     Principia Press, pp. 179, 309-10, 327-29, 335, 341.
         Discusses the treatment of the theme of feigned friendship
     in The Malcontent, and credits Marston with introducing to the
     English stage the plot device of a woman demanding of her lover
     that he kill his best friend.
         The Dutch Courtezan

11   SCHÜCKING, LEVIN LUDWIG. The Meaning of Hamlet. Oxford:
     Clarendon Press, pp. 26-27 and passim. Reprint. New York:
     Barnes & Noble, 1966.

Points out traditional elements of the revenge play in
Antonio's Revenge.

1938

1   ANON. "The Plays of John Marston: Tragedy and Social
    Satire." TLS, 26 March, p. 209.
        Reviews vol. 2 of Wood's edition of Marston's plays (Col-
lected edition 1938.1). Attempts to evaluate Marston's plays.
Sees Sophonisba as a true tragedy, faults The Dutch Courtezan for
its obscenity and extravagant farce, but finds The Fawn a de-
lightful, easygoing comedy. Views What You Will as faulty, too
absorbed in satirizing contemporaries of Marston.

2   CAMPBELL, OSCAR JAMES. Comicall Satire and Shakespeare's
    Troilus and Cressida. San Marino, Calif.: Huntington
    Library, pp. 135-84.
        Concentrates upon the satirical elements in Marston's early
plays, such as the portraits of fools representing various follies and proclivities toward vice, and sees Marston as inferior
to Jonson as a satirist. Suggests that Marston's problem as a
dramatist was his inability to express his satiric impulse in a
suitable dramatic form. Observes that his plots drew upon
farce and melodrama and holds that Marston could not harmonize
these dramatic styles with his compulsion to write diatribes.
Reprinted: 1971.40. For a discussion of Campbell's views, see
1949.6.
        Antonio and Mellida, Antonio's Revenge, Jack Drum's
Entertainment, The Scourge of Villainy, Satiromastix, What You
Will

3   CAWLEY, ROBERT RALSTON. The Voyagers and Elizabethan Drama.
    Boston: Heath, passim. Reprint. New York: Kraus Reprint,
    1966.
        Provides passing comments and observations upon Marston's
attitudes toward travel and the exploration of the new world.

4   HOWARTH, R.G. "Dipsas in Lyly and Marston." NQ 174:24-25.
        Discusses the origin of the name "Dipsas," used as that of
the witch in Lyly's Endymion and as an epithet applied to
Maquerelle in The Malcontent.

5   KOSZUL, A. Review of Vol. 2 of Wood's edition of Marston's
    plays. EA 3:147-48.
        Believes that Wood (Collected edition 1938.1) should have
taken greater pains to emend the text, particularly its punctuation. Also faults Wood for not attempting to explain numerous
obscurities.

6   McGINN, DONALD J. "A New Date for Antonio's Revenge." PMLA
    53:129-37.

Suggests that the date of the composition of <u>Antonio's</u> <u>Revenge</u> would be either the winter or spring of 1601. Bases this theory of Jonson's attack upon the play in <u>The</u> <u>Poetaster</u> and other evidence. Concludes, then, that Shakespeare, not Marston, revitalized the revenge play and that Marston, having seen Shakespeare's <u>Hamlet</u>, revamped his plans for a sequel to <u>Antonio</u> <u>and</u> <u>Mellida</u> and thus created a revenge play. For a discussion of some of the ideas touched upon in this essay, see 1938.7.

7 _____. <u>Shakespeare's</u> <u>Influence</u> <u>on</u> <u>the</u> <u>Drama</u> <u>of</u> <u>His</u> <u>Age:</u> <u>Studied</u> <u>in</u> <u>Hamlet</u>. New Brunswick: Rutgers University Press, passim.
Provides numerous comments on Marston's career and his debt to Shakespeare, and cites Marston's borrowings from Shakespeare. Expands the treatment of some of the ideas in 1938.6.
<u>Antonio</u> <u>and</u> <u>Mellida</u>, <u>Antonio's</u> <u>Revenge</u>

*8 MERES, FRANCIS. <u>Palladis</u> <u>Tamia</u>. <u>Wits</u> <u>Treasury</u> <u>Being</u> <u>the</u> <u>Second</u> <u>Parts</u> <u>of</u> <u>Wits</u> <u>Common</u> <u>Wealth</u>. New York: Scholars Facsimiles and Reprints.
Cited in Tannenbaum 1940.5. Facsimile edition of 1598.2. For a selection from this work, see 1904.8.

9 NICOLL, ALLARDYCE. <u>Stuart</u> <u>Masques</u> <u>and</u> <u>the</u> <u>Renaissance</u> <u>Stage</u>. New York: Harcourt, Brace, pp. 40, 43, 67, 158, 215, 216.
Provides passing comments upon the <u>Entertainment</u> <u>of</u> <u>Alice,</u> <u>Dowager-Countess</u> <u>of</u> <u>Derby</u>.

10 SCHÜCKING, LEVIN LUDWIG. "The Baroque Character of the Elizabethan Tragic Hero." <u>PBA</u> 24:85-111.
Provides passing comments upon the baroque treatment of Marston's characters. Reprinted: 1938.11.

11 _____. <u>The</u> <u>Baroque</u> <u>Treatment</u> <u>of</u> <u>the</u> <u>Elizabethan</u> <u>Tragic</u> <u>Hero</u>. London: H. Milford, passim. Reprint. Folcroft, Penn.: Folcroft Press, 1969.
Hardcover edition: 1938.10.

12 TILLEY, M.P. "Charles Lamb, Marston, and Du Bartas." <u>MLN</u> 53:494-98.
Points out Marston's borrowings in <u>The</u> <u>Malcontent</u> from Du Bartas.

<u>1939</u>

1 DRAPER, JOHN. <u>The</u> <u>Hamlet</u> <u>of</u> <u>Shakespeare's</u> <u>Audience</u>. Durham: Duke University Press, p. 178. Reprint. New York: Octagon Books, 1966.
Discusses the cause of Lampatho's melancholy in <u>What</u> <u>You</u> <u>Will</u>.

2   PERRY, HENRY TEN EYCK. <u>Masters</u> <u>of</u> <u>Dramatic</u> <u>Comedy</u> <u>and</u> <u>Their</u>
      <u>Social</u> <u>Themes</u>. Cambridge, Mass.: Harvard University Press,
      pp. 95-97.
        Discusses Jonson's <u>Poetaster</u> and the War of the Theaters.

3   PRAZ, MARIO. Review of Vol. 2. of Wood's edition of Marston's
      Plays. <u>ES</u> 21:24-26.
        Sees <u>Sophonisba</u> as an interesting play, but not great art.
      Judges it weakened by abstract characterizations, stilted dic-
      tion, and a puerile imagination. Sees <u>The</u> <u>Fawn</u> and <u>What</u> <u>You</u> <u>Will</u>
      as lacking interest. Suggests that in some instances Wood (Col-
      lected edition 1938.1) has provided a very good text of the
      plays.

4   STOLL, ELMER EDGAR. "Jaques and the Antiquaries." <u>MLN</u> 54:
      79-85.
        A criticism in part of 1935.4. Attacks those critics who
      would seek to analyze and understand the characters of such
      malcontents as Shakespeare's Jaques in <u>As</u> <u>You</u> <u>Like</u> <u>It</u> and
      Marston's Malevole in <u>The</u> <u>Malcontent</u> by consulting Elizabethan
      medical books and stresses that these dramatic creations are
      characters, not case histories. Supports author's earlier views
      in 1906.11. Reprinted: 1944.8.

5   WELLS, HENRY WILLIS. <u>Elizabethan</u> <u>and</u> <u>Jacobean</u> <u>Playwrights</u>.
      New York: Columbia University Press, pp. 25-31 and passim.
      Reprint. Westport, Conn.: Greenwood Press, 1975.
        Presents a general discussion of Marston.
      <u>Antonio</u> <u>and</u> <u>Mellida</u>, <u>Antonio's</u> <u>Revenge</u>, <u>The</u> <u>Malcontent</u>

6   WEST, ROBERT HUNTER. <u>The</u> <u>Invisible</u> <u>World</u>: <u>A</u> <u>Study</u> <u>of</u>
      <u>Pneumatology</u> <u>in</u> <u>Elizabethan</u> <u>Drama</u>. Athens: University of
      Georgia Press, passim. Reprint. New York: Octagon Books,
      1969.
        Provides comments upon Renaissance superstitions as evi-
      denced in Elizabethan plays and upon the use in the plays of such
      supernatural characters as ghosts and witches.
      <u>Antonio's</u> <u>Revenge</u>, <u>Sophonisba</u>

1940

1   BOWERS, FREDSON. <u>Elizabethan</u> <u>Revenge</u> <u>Tragedy,</u> <u>1587-1642</u>.
      Princeton: Princeton University Press, pp. 118-25, 130-32,
      and passim. Reprint. 1966.
        Discusses <u>Antonio's</u> <u>Revenge</u> within the tradition of the
      revenge play, sees Marston borrowing from Kyd and Shakespeare,
      and praises the portrait of Piero as being more realistic than
      that of other revenge play villains, but feels that near the end
      of the play Marston turns him into a caricature. Suggests that
      Marston does not condemn Antonio's exacting vengeance, but views
      him as a dutiful son avenging his father's murder. Pronounces

the play weakened by Marston's straining for heightened effects,
a practice that leads him to write melodrama and to produce
extravagant emotionalism. Sees The Malcontent as a comedy, but
points out revenge play elements in this work, such as Altofronto's
disguise, and suggests that Marston was one of the first to base
a plot upon multiple intrigues. Sees the portrayal of Mendoza, a
Machiavellian who attempts to gain power by overthrowing his vil-
lainous master, as a force popularizing this character type on
the Elizabethan stage.

2   CAWLEY, ROBERT RALSTON. Unpathed Waters: Studies in the
      Influence of the Voyagers in Elizabethan Literature.
      Princeton: Princeton University Press, passim. Reprint. New
      York: Octagon Books, 1967.
         Provides comments and observations upon Marston's attitudes
      toward travel and the exploration of the New World.

3   HARBAGE, ALFRED, ed. Annals of English Drama, 975-1700.
      Philadelphia: University of Pennsylvania Press, passim.
         Lists plays by the year in which they were probably pro-
      duced, gives the name of the theater in which the first produc-
      tion of the play was given, provides the play's generic
      classification, and presents the date of the first printed
      edition. Revised edition: 1964.3.
         Antonio and Mellida, Antonio's Revenge, The Dutch
      Courtezan, Eastward Hoe, The Fawn, Jack Drum's Entertainment,
      Histriomastix, The Insatiate Countess, The Malcontent,
      Satiromastix, Sophonisba, What You Will

4   SOBEL, BERNARD. The Theatre Handbook and Digest of Plays.
      New York: Lathrop, Lee, & Shepard, pp. 522-23.
         Provides a general article on Marston.

5   TANNENBAUM, SAMUEL A., ed. John Marston, A Concise
      Bibliography. Elizabethan Bibliographies, no. 15.
      New York: Samuel A. Tannenbaum, 42 pp.
         Provides a basic bibliography of Marston, including edi-
      tions of his works, books and articles about Marston, and discus-
      sions of Marston in books on Elizabethan drama, Shakespeare, and
      social and cultural history. Provides sparse annotations and
      does not supply full titles of works listed. At times provides
      books and articles with titles chosen by the editor, titles he
      apparently feels are more indicative of the subject matter than
      the original titles.

6   WELLS, HENRY WILLIS, ed. A Chronological List of Extant Plays
      Produced in or about London, 1581-1642. New York: Columbia
      University Press, passim.
         Provides a listing of these plays and gives the dates when
      they were first performed.

1941

1 CLARK, A.M. <u>Thomas</u> Heywood: <u>Playwright</u> and <u>Miscellanist</u>.
Oxford: Blackwell, passim. Reprint. New York: Russell &
Russell, 1967.
Provides general comments upon Marston.

2 CLARK, ELEANOR GRACE. <u>Raleigh</u> and <u>Marlowe</u>: <u>A Study</u> in <u>Eliza-</u>
<u>bethan</u> <u>Fustian</u>. New York: Fordham University Press, passim.
Reprints 1937.4 as the first part of this study.

3 HARRISON, G.B. <u>A Jacobean</u> <u>Journal</u>: <u>Being a Record of Those</u>
<u>Things</u> <u>Most</u> <u>Talked</u> <u>of</u> <u>during</u> <u>the</u> <u>Years</u> <u>1603-1606</u>. London:
G. Routledge, passim.
Written as though the author were a Jacobean recording
events of prominence and interest. The goal is to give the
student of literature a sense of what living in the time of
Shakespeare was like. Provides plot summaries of Marston's plays
and discusses the controversy surrounding <u>Eastward Hoe</u>.
The <u>Dutch</u> <u>Courtezan</u>, The <u>Fawn</u>, The <u>Malcontent</u>, Sophonisba

4 KING, ARTHUR H. <u>The Language</u> of <u>Satirized Characters</u> in
<u>Poetaster</u>: <u>A Socio-Stylistic</u> <u>Analysis,</u> <u>1597-1602</u>. London:
Williams & Norgate, passim.
Provides passing comments on Marston.

5 MUNCE, T. EDWARD, Jr. "Southey and Marston." <u>TLS</u>,
25 October, p. 536.
Suggests that Southey drew from <u>The Scourge</u> of <u>Villainy</u> as
a source of a quip recorded in one of <u>Coleridge's</u> letters. For a
response to this article, see 1942.2.

6 NESS, FREDERIC W. <u>The Use of Rhyme</u> in <u>Shakespeare's</u> <u>Plays</u>.
New Haven: Yale University Press, p. 24. Reprint. Hamden,
Conn.: Shoestring Press, 1969.
Comments upon Marston's fondness for rhyme.

7 PRAZ, MARIO. Review of Vol. 3. of Wood's edition of Marston's
plays. <u>ES</u> 23:55-58.
Faults Wood's sparsity of notes for <u>The Insatiate Countess</u>
and lack of notes for other plays in the volume (Collected edition 1939.1). Discusses <u>The Insatiate Countess,</u> points out
faults, sees its dramatic style verging upon parody, but concludes that it is neither parody nor tragedy, but a "hybrid
product," typical of Marston's "hybrid talent."

8 RANDOLPH, MARY CLAIRE. "The Medical Concept in English
Renaissance Satiric Theory: Its Possible Relationships and
Implications." <u>SP</u> 38:125-57.
Provides passing comments on Marston.

9   ____. "Thomas Drant's Definition of Satire." NQ 180:416-18.
     Calls attention to an Elizabethan definition of satire and discusses the satirical climate in which Marston wrote.

10   SAMPSON, GEORGE. The Concise Cambridge History of English
     Literature. Cambridge: Cambridge University Press, pp. 303-4.
     Presents a general discussion of Marston. Revised edition: 1970.23.

1942

1   BAKELESS, JOHN. The Tragicall History of Christopher Marlowe.
     Vol. 2. Cambridge, Mass.: Harvard University Press, pp. 45, 117-19, 170, 187, 285.
     Discusses possible influences of Marlowe's Hero and Leander upon Marston's The Metamorphosis of Pigmalion's Image.

2   COON, ARTHUR M. "Southey and Marston." TLS, 31 January, p. 55.
     Seeks to refute Edward Munce's belief (1941.5) that Southey in making a quip drew upon Marston.

3   DAVENPORT, ARNOLD. "An Elizabethan Controversy: Harvey and
     Nashe." NQ 182:116-19.
     Suggests that themes and subjects of quarrels between Gabriel Harvey and Thomas Nashe were picked up by Marston and Hall.

4   ____. "The Quarrel of the Satirists." MLR 37:123-30.
     Discusses John Weever's role in the Marston-Hall quarrel and points out that in 1599 Weever was on Marston's side, but that in 1600 he was on Hall's. Discusses Weever's Faunus and Melliflora and points out criticisms of and references to Marston in this work. Also suggests that Weever wrote The Whipping of the Satyre in which Marston, Guilpin, and Jonson were attacked.

5   RANDOLPH, MARY CLAIRE. "The Structural Design of the Formal
     Verse Satire." PQ 21:368-84.
     Discusses Marston and the practice of grouping satires into books.

1943

1   BABB, LAWRENCE. "Scientific Theories of Grief in Some Eliza-
     bethan Plays." SP 40:502-19.
     Discusses the effect of grief upon Piero in The Malcontent within the context of Elizabethan theories of this emotion.

2   No entry.

3 BENTLEY, GERALD EADES. "John Cotgrave's English Treasury of
   Wit and Language and the Elizabethan Drama." SP 40:186-202.
        Provides passing references to Marston's plays quoted in
   this collection.

4 BERRINGER, RALPH W. "Jonson's Cynthia's Revels and the War of
   the Theatres." PQ 22:1-22.
        Suggests that Hedon in Cynthia's Revels is not a portrait
   of Marston and that the War of the Theaters was more limited than
   many scholars believe.

5 BROOKS, ALDEN. Will Shakespeare and the Dyer's Hand. New
   York: Scribner's, passim.
        Provides passing comments on Marston.

6 CAMPBELL, OSCAR JAMES. Shakespeare's Satire. London: Oxford
   University Press, passim.
        Provides general comments on Marston, the satire in his
   plays, and his influence upon Elizabethan satire.
        The Malcontent

7 COLEMAN, EDWARD, ed. The Jew in English Drama: An Annotated
   Bibliography. New York: New York Public Library, pp. 243,
   244. Reprint. New York: Ktav Publishing House, 1970.
        Cites Eastward Hoe and Jack Drum's Entertainment as plays
   containing Jewish characters.

8 CRUNDELL, H.W. "John Marston." NQ 184:175.
        Comments briefly upon the collected editions of Marston's
   works (Collected edition 1856.1; Collected edition 1887.1). A
   response to 1943.9. For emendations to Bullen's edition, see
   1887.1; 1893.2; 1896.2; 1903.2; 1906.4; 1908.2; 1943.10; 1948.6.

9 HALSTEAD, W.L. "An Explanation for the Two Editions of
   Marston's Fawne." SP 40:25-32.
        Argues that the second printing of the play should be
   considered a separate edition.

10 LOANE, GEORGE. "Notes on Marston." NQ 184:71-74.
        Supplies textual emendations to Bullen's edition of
   Marston's works (Collected edition 1887.1). For a response to
   this article, see 1943.7. For other emendations to Bullen's
   edition, see 1887.1; 1893.2; 1896.2; 1903.2; 1906.4; 1908.8;
   1943.8; 1948.6.

11 PARROTT, THOMAS MARC, and ROBERT HAMILTON BALL. A Short View
   of Elizabethan Drama. New York: Scribner's, pp. 153-58, 210-
   12, and passim.
        Provides a general discussion of Marston and gives plot
   summaries of his plays.
        Antonio and Mellida, Antonio's Revenge, The Dutch
   Courtezan, The Fawn,The Malcontent, Sophonisba, What You Will

12   STEIN, ARNOLD. "The Second English Satirist." MLR 38:273-78.
     Argues that despite his quarrel with Joseph Hall, Marston
had little firsthand knowledge of Latin satirists such as Juvenal
and Persius and turned to Hall's satires as sources of inspiration and content for his own. Stresses that, therefore, Marston
imitates Hall in cultivating obscurity in choosing names for
satirized characters, in selecting character types for satire,
and in various other ways. Judges that much of the ineptitude of
Marston's verse satires can be traced to his attempt to imitate
Hall.
     Certain Satires, The Scourge of Villainy

                              1944

1   GORDON, GEORGE. Shakespearean Comedy and Other Studies.
     London: Oxford University Press, pp. 136-37.
     Discusses Marston's vocabulary as depicted by Jonson in
Poetaster.

2   GRIERSON, HERBERT C.J., and J.C. SMITH. A Critical History of
     English Poetry. London: Chatto & Windus, pp. 80, 88, 134.
     Reprint. 1965.
     Provides passing comments on Marston.

3   HIGGINS, MICHAEL. "The Convention of the Stoic Hero as
     Handled by Marston." MLR 39:338-46.
     Suggests that Marston, like many of his contemporaries who
felt themselves threatened by a world of evil and corruption,
turned to Stoicism as a means of finding a code of behavior that
would enable them to confront an evil world and that Marston
introduced the Stoical type to the world of tragedy. Suggests,
however, that Marston's satirical bent, his moralism and didacticism, and his interest in ideas rather than persons led him to
create not engaging human beings but lifeless mouthpieces for
ideas and examples of conduct. Hence, his stoical characters
such as Antonio, Pandulpho, and Andrugio are merely walking
abstractions. Also contrasts Marston's failure with this character type with Shakespeare's success in creating Stoical men whose
tragedies powerfully engage our sympathies and other emotions.

4   LeCOMTE, EDWARD. Endymion in England: The Literary History
     of a Greek Myth. Morningside Heights, N.Y.: King's Crown
     Press,pp. 7, 41, 45, 60.
     Points out references to the myth of Endymion in Marston's
plays.

5   SIMPSON, PERCY. "The Problem of Authorship of Eastward Hoe."
     PMLA 59:715-25.
     Discusses various theories as to the shares of authorship
of Eastward Hoe, then presents a new theory as to which portions

were written by Chapman, Marston, and Jonson. Assigns the initial idea for the play, act one, and scenes and passages from the rest of the play to Marston.

6   STEIN, ARNOLD. "Donne and the Satiric Spirit." <u>ELH</u> 11: 266-82.
     Provides passing comments on Marston.

7   _____. "Donne's Harshness and the Elizabethan Tradition." <u>SP</u> 42:390-409.
     Discusses Marston's poetic style.

8   STOLL, ELMER EDGAR. "Jaques and Antiquaries." In <u>From Shakespeare to Joyce: Authors, Critics, Literature and Life</u>. Garden City, N.Y.: Doubleday, Doran, pp. 138-64.
     Reprint of 1939.4.

1945

1   BENTLEY, GERALD EADES, ed. <u>Shakespeare and Jonson</u>. Chicago: University of Chicago Press, pp. 16, 88, 189, 200, 211, 263.
     Reprints contemporary references to <u>Eastward Hoe</u> and Langbaine's account (1691.1) of Marston's and Jonson's relationship.

2   BUSH, DOUGLAS. <u>English Literature in the Earlier Seventeenth Century</u>. Oxford History of English Literature. Oxford: Clarendon Press, passim.
     Provides passing comments on Marston. Revised edition: 1962.8.

3   TALBERT, ERNEST WILLIAM. "The Purpose and Technique of Jonson's <u>Poetaster</u>." <u>SP</u> 42:225-52.
     Provides passing comments on Marston satirized as the character Crispinus.

1946

1   BOAS, FREDERICK S. <u>An Introduction to Stuart Drama</u>. Oxford: Oxford University Press, pp. 132-47 and passim.
     Provides a general article on Marston.
     <u>Antonio and Mellida</u>, <u>Antonio's Revenge</u>, <u>The Dutch Courtezan</u>, <u>Eastward Hoe</u>, <u>The Fawn</u>, <u>Histriomastix</u>, <u>The Insatiate Countess</u>, <u>The Malcontent</u>, <u>Sophonisba</u>

2   BOWERS, FREDSON. "Notes on Standing Type in Elizabethan Printing." <u>PBSA</u> 40:204-24.
     Discusses early editions of <u>The Fawn</u> and <u>The Malcontent</u>.

3   ELLIS-FERMOR, UNA. The Frontiers of Drama. London: Methuen,
     p. 86.
          Compares imagery in Antonio and Mellida with that in
     Webster's plays and Tourneur's The Revenger's Tragedy.

4   HARRISON, G.B. A Jacobean Journal: Being a Record of Those
     Things Most Talked of during the Years 1603-1606. Rev. ed.
     London: G. Routledge, passim.
          Revised edition of 1941.3.

5   HODGES, C. WALTER. Shakespeare and the Players. London:
     Benn, passim.
          Provides passing comments on Marston.

6   HUGHES, LEO, and ARTHUR H. SCOUTEN. "Some Theatrical Adapta-
     tions of a Picaresque Tale." Texas Studies in English,
     1945-46:98-114.
          Discusses the similarities and differences among the adap-
     tations of the Cocledemoy subplot of The Dutch Courtezan.

7   NICOLL, ALLARDYCE. British Drama: An Historical Survey from
     the Beginning to the Present Time. New York: Barnes & Noble,
     pp. 117, 152, 154, 172-73.
          Provides a general discussion of Marston.

8   ORSINI, NAPOLEONE. "'Policy' or the Language of Elizabethan
     Machiavellianism." JWCI 9:122-34.
          Quotes from Marston to illustrate Elizabethan ideas of
     Machiavellianism.

9   PERRY, WILLIAM. "A Latin Quotation in Wonder of Women and
     Woman Is a Weathercock." NQ 191:33-34.
          Points out a quotation from Persius used in Field's play
     and in Sophonisba.

                              1947

1   GRAY, HENRY DAVID. "The Chamberlain's Men and the Poetaster."
     MLR 47:173-79.
          Discusses the War of the Theaters.

2   HOLZKNECHT, KARL J. Outlines of Tudor and Stuart Plays. New
     York: Barnes & Noble, pp. 228-39.
          Provides detailed plot summaries of The Dutch Courtezan and
     The Malcontent.

3   PERRY, WILLIAM. "Eastward Ho! and A Woman Is a Weathercock."
     MLN 62:131-32.
          Suggests that Nathan Field knew Eastward Hoe and drew upon
     it in composing his own play.

4   SCHÜCKING, LEVIN LUDWIG. Shakespeare und der Tragödienstil
     seiner Zeit. Bern: A. Francke, passim.
     Provides passing comments on Marston.

5   WALLACE, LAWRENCE B. Fletcher, Beaumont, and Company:
     Entertainers to the Jacobean Gentry. Morningside Heights,
     N.Y.: King's Crown Press, passim.
     Provides passing comments on Marston.

1948

1   ARMSTRONG, WILLIAM A. "The Influence of Seneca and
     Machiavelli on the Elizabethan Tyrant." RES 24:19-35.
         Discusses Piero of Antonio and Mellida and Antonio's
     Revenge as an example of a certain type of Machiavellian stage
     villain who performs his evils out of purely personal motives and
     whose actions have little or nothing to do with politics and
     political realities.

2   BRERETON, JOHN Le GAY. "John Marston." In Writings on
     Elizabethan Drama. Melbourne: Melbourne University Press,
     pp. 41-64.
         Reprint of 1904.4.

3   BROOKE, C.F. TUCKER. "The Renaissance." In A Literary
     History of England. Edited by Albert C. Baugh. New York:
     Appleton-Century-Crofts, pp. 563-65.
         Provides a general discussion of Marston. Revised edition:
     1967.2.

4   CRAIG, HARDIN. An Interpretation of Shakespeare. New York:
     Dryden Press,pp. 116, 179, 237, 338.
         Provides passing comments on Marston.

5   JOHNSON, FRANCIS R. "Shakespearean Imagery and Senecan Imita-
     tion." In Joseph Quincy Adams Memorial Studies. Washington,
     D.C.: Folger Shakespeare Library, pp. 33-53.
         Discusses the use of a Senecan sententia in The Malcontent.

6   KRZYZANOWSKI, J. "Some Conjectural Remarks on Elizabethan
     Dramatists." NQ 193:233-34.
         Provides emendations to both Certain Satires and The
     Scourge of Villainy as given in Bullen's edition (Collected
     edition 1887.1). For other suggested emendations to Bullen's
     edition, see 1887.1; 1893.2; 1896.2; 1903.2; 1906.4; 1943.7, 9;
     1948.6.

7   PAUL, HENRY N. The Royal Play of Macbeth: When, Why, and How
     It Was Written by Shakespeare. New York: Macmillan, pp. 324,
     361, 403. Reprint. New York: Octagon Books, 1971.
         Sophonisba discussed.

8   SPENCER, THEODORE.   "The Elizabethan Malcontent."   In Joseph
    Quincy Adams Memorial Studies. Washington, D.C.:   Folger
    Shakespeare Library, pp. 523-35.
        Considers the question of why malcontent characters became
    so prominent in late Elizabethan and Jacobean drama and suggests
    that the appearance of this character type in the 1590s reflects
    an intensifying pessimism in the English consciousness. Contains
    much information on traditions of pessimistic thought and Eliza-
    bethan medical theories of melancholy. Divides the character
    type of the melancholy man as portrayed in Elizabethan drama into
    five classifications: the naturally melancholy men; the diseased
    melancholy man; the man who affects melancholy; the malcontent,
    who feels himself an outcast from the social order; and the
    satirical railer, who attacks vices and crimes. Points out that
    these types are not mutually exclusive. Discusses Marston's
    Antonio from Antonio's Revenge as an example of the naturally
    melancholy man and Malevole from The Malcontent as an example of
    the malcontent. Includes other observations on Marston and the
    portrayal of melancholy characters. Reprinted:: 1966.30.

9   WEEVER, JOHN. Faunus and Melliflora. Edited by Arnold
    Davenport. Liverpool: University Press of Liverpool; London:
    Hodder & Stoughton, passim.
        Modern edition of 1600.1.

                                    1949

1   ANON. The Return from Parnassus. In The Three Parnassus
    Plays. Edited by J.B. Leishman. London: Ivor Nicholson &
    Watson, pp. 3-12, 215-367, 369-71.
        Presents a detailed discussion of the satirical climate in
    which the Parnassus plays were written and in which Marston
    penned his satires. Also gives attention to the possible satiri-
    zation of Marston in The Return from Parnassus. An appendix
    discusses the War of the Theaters and the purge Shakespeare
    supposedly gave Jonson. For other editions, see 1606.1; 1874.1;
    1879.1; 1886.1; 1904.1 (selection); 1905.1; 1907.1.

2   CHUTE, MARCHETTE Shakespeare of London. New York: Dutton,
    passim.
        Provides passing comments on Marston.

3   GRAVES, ROBERT. "The Sources of the Tempest." In The Common
    Asphodel: Collected Essays on Poetry, 1922-1949. London:
    Hamish Hamilton, pp. 27-49.
        Presents in more detail the idea first given in 1925.3.

4   HYDE, MARY CRAPO. Playwriting for Elizabethans, 1600-1605.
    New York: Columbia University Press passim.
        Provides passing comments on Marston.

5   LEVIN, HARRY. "An Echo from The Spanish Tragedy." MLN
     64:297-302.
         On the basis of the relationship of the scenes involving
     painters in Antonio and Mellida and The Spanish Tragedy and of
     verbal echoes in the two plays, suggests that Marston was imitat-
     ing the unknown author who wrote additions to the latter play.

6   TILLYARD, E.M.W. Shakespeare's Problem Plays. Toronto:
     University of Toronto Press, pp. 46-48. Reprint. 1971.
         Discusses Oscar James Campbell's view (1938.2) that Troilus
     and Cressida was influenced by the satirical plays of Marston and
     Jonson.

7   URE, PETER. "John Marston's Sophonisba: A Reconsideration."
     DUJ 10:81-90.
         Concurs with T.S. Eliot's view (1934.2) that Sophonisba is
     a successful play and analyzes it. Sees the question of situa-
     tional ethics as central to the play and suggests that Marston
     ultimately decides that virtuous conduct in some situations
     should never be compromised. Also comments upon Marston's preoc-
     cupation with Stoical heroes and believes that in Massinissa and
     Sophonisba, Marston has finally succeeded in creating forceful
     and dramatic Stoical characters. Views the play as a powerful
     tragedy and the dramatic culmination of Marston's preoccupations
     with Stoicism, morality, and lust. Also gives attention to
     Marston's poetic style, the intellectual traditions that influ-
     enced his writing of the play, and stylistic and thematic paral-
     lels with other Elizabethan plays.

8   WILCOX, JOHN. "Informal Publication of Late Sixteenth-Century
     Verse Satire." HLQ 13:191-200.
         Provides passing comments on Marston.

                              1950

1   CRAIG, HARDIN. The Literature of the English Renaissance,
     1485-1600. A History of English Literature, no. 2. Oxford:
     Oxford University Press, pp. 159-61 and passim. Reprint. New
     York: Collier Books, 1962.
         Provides a general discussion of Marston and plot summaries
     of Antonio and Mellida, Antonio's Revenge, The Dutch Courtezan,
     The Malcontent.

2   DOWNER, ALAN. The British Drama: A Handbook and Brief
     Chronicle. New York: Appleton-Century-Crofts, pp. 113-15
     and passim.
         Provides a general discussion of Antonio and Mellida,
     Antonio's Revenge, and The Malcontent.

3   HAYDN, HIRAM. The Counter-Renaissance. New York:
     Scribner's, passim.
         Provides passing comments on Marston.

4   HOLZKNECHT, KARL J. The Backgrounds of Shakespeare's Plays.
    New York: American Book Co., passim.
    Provides passing comments on Marston.

5   LEECH, CLIFFORD. Shakespeare's Tragedies and Other Studies in
    Seventeenth Century Drama. London: Chatto & Windus, passim.
        Provides passing comments on Antonio and Mellida and
    Antonio's Revenge.

6   McNEIR, WALDO. "Marston versus Davies and Terpsichore." PQ
    29:430-34.
        Suggests that in The Scourge of Villainy Marston attacks
    Sir John Davies and his poem Orchestra.

7   MASON, EUDO C. "Satire on Women and Sex in Elizabethan
    Tragedy." ES 31:1-10.
        Discusses the disillusioned view of women as vile, lecher-
    ous creatures and the obsessional view of sex as a degrading,
    ultimately meaningless experience, which appear in Jacobean lit-
    erature, particularly the drama. Suggests that the disillusion-
    ment with women and sex tormented writers because it made life
    seem meaningless and that the disillusionment was particularly
    acute because these writers felt a need to idealize women and
    romantic love. Provides passing comments upon Marston and quota-
    tions from his writings to illustrate these ideas.

8   PARKES, HENRY BAMFORD. "Nature's Diverse Laws: The Double
    Vision of the Elizabethans." SR 58:402-18.
    Provides passing comments on Marston.

9   PETER, J.D. "John Marston's Plays." Scrutiny 17:132-53.
        Gives considerable attention to Marston's poetic abilities,
    pointing out strengths and weaknesses, and to his dramatic abili-
    ties, showing that Marston often wrote very effectively for the
    stage, but concludes that Marston had difficulty in welding the
    disparate elements of his plays into artistic wholes. Suggests
    that this problem is especially evidenced in Marston's continued
    and widespread use of sexual and scatological humor, which under-
    cuts his avowed purpose as a moral satirist and indicter of man's
    lusts and perversions.
        Antonio and Mellida, Antonio's Revenge, The Dutch
    Courtezan, The Fawn, The Malcontent, Sophonisba

10 ROSSITER, A.P. English Drama from Early Times to the Eliza-
    bethans: Its Background, Origin, and Development. New York:
    Hutchinson's University Library, passim. Reprint. New York:
    Barnes & Noble, 1967.
    Provides passing comments on Marston.

11 WEDGWOOD, C.V. Seventeenth-Century English Literature.
    London: Oxford University Press, pp. 34, 35, 40, 41-42.
    Provides a general discussion of Marston.

12   ZOCCA, LOUIS. Elizabethan Narrative Poetry. New Brunswick:
      Rutgers University, pp. 123, 174, 193, 279-82. Reprint: New
      York: Octagon Books, 1970.
          Discusses The Metamorphosis of Pigmalion's Image as a
      satire upon Elizabethan amatory verse.

                                  1951

1   BABB, LAWRENCE. The Elizabethan Malady: A Study of Melan-
      cholia in English Literature from 1580 to 1642. East Lansing:
      Michigan State University Press, passim.
          Provides numerous comments upon Marston's treatments of
      malcontents, love melancholy, and various psychological disturb-
      ances. Also quotes from Marston to illustrate Elizabethan ideas
      concerning these problems.

2   BOWDEN, WILLIAM R. The English Dramatic Lyric, 1603-1642: A
      Study in Stuart Dramatic Technique. New Haven: Yale Univer-
      sity Press, pp. 180-85.
          Provides passing comments upon the songs in Antonio and
      Mellida, Antonio's Revenge, The Dutch Courtezan, Eastward Hoe,
      The Fawn, Histriomastix, The Insatiate Countess, Jack Drum's
      Entertainment, The Malcontent, Sophonisba.

3   [BRETON, NICHOLAS.] No Whippinge, nor Trippinge: but a Kinde
      Friendly Snippinge. In The Whipper Pamphlets, Part 2. Edited
      by Arnold Davenport. Liverpool: University Press of
      Liverpool, pp. 1-34.
          An original spelling edition of 1601.1.

4   CARRIÈRE, FÉLIX. Le Théâtre de Thomas Kyd: Contribution à
      l'étude du drame élizabéthain. Toulouse: Edouard Privat,
      pp. 55, 170, 297, 385.
          Provides general comments on Marston.

5   ELIOT, T.S. "John Marston." In Selected Essays. 3d ed.
      London: Faber & Faber, pp. 221-33.
          Reprint of 1934.2. Reprinted: 1934.3; 1956.11.

6   [GUILPIN, EVERARD.] The Whipper of Satyre his Pennance in a
      White Sheete: Or the Beadles Confutation. In The Whipper
      Pamphlets, Part 2. Edited by Arnold Davenport. Liverpool:
      University Press of Liverpool, pp. 35-49.
          An original spelling edition of 1601.2.

7   HUNTER, G.K. "The Marking of Sententiae in Elizabethan
      Printed Plays, Poems, and Romances." Library, 5th ser.
      6:71-88, 183-85.
          Suggests that at times Marston took an active hand in
      marking sententiae in the printed versions of his plays.
      The Dutch Courtezan, The Malcontent

8   I[NGRAM], W[ILLIAM.] The Whipping of the Satyre. In The
     Whipper Pamphlets, Part 1. Edited by Arnold Davenport.
     Liverpool: University Press of Liverpool, pp. 1-61.
         An original spelling edition of 1601.3. Davenport, how-
     ever, suggests that John Weever, not Ingram, authored this work.

9   JACQUOT, JEAN. George Chapman, sa vie, sa poésie, son
     théatre, sa pensée. Paris: Société D'Edition les Belles
     Lettres, passim.
         Provides passing comments on Eastward Hoe.

10   JOSEPH, B.L. Elizabethan Acting. London: Oxford University
     Press, pp. 144, 145. Reprint. New York: Octagon Books,
     1979.
         Suggests that the actor portraying Malevole in The
     Malcontent would have to use his imagination and experience to
     overcome bad writing and suggests that the acting was responsible
     for the initial success of The Fawn.

11   LEECH, CLIFFORD. John Webster, A Critical Study. London:
     Hogarth Press, pp. 5, 6, 58, 79-80. Reprint. New York:
     Haskell House, 1966.
         Compares Malheureux's longing for freedom in The Dutch
     Courtezan to that of the Duchess in Webster's The Duchess of
     Malfi.

*12 MAUGERI, ALDO. John Marston--Antonio and Mellida. Messina:
     Edizioni La Editrice Universitaria, 199 pp.
         Cited in The Annual Bibliography of English Language and
     Literature, 1951-1952.

13   VENEZKY, ALICE S. Pageantry on the Shakespearean Stage. New
     York: Twayne, pp. 122-23 and passim.
         Discusses the employment of and symbolical groupings of
     allegorical characters in Histriomastix.

                                  1952

1   BAKER, HERSCHEL. The Wars of Truth: Studies in the Decay of
     Christian Humanism in the Earlier Seventeenth Century.
     Cambridge, Mass.: Harvard University Press, pp. 51-56.
     Reprint. Gloucester, Mass.: Peter Smith, 1966.
         Sees Marston as departing from the true aim of satire,
     which is to reform evil, because of his conviction that man is
     innately evil; discusses Marston's obsession with sex and judges
     that Marston tends to see sex as a sterile, bestial, degrading
     act without love or joy. Also suggests that Marston's concentra-
     tion upon sexual evil reflects his age's morbid fascination with
     license.

2   BRADBROOK, M.C. Shakespeare and Elizabethan Poetry: A Study
     of His Earlier Work in Relation to the Poetry of His Time.
     New York: Oxford University Press, pp. 43, 66, 126, 226, 244,
     248. Reprint: New York: Cambridge University Press, 1979.
     Provides passing comments on Marston.

3   CAZAMIAN, LOUIS. The Development of English Humor. Durham:
     University of North Carolina Press, pp. 112, 336, 342-44.
         Suggests that basically Marston's humor is bitter, black-
     natured, but that at times a lighter vein of humor appears in his
     works. Part 1 of this study was written in 1930; Part 2, dealing
     with Marston, in 1952. Both parts reprinted: 1965.6.

4   HALLIDAY, F.E. "Marston, John." In A Shakespeare Companion.
     London: Duckworth, pp. 396-97.
         Presents a general discussion of Marston. Revised edition:
     1965.18.

5   HARBAGE, ALFRED. Shakespeare and the Rival Traditions. New
     York: Macmillan, passim. Reprint. New York: Barnes &
     Noble, 1968.
         Suggests that Marston as a coterie dramatist writing for
     the private theaters opposed the orthodox ideals and values of
     Shakespeare and the popular dramatic tradition. Also stresses
     that Marston and other private theater writers dealt with un-
     seemly subjects and humor, which were largely excluded from the
     public stage.
         Antonio and Mellida, Antonio's Revenge, Certain Satires,
     The Dutch Courtezan, Eastward Hoe, The Fawn, Histriomastix, The
     Insatiate Countess, Jack Drum's Entertainment, The Malcontent,
     The Metamorphosis of Pigmalion's Image, Satiromastix, The Scourge
     of Villainy, Sophonisba, What You Will

6   HELTON, TINSLEY. "The Concept of a Woman's Honor in Jacobean
     Drama." Ph.D. diss., University of Minnesota.
         Discusses the change in the treatment of a woman's honor in
     Elizabethan-Jacobean drama and suggests that authors began to
     write sympathetic and fascinating treatments of women who did not
     live by strict laws of chastity. Sees Marston creating women
     who, although they step outside the bounds of honor and are
     suitably punished, fascinate the reader and command respect.

7   HOWARTH, R.G. "John Marston." NQ 197:518.
         Prints two hitherto unpublished epigrams on Marston.

8   JACKSON, JAMES L. "Sources of the Subplot of Marston's The
     Dutch Courtesan." PQ 31:223-24.
         Suggests that the comic shaving scene in The Dutch
     Courtezan derives from similar scenes in Promos and Cassandra and
     Damon and Pithias, two earlier Elizabethan plays, and that the
     episode involving Mulligrub and the cloak was borrowed from
     Plautus's Menaechmi.

9   KUNITZ, STANLEY J., and HOWARD HAYCRAFT. "Marston, John." In
     British Authors before 1800. New York: H.W. Wilson,
     pp. 344-46.
        Presents a general discussion of Marston.

10   OTIS, WILLIAM BRADLEY, and MORRISS H. NEEDLEMAN. An Outline
     History of English Literature, Vol. 1, To Dryden. New York:
     Barnes & Noble, p. 240.
        Provides a general discussion of Marston.

11   PELLIGRINI, GIULIANO. Il Teatro di John Marston. Pisa:
     Libraria Goliardica Editrice, 219 pp.
        Presents a favorable study and judgment of Marston. Sees
     Marston not as a thwarted satirist forced into writing for the
     stage but as a skillful man of the theater. Suggests that
     Marston's understanding of theatrical skills and the human
     condition matured throughout his career. Reviews the course of
     Marston's reputation throughout the ages and discusses much crit-
     icism of this poet and playwright. Review: 1955.1.
        Antonio and Mellida, Antonio's Revenge, Certain Satires,
     The Dutch Courtezan, The Fawn, The Insatiate Countess, Jack
     Drum's Entertainment, The Malcontent, The Metamorphosis of
     Pigmalion's Image, Sophonisba

12   REED, ROBERT RENTOUL. Bedlam on the Jacobean Stage.
     Cambridge, Mass.: Harvard University Press, passim. Reprint.
     New York: Octagon Books, 1969.
        Provides comments on Marston's treatment of malcontents,
     love melancholy, and other topics concerning mental problems and
     disorders.

13   SCHOENBAUM, S. "The Precarious Balance of John Marston."
     PMLA 67:1069-78.
        Sees Marston as an author whose writings are continuously
     bedeviled by incoherence and suggests that comedy, hysteria,
     crude violence, satire, and romance vie with one another for
     dominance within single scenes and entire plays. Observes that
     Marston's imagery reveals a tormented fascination with violence,
     sexual license, and excremental bodily functions. Stresses that
     Marston's central problem was that he could not come to terms
     with a conflict between his powerful attraction to the vices he
     dramatized and an overwhelming need to see them eradicated from
     society. Concludes that Marston is of interest not because of
     what he reveals about humanity but because of what he reveals
     about his own complex and tormented personality.

14   SCHRICKX, W. "The Portraiture of Gabriel Harvey in the
     Parnassus Plays and John Marston." Neophil 36:225-34.
        Suggests that Gabriel Harvey is satirized as Luxurio in the
     Parnassus plays and in satires, VI, IX, XV of The Scourge of
     Villainy. Points out that Marston caricatures him as a pedantic
     fool, given to wearing satin clothing, wishing to introduce

classical hexameters into English verse, and assuming wisdom and
literary knowledge, which indeed he lacks.

15 SMITH, HALLETT. Elizabethan Poetry: A Study in Conventions,
    Meaning, and Expression. Cambridge, Mass.: Harvard Univer-
    sity Press, pp. 238-47, 253-54, and passim. Reprint. Ann
    Arbor: University of Michigan Press, 1968.
        Stresses Marston's use of the persona of the malcontent in
    his verse satires and highlights his emphasis on lust. Finds the
    value of Marston's verse difficult to assess but underscores his
    importance as a source of information about the Jacobean intel-
    lectual climate.
        Certain Satires, The Metamorphosis of Pigmalion's Image,
    The Scourge of Villainy

16 WAITH, EUGENE. The Pattern of Tragicomedy in Beaumont and
    Fletcher. New Haven: Yale University Press, pp. 64-70 and
    passim. Reprint. Hamden, Conn.: Archon Books, 1969.
        Discusses the backgrounds and elements of Elizabethan
    satire and studies Marston as an example of the satirical writer.
    Concentrates on The Malcontent and analyzes its atmosphere,
    characters, themes, and outlook. Sees its structure as that of
    tragicomedy and suggests that elements of Jonson's and Marston's
    plays became important ingredients in the tragicomedy of Beaumont
    and Fletcher.

1953

*1 BALDINI, GABRIELE. John Webster e il linguaggio della
    tragedia. Rome: Edizioni dell' Ateneo, passim.
        Provides passing comments on Marston.

2   CHUTE, MARCHETTE. Ben Jonson of Westminster. New York:
    Dutton, pp. 96-100, 149-54, and passim.
        Provides a general discussion of the War of the Theaters
    and the controversy involving Eastward Hoe.

3   HARRISON, G.B. Shakespeare's Tragedies. New York: Oxford
    University Press, pp. 12, 89-91, 161, 264.
        Provides a plot summary of Antonio's Revenge in order to
    point out fundamental conventions of the Elizabethan revenge
    play.

4   O'DONNELL, NORBERT F. "Shakespeare, Marston, and the Univer-
    sity: The Sources of Thomas Goffe's Orestes." SP 50:476-84.
        Suggests that Goffe in writing his Orestes was indebted
    both to Shakespeare's Hamlet and Marston's Antonio's Revenge.
    Sees the borrowing from Marston in the scene in which Orestes
    murders his small stepbrother--a parallel with Antonio's killing
    Julio, Piero's small son.

5   PALMER, RALPH GRAHAM. <u>Seneca's De Remediis Fortuitorum and</u>
     <u>the Elizabethans</u>. Chicago: Institute of Elizabethan Studies,
     passim.
         Points out Marston's adaptations from this work.

6   PELLEGRINI, GIULIANO. <u>Barocco inglese</u>. Messina: Casa
     Editrice G. D'Anna, pp. 49, 80, 87, 107, 199.
         Provides passing comments on Marston.

7   REESE, M.M. <u>Shakespeare, His World and His Work</u>. London:
     Edward Arnold, passim. Reprint. 1964.
         Provides general comments on Marston and his plays.

8   WADSWORTH, FRANK W. "The Relationship of <u>Lust's Dominion</u> and
     John Mason's <u>The Turke</u>." <u>ELH</u> 20:194-99.
         Suggests that <u>Lust's Dominion</u> was the inspiration for and
     source of Mason's <u>The Turke</u>. Bases this argument upon close
     parallels in the portrayals of the Muslim villains and the queens
     with whom these men are having affairs. Adduces further evidence
     from the use of similar plot devices such as echoes, disguises,
     and sleeping potions.

*9   WARD, A.C. <u>Illustrated History of English Literature</u>. Vol.
     2. London: Longmans, Green. Reprint. New York: David
     McKay, 1967.
         Cited in <u>The National Union Catalogue</u>.

10   WILSON, F.P. <u>Marlowe and the Early Shakespeare</u>. Oxford:
     Clarendon Press, p. 26.
         Discusses Marston's use of the practice of writing intro-
     ductions to printed versions of plays.

11   ZALL, PAUL M. "John Marston, Moralist." <u>ELH</u> 20:186-93.
         Suggests that a concern with human sexuality is a central
     theme in all of Marston's plays and that the problem that con-
     fronted Marston again and again was how to distinguish between
     the just enjoyment of passion and a violent, unrestrained submis-
     sion to sexual desire, which could be potentially tragic. Sug-
     gests that Marston honors those persons who can accept love and
     sexuality as natural, yet who are able to maintain virtue. Thus
     concludes that Marston upholds orthodox moral values and condemns
     the lawless eroticism of such characters as Syphax in <u>Sophonisba</u>.
     Adds that Marston, however, realizes that no moral system can
     guarantee man happiness.

                                1954

1   BOUGHNER, DANIEL. <u>The Braggart in Renaissance Comedy: A</u>
     <u>Study in Comparative Drama from Aristophanes to Shakespeare</u>.
     Minneapolis: University of Minnesota Press, p. 306.

Comments upon the possible source of Matzagente's name in
Antonio and Mellida.

2   CAPUTI, ANTHONY. "'Certain Satires' and the Hall-Marston
    Quarrel." NQ, n.s. 1:235-36.
        Suggests that one of the causes of the Marston-Hall quarrel
    was that Hall, a Cambridge scholar, wrote of London, which
    Marston felt he did not know. Suggests that to Marston, Hall's
    describing London was presumptuous.

3   CROSS, GUSTAV. "Some Notes on the Vocabulary of John
    Marston." NQ, n.s. 1:425-27.
        Presents a listing of words coined by Marston and words
    that have their earliest appearances in his plays. Points out
    that many of these words are not recorded in the Oxford English
    Dictionary. Supplies definitions for the words omitted in this
    work. For continuations of this article, see 1955.6; 1956.8;
    1957.8; 1958.7; 1959.2; 1960.5; 1961.8; 1963.3.

4   DAVRIL, ROBERT. Le Drame de John Ford. Paris: Didier,
    passim.
        Provides passing comments on Marston.

5   DORAN, MADELEINE. Endeavors of Art: A Study of Form in
    Elizabethan Drama. Madison: University of Wisconsin Press,
    passim.
        Studies Elizabethan drama from the standpoint of dramatic
    conventions, rhetorical practices, the taste of the audience and
    other factors that created the aesthetic of English Renaissance
    drama. Considers plays of Marston in this light and contains
    information on Marston's critical theories, the use of satire in
    his dramas, his tragic sense, his use of imagery, and other
    aspects of his dramatic career.
        Antonio and Mellida, Antonio's Revenge, The Dutch
    Courtezan, Eastward Hoe, The Insatiate Countess, The Malcontent,
    What You Will

*6 FINKELPEARL, PHILIP J. "The Works of John Marston: A
    Critical Study." Ph.D. diss., Harvard University.
        Cited in Lawrence McNamee, Dissertations in English and
    American Literature, 1865-1964.

7   GASSNER, JOHN. Masters of the Drama. New York: Dover,
    pp. 231, 241-42, 243, 251-52, 259, 260.
        Provides a general discussion of Marston.

*8 HALLIDAY, F.E. The Poetry of Shakespeare's Plays. London:
    Duckworth.
        Cited in The National Union Catalogue.

9   HUNTER, G.K. "Henry IV and the Elizabethan Two-Part Play."
    RES 5:236-48.

Discusses <u>Antonio</u> <u>and</u> <u>Mellida</u> and <u>Antonio's</u> <u>Revenge</u> and
sees the structure of the two plays as complementary.

*10   KERNAN, ALVIN. "John Marston's Concept and Use of Satire,
      Formal and Dramatic." Ph.D. diss., Yale University.
          Cited in Lawrence McNamee, <u>Dissertations</u> <u>in</u> <u>English</u> <u>and</u>
      <u>American</u> <u>Literature,</u> <u>1865-1964.</u>

11   KIEFER, CHRISTIAN. "Music and Marston's <u>The</u> <u>Malcontent</u>." <u>SP</u>
      51:163-71.
          Points out that music is used to unify the play and to
      comment on the characters and their behavior. Suggests that
      disharmonious music is used to characterize Malevole and the
      corrupt court and that harmonious music implied the hiding of
      vice and sin.

12   LEWIS, C.S. <u>English</u> <u>Literature</u> <u>in</u> <u>the</u> <u>Sixteenth</u> <u>Century</u>
      <u>Excluding</u> <u>Drama</u>. Oxford History of English Literature.
      Oxford: Clarendon Press, pp. 472-74 and passim.
          Sees Marston as an uneven writer, at times an extremely
      poor writer. Views <u>The</u> <u>Metamorphosis</u> <u>of</u> <u>Pigmalion's</u> <u>Image</u> as an
      unsuccessful attempt to write erotic poetry and believes that
      Marston's claim that he was parodying such verse is a falsifica-
      tion. Sees <u>Certain</u> <u>Satires</u> and <u>The</u> <u>Scourge</u> <u>of</u> <u>Villainy</u> as often
      tedious and awkward, but holds that at times in these works,
      Marston provides passages of force, skill, and insight.

13   MEADER, WILLIAM G. <u>Courtship</u> <u>in</u> <u>Shakespeare:</u> <u>Its</u> <u>Relation</u> <u>to</u>
      <u>the</u> <u>Tradition</u> <u>of</u> <u>Courtly</u> <u>Love</u>. New York: King's Crown Press,
      p. 82.
          Points out that <u>The</u> <u>Dutch</u> <u>Courtezan</u> illustrates the belief
      in love at first sight and quotes the passage in which this idea
      appears.

14   PETER, J.D. "Marston's Use of Seneca." <u>NQ</u>, n.s. 1:145-49.
          Compares a passage in <u>Antonio</u> <u>and</u> <u>Mellida</u> translated from
      Seneca with translations of these lines by Leigh Hunt and Jasper
      Heywood.

15   RACE, SYDNEY. "Manningham's Diary: The Case for Reexamina-
      tion." <u>NQ</u>, n.s. 1:380-83.
          Suggests that the anecdote about Marston's insult to Alder-
      man More's wife's daughter (1868.1) may be spurious. For further
      treatments of this idea, see 1956.5; 1957.15, 20.

16   RATLIFF, JOHN DAVID. "The Kydian Revenge Play." Ph.D. diss.,
      Stanford University.
          Discusses ten revenge plays in the light of Kydian devices
      and points out changes and evolutions in the conventions of this
      kind of drama. Sees <u>Antonio's</u> <u>Revenge</u> as a traditional revenge
      play and <u>The</u> <u>Malcontent</u> as a development in the genre in which
      Malevole acts immediately against his enemies instead of delaying
      action and in which new enemies arise to replace old ones.

<u>1955</u>

1   ARMSTRONG, WILLIAM A. Review of Giuliano Pelligrini's <u>Il</u>
     <u>teatro di</u> John <u>Marston</u>. <u>ES</u> 36:169-70.
          Presents a favorable review and outlines major achievements
     of Pelligrini's work (1952.11).

2   AXELRAD, A. JOSÉ. <u>Un</u> <u>Malcontent</u> élizabéthain: John
     <u>Marston</u> (1576-1634). Paris: Didier, 351 pp.
          Presents a detailed and ambitious study of Marston. Sees
     him as a satirist driven into writing for the stage. Discusses
     Marston's life, then considers his works. Stresses that at times
     Marston can be forceful and skilled as a dramatist, yet sees
     mediocrity as a recurring blemish upon his plays. Gives consid-
     erable attention to character types that appear again and again
     in Marston's dramas. Concludes by delving into psychological
     speculations about Marston, suggesting that he was torn between
     hating mankind and needing to reform it. Speculates that this
     conflict along with other problems eventually forced him to
     retire from the theater and to find solace as a clergyman.
     Review: 1958.2.
          <u>Antonio</u> <u>and</u> <u>Mellida</u>, <u>Antonio's</u> <u>Revenge</u>, <u>Certain</u> <u>Satires</u>,
     <u>The</u> <u>Dutch</u> <u>Courtezan</u>, <u>The</u> <u>Fawn</u>, <u>Histriomastix</u>, <u>The</u> <u>Insatiate</u>
     <u>Countess</u>, <u>Jack</u> <u>Drum's</u> <u>Entertainment</u>, <u>The</u> <u>Malcontent</u>, <u>The</u>
     <u>Metamorphosis</u> <u>of</u> <u>Pigmalion's</u> <u>Image</u>, <u>The</u> <u>Scourge</u> <u>of</u> <u>Villainy</u>,
     <u>Sophonisba</u>, <u>What</u> <u>You</u> <u>Will</u>

3   BENÉT, WILLIAM ROSE. "Marston, John (1575?-1634)." In <u>The</u>
     <u>Reader's</u> <u>Encyclopedia</u>: <u>An</u> <u>Encyclopedia</u> <u>of</u> <u>World</u> <u>Literature</u>
     <u>and</u> <u>the</u> <u>Arts</u>. New York: Crowell, p. 695.
          Provides a general article on Marston.

4   BOGARD, TRAVIS. <u>The</u> <u>Tragic</u> <u>Satire</u> <u>of</u> John <u>Webster</u>. Berkeley:
     University of California Press, pp. 85-98. Reprint. New
     York: Russell & Russell, 1965.
          Discusses Marston's influence upon Webster's <u>The</u> <u>White</u>
     <u>Devil</u> and <u>The</u> <u>Duchess</u> <u>of</u> <u>Malfi</u>.
          <u>Antonio</u> <u>and</u> <u>Mellida</u>, <u>Antonio's</u> <u>Revenge</u>, <u>The</u> <u>Malcontent</u>

5   BRADBROOK, M.C. <u>The</u> <u>Growth</u> <u>and</u> <u>Structure</u> <u>of</u> <u>Elizabethan</u>
     <u>Comedy</u>. London: Chatto & Windus, pp. 95-103, 147-54, and
     passim. Reprint. 1962.
          Discusses the War of the Theaters and Marston's dramatic
     career and sees him as a limited but highly influential writer.

6   CROSS, GUSTAVE. "Some Notes on the Vocabulary of John
     Marston." <u>NQ</u>, n.s. 2:20-21, 57-58, 186-87, 335-36, 427-29,
     480-82.
          A continuation of 1954.3. For other continuations, see
     1956.8; 1957.8; 1958.7; 1959.2; 1960.5; 1961.8; 1963.3.

7 CURRY, JOHN V. Deception in Elizabethan Comedy. Chicago:
   Loyola University Press, passim.
      Provides passing comments upon The Dutch Courtezan,
   Eastward Hoe, The Malcontent.

8 FORD, BORIS, ed. The Age of Shakespeare. Pelican Guide to
   English Literature, no. 2. Harmondsworth, Middlesex: Penguin
   Books, passim. Reprint. London: Cassell, 1955.
      Presents passing comments on Marston amid articles on
   Elizabethan-Jacobean literature. For information on the article
   in this collection dealing specifically with Marston, see
   1955.14.

*9 FRIEDMAN, LILA H. "Satiric Personae: A Study of Point of
   View in Formal Verse Satire in the English Renaissance from
   Wyatt to Marston." Ph.D. diss., University of Wisconsin.
      Cited in Lawrence McNamee, Dissertations in English and
   American Literature, 1865-1964.

10 HERRICK, MARVIN T. Tragicomedy: Its Origin and Development
   in Italy, France, and England. Illinois Studies in Language
   and Literature, no. 39. Urbana: University of Illinois
   Press, pp. 241-45 and passim.
      Provides plot summaries of and discusses the tragicomic
   elements in Antonio and Mellida, Antonio's Revenge, The Dutch
   Courtezan, and The Malcontent. Sees The Dutch Courtezan as
   Marston's best comedy.

11 KNIGHT, G. WILSON. The Mutual Flame: On Shakespeare's
   Sonnets and The Phoenix and the Turtle. London: Methuen,
   pp. 182-84 and passim.
      Discusses and interprets the verses Marston contributed to
   Robert Chester's Love's Martyr and sees it as a celebration of a
   perfect being; finds Platonic elements in the poem, but stresses
   that the poet goes beyond philosophy to create an expression of
   ideal love.

12 LAIRD, DAVID. "The Inserted Masque in Elizabethan and
   Jacobean Drama." Ph.D. diss., University of Wisconsin.
      Discusses the use of the masque in Elizabethan and Jacobean
   drama and finds it serves four functions: the spectacular or
   scenic; the dramatic; the thematic; and the illusional. Views
   the masque in Antonio's Revenge as dramatic.

13 MAXWELL, J.C. "The Relation of Macbeth to Sophonisba." NQ,
   n.s. 2:373-74.
      Suggests that Shakespeare borrowed a line from Marston,
   which the latter found in Jonson's Sejanus.

14 SALINGAR, L.G. "Tourneur and the Tragedy of Revenge." In The
   Age of Shakespeare. Edited by Boris Ford. Pelican Guide to

English Literature, no. 2. Harmondsworth, Middlesex: Penguin
Books, pp. 334-54.   Reprint.   London: Cassell, 1961.
   Discusses Marston and finds him a talented, but misdirected
writer.
   Antonio's Revenge, The Malcontent

15   SCHOENBAUM, S.   Middleton's Tragedies: A Critical Study.   New
     York: Columbia University Press, passim.
     Provides passing comments on Marston.

16   SIMPSON, PERCY.   "The Theme of Revenge in Elizabethan
     Tragedy."   In Studies in Elizabethan Drama.   Oxford:
     Clarendon Press, pp. 138-78.
        Provides a detailed plot summary of Antonio's Revenge and
     makes comments upon its relationship to the revenge tradition;
     sees Marston copying Seneca's rhetorical style more than any
     other Elizabethan playwright.

1956

1   ANON.   "Marston, John."   In The New Century Handbook of
    English Literature.   New York: Appleton-Century-Crofts,
    p. 730.
       Provides a general article on Marston.

2   APPLETON, WILLIAM A.   Beaumont and Fletcher: A Critical
    Study.   London: George Allen & Unwin, passim.
       Provides general comments on Marston.

*3   AXELRAD, A. JOSÉ.   Le Theme de Sophonisbe dans les principales
     tragédies de la littérature occidentale.   Lille: Bibliothèque
     Univérsitaire, pp. 28-45.
        Cited in the Annual Bibliography of English Language and
     Literature, 1955-56.

4   CAPUTI, ANTHONY.   "The Satires and Satirical Comedies of John
    Marston."   Ph.D. diss., Cornell University.
       Traces Marston's use of satire from the early nondramatic
    satires to his satirical plays and finds his later comedies to be
    successful adaptations of satire to the dramatic form.   For
    Caputi's book on Marston, see 1961.5.
       Antonio and Mellida, The Dutch Courtezan, Eastward Hoe, The
    Fawn, Histriomastix, Jack Drum's Entertainment, The Malcontent,
    The Metamorphosis of Pigmalion's Image, The Scourge of Villainy,
    What You Will

5   CROSS, GUSTAV.   "Manningham's Libel on Marston."   NQ, n.s.
    3:377-78.
       Casts doubt on the verity of Manningham's anecdote (1868.1)
    about Marston's insulting Alderman More's wife's daughter.   Sug-
    gests that the story is simply an old folk tale that was con-
    nected with Marston.   For other discussions of this issue, see
    1954.15; 1957.15, 20.

6 _____. "Ovid Metamorphosed." NQ, n.s. 3:508-9.
    Adds a further suggestion to support his view (1956.7) that
Marston drew upon Arthur Golding's translation of Ovid's
Metamorphoses.

7 _____. "Ovid Metamorphosed: Marston, Webster, and Nathaniel
Lee." NQ, n.s. 3:244-45.
    Suggests that these three authors drew upon Arthur
Golding's translation of Ovid's Metamorphoses in describing death
as a city with many entrances. A continuation of 1956.6.

8 _____. "Some Notes on the Vocabulary of John Marston." NQ,
n.s. 3:331-32, 470-71.
    A continuation of 1954.3. For other continuations, see
1955.6; 1957.8; 1958.7; 1959.2; 1960.5; 1961.8; 1963.3.

9 CROTTY, JOHN. "The Language in the Plays of John Marston."
Ph.D. diss., University of Notre Dame.
    Suggests that Marston tired of the literary style of such
Elizabethans as Lyly, Sidney, and Spenser and that he sought to
create a new means of verbal expression that would be supple and
well suited for dramatic presentation. Marston, consequently,
creates his dialogue to reveal characters pondering issues or
plotting crimes, experiencing abnormal psychological reactions,
or undergoing personality adjustments. Sees Marston as having a
vital sense of what makes good theater.

*10 EGLI, WILLY. John Marstons Dramen. Winterthur: G.P. Keller.
    Cited in the Annual Bibliography of English Language and
Literature, 1955-56.

11 ELIOT, T.S. "John Marston." In Essays on Elizabethan Drama.
New York: Harcourt, Brace, pp. 162-78.
    Reprint of 1934.2.

12 FLUCHÈRE, HENRI. Shakespeare and the Elizabethans. Translated by Guy Hamilton. New York: Hill & Wang, pp. 60, 64,
139-40, 142.
    Provides passing comments on Marston.

13 HALLIDAY, F.E. Shakespeare: A Pictorial Biography. New
York: Crowell, pp. 62, 86-87.
    Provides a general discussion of Marston.

14 HARRISON, G.B. Elizabethan Plays and Players. Ann Arbor:
University of Michigan Press, pp. 208-21, 231-32, 241-45,
250-81.
    Outlines the War of the Theaters and defends Marston as a
dramatist. Sees him as a bold experimenter, ushering new ideas
and techniques onto the Elizabethan stage. Presents a favorable
evaluation of Antonio's Revenge and an extended analysis of the
dramatic style of this play.

Antonio and Mellida, Jack Drum's Entertainment, What You
Will

*15   HEUSER, GEORG. Die aktlose Dramaturgie William Shakespeares.
       Marburg: n.p., pp. 421-23.
       Cited in the introduction to George K. Hunter's edition of
       The Malcontent (The Malcontent 1975.1).

16   HUGHES, LEO. A Century of English Farce. Princeton:
       Princeton University Press, passim.
       Provides passing comments on Marston.

17   INGRAM, R.W. "The Use of Music in the Plays of Marston." M&L
       37:154-56.
       Points out that Marston skillfully used music to enhance
       dramatic effects, create atmosphere, establish mood, and motivate
       actions. Concentrates upon the use of incidental music and song
       and sees Marston's use of song approaching something like the
       techniques of Richard Wagner's music dramas.
       Antonio and Mellida, Antonio's Revenge, The Dutch
       Courtezan, The Insatiate Countess, Jack Drum's Entertainment, The
       Malcontent, Sophonisba

18   LACY, MARGARET SWANSON. "The Jacobean Problem Play: A Study
       of Shakespeare's Measure for Measure and Troilus and Cressida
       in Relation to Selected Plays of Chapman, Dekker, and
       Marston." Ph.D. diss., University of Wisconsin.
       Sees the essence of the problem play residing in an incom-
       patible fusion of a romantic plot and a realistic treatment of
       serious issues. Studies Marston in this light and sees the
       conclusion of The Dutch Courtezan weakening the play and the
       romantic elements in The Fawn reducing Duke Hercules's role in
       the action to incoherence.

19   McDIARMID, MATTHEW P. "The Stage Quarrel in Wily Beguiled."
       NQ, n.s. 3:380-83.
       Suggests that the play satirizes Marston and Dekker as well
       as Jonson. Views Churms, the unscrupulous lawyer, as a carica-
       ture of Marston.

20   PETER, J.D. Complaint and Satire in Early English Literature.
       Oxford: Clarendon Press, pp. 219-54.
       Discusses the development of English satire from the Middle
       Ages to the Renaissance and its influence upon Elizabethan-
       Jacobean drama. Devotes considerable space to Marston's use of
       satire and provides in-depth commentary upon most of Marston's
       plays. Concludes that his complex and disturbed personality made
       it difficult for him to use effectively the Juvenalian satire
       that he favored and that the later plays, like The Dutch
       Courtezan and The Fawn in which satiric elements are indirect and
       subtle, are better plays. Sees Marston as a limited, but reward-
       ing dramatist.

Antonio and Mellida, Antonio's Revenge, The Malcontent,
Jack Drum's Entertainment, What You Will

21   PRESSON, ROBERT K. "Marston's Dutch Courtezan: The Study of
     an Attitude in Adaptation." JEGP 55:406.13.
        Accepts Matteo Bandello's novella "The Countess of Celant"
     as the play's source and suggests that Marston refashioned the
     tale into a Jacobean version of the morality play with Malheureux
     representating Mankind or the Humanum Genus, Franceschina the
     devil, and Beatrice the spirit of salvation.

22   SCHRICKX, W. Shakespeare's Early Contemporaries: The Back-
     ground of the Harvey-Nashe Polemic and Love's Labour's Lost.
     Antwerp: De Nederlandsche Boekhandel, pp. 5-6, 58, 106, 110.
        Quotes from The Metamorphosis of Pigmalion's Image to
     illustrate the Jacobean interest in and use of Natalis Comes's
     Mythologiae sive explicationum fabularum libri decem and to pro-
     vide a basis for the discussion of the influence of this work
     upon English Renaissance writing.

23   SMITH, GROVER, Jr. T.S. Eliot's Poetry and Plays: A Study in
     Sources and Meaning. Chicago: University of Chicago Press,
     pp. 52, 53, 111, 112, 138.
        Discusses Eliot's use of Marston's Entertainment of Alice,
     Dowager-Countess of Derby in "Burbank with a Baedeker; Bleistein
     with a Cigar"; quotes the passage from Eliot's essay on Marston
     (1934.2) on levels of meaning in Sophonisba and applies this
     theory to Eliot's own plays.

                              1957

1   ANON. Review of A. José Axelrad's Un Malcontent élizabéthain:
     John Marston (1576-1634). SCN 15:34.
        Sees the work (1955.2) as the best study to date of
     Marston, but feels that it is too detailed, at times laborious.

2   BOKLUND, GUNNAR. The Sources of The White Devil. Uppsala:
     Lundequistska Bokhandeln, passim. Reprint. New York:
     Haskell House, 1966.
        Provides passing comments on Marston.

3   BRUSTEIN, ROBERT SANFORD. "Italianate Court Satire and the
     Plays of John Marston." Ph.D. diss., Columbia University.
        Traces the development in Elizabethan literature of the use
     of the Italian court as a center of vice, intrigue, and power
     politics. Concentrates upon portrayals of the courtier and court
     lady and shows that Marston's treatment of these character types
     became a convention.

4   BURKE, Brother FIDELIAN. Metrical Roughness in Marston's
     Formal Satire. Washington, D.C.: Catholic University of
     America, 98 pp.

Studies the means by which Marston gave the effect of
roughness to <u>Certain</u> <u>Satires</u> and <u>The</u> <u>Scourge</u> <u>of</u> <u>Villainy</u>.

5   COPE, JACKSON I. "<u>Volpone</u> and the Authorship of <u>Eastward</u>
    <u>Hoe</u>." <u>MLN</u> 72:253-56.
        On the basis of a comparison with speeches in <u>Volpone</u>,
    suggests that Jonson wrote the second scene of Act II of <u>Eastward</u>
    <u>Hoe</u>.

6   CROSS, GUSTAV. "The Date of Marston's <u>Antonio</u> <u>and</u> <u>Mellida</u>."
    <u>MLN</u> 72:328-32.
        Suggests that the play was written between September 1599
    and March 1600.

7   _____. "More's <u>Historie</u> <u>of</u> <u>Kyng</u> <u>Rycharde</u> <u>the</u> <u>Thirde</u> and <u>Lust's</u>
    <u>Dominion</u>." <u>NQ</u>, n.s. 4:198-99.
        Suggests that Eleazar's plot in <u>Lust's</u> <u>Dominion</u> to dis-
    credit the rightful heir as a bastard was derived from More's
    history.

8   _____. "Some Notes on the Vocabulary of John Marston." <u>NQ</u>,
    n.s. 4:65-66, 221-23, 283-85, 524-26.
        A continuation of 1954.3. For other continuations, see
    1955.6; 1956.8; 1958.7; 1959.2; 1960.5; 1961.8; 1963.3.

*9 _____. "Retrograde Genius: A Study of John Marston." Ph.D.
    diss., Trinity College, Dublin.
        Cited in the <u>Annual</u> <u>Bibliography</u> <u>of</u> <u>English</u> <u>Language</u> <u>and</u>
    <u>Literature,</u> <u>1957-58</u>.

10 De CHAMBRUN, CLARA LONGWORTH. <u>Shakespeare:</u> <u>A</u> <u>Portrait</u>
    <u>Restored</u>. London: Hollis & Carter, passim.
        Provides passing comments on Marston.

11 FRYE, NORTHROP. <u>Anatomy</u> <u>of</u> <u>Criticism,</u> <u>Four</u> <u>Essays</u>.
    Princeton: Princeton University Press, pp. 176, 236. Reprint.
    New York: Atheneum, 1966.
        Sees Malevole as part of his society's evil.

12 GEORGE, J. "John Marston in the Trumbull Correspondence."
    <u>NQ</u>, n.s. 4:226.
        Points out a reference to Marston as a minister in a letter
    to William Trumbull.

13 GREG, W.W., ed. <u>A</u> <u>Bibliography</u> <u>of</u> <u>the</u> <u>English</u> <u>Printed</u> <u>Drama</u>
    <u>to</u> <u>the</u> <u>Restoration</u>. Vol. 3. London: Printed for the Biblio-
    graphical Society, pp. 1089-90.
        Provides bibliographical data on the seventeenth-century
    collected editions of Marston's plays (Collected edition 1633.1;
    Collected edition 1633.2; Collected edition 1652.1).

14   HIGHET, GILBERT. The Classical Tradition: Greek and Roman
     Influence on Western Literature. New York: Oxford University
     Press, p. 311.
          Provides passing references to The Scourge of Villainy and
     the controversy it stirred up.

15   JENKINS, GLADYS. "Manningham, Marston, and Alderman More's
     Wife's Daughter." NQ, n.s. 4:243-44.
          Criticizes Sydney Race's skeptical suggestion (1957.20)
     that the Marston anecdote in Manningham's diary (1868.1) was
     forged by John Payne Collier and presents evidence that Alderman
     More and his wife's daughter did indeed exist. For other discus-
     sions of this topic, see 1954.15; 1956.5.

16   LEVIN, HARRY. Christopher Marlowe: The Overreacher. London:
     Faber & Faber, p. 96. Reprint. 1961.
          Comments upon similarities between Marlowe and Marston.

17   McCOLLUM, WILLIAM G. Tragedy. New York: Macmillan, p. 97.
          Cites Lust's Dominion as a typical tragedy of blood.

18   MUIR, KENNETH. Shakespeare's Sources (1): Comedies and
     Tragedies. London: Methuen, pp. 116-17. Reprint. 1961.
          Discusses Antonio's Revenge as a revenge play and its
     possible influence upon Hamlet.

19   O'CONNOR, JOHN J. "The Chief Source of Marston's Dutch
     Courtezan." SP 54:509-15.
          Suggests that the source of the main plot involving
     Freevill and Malheureux is a tale in Nicholas de Montreux's Le
     premier livre des bergeries de Julliette. Summarizes the story
     and compares Marston's changes in it with the original. Stresses
     that many of these alterations were brought about because of
     Marston's concern with sin and the need to enforce traditional
     morality. Suggests that these changes weaken his adaptation.

20   RACE, SYDNEY. "Manningham and Marston." NQ, n.s. 4:147.
          Suggests that the tale in Manningham's diary (1868.1) of
     Marston's insult to Alderman More's wife's daughter is a forgery
     by John Payne Collier. For a criticism of this essay, see
     1957.15. For other discussions, see 1954.15; 1956.5.

21   RIBNER, IRVING. The English History Play in the Age of
     Shakespeare. Princeton: Princeton University Press,
     pp. 66-67.
          Sees Marston's style of writing as weakening the vogue of
     the history play.

22   SIEGEL, PAUL N. Shakespearean Tragedy and the Elizabethan
     Compromise. New York: New York University Press, pp. 63-65
     and passim. Reprint. Freeport, N.Y.: Books for Libraries,
     1972.

Discusses the portrayal in The Scourge of Villainy of
Marston's acute sense of the disparity between idealized views of
human nature and the reality of depravity in London.

23   TAYLOR, WILLIAM EDWARDS. "The Villainess in Elizabethan
     Drama." Ph.D. diss., Vanderbilt University.
     Traces the development of the character of the villainess
in Elizabethan drama and finds the countess in The Insatiate
Countess representing this character type in "almost pure form."

24   UNDERWOOD, DALE. Etherege and the Seventeenth-Century Comedy
     of Manners. New Haven: Yale University Press, pp. 125, 126-
     29, 149. Reprint. Hamden, Conn.: Archon Books, 1969.
     Discusses The Dutch Courtezan as representing certain dra-
matic trends in the treatment of sexuality, which continued in
the drama until the end of the seventeenth century.

                              1958

1   ANON. "Marston, John." In Cyclopedia of World Authors.
     Edited by Frank N. Magill. New York: Harper & Row,
     pp. 717-19.
     Provides a general article on Marston.

2   ARMSTRONG, WILLIAM A. Review of A. José Axelrad's Un
     Malcontent élizabéthain: John Marston (1576-1634). ES
     39:263-65.
     Provides a sympathetic detailed report on the book
     (1955.1).

3   BARKER, RICHARD HINDRY. Thomas Middleton. New York:
     Columbia University Press, passim. Reprint. Westport, Conn.:
     Greenwood Press, 1975.
     Provides passing comments on Marston.

4   CHAMETZKY, JULES. "Reason and Desire in the Plays of John
     Marston." Ph.D. diss., University of Minnesota.
     Sees the conflict between reason and desire as a central
theme in Marston's plays and points out that this preoccupation
gives birth to two prominent character types in his dramas—the
malcontent and the Machiavel. Also suggests that Marston, though
railing against evil in his writings, is both fascinated and
repelled by it and, furthermore, has trouble in dramatizing and
making convincing the moral ideals that would offset the evil.

5   COOKMAN, A.V. "Shakespeare's Contemporaries on the Modern
     English Stage." SJ 94:29-41.
     Discusses productions of The Dutch Courtezan and Eastward
Hoe.

                              121

6   CROSS, GUSTAV. "The Authorship of Lust's Dominion." SP
    55:39-61.
       Suggests that Marston had a hand in this play, along with
    Day, Dekker, and Haughton. For additional support for this view,
    see 1972.21.

7   _____. "Some Notes on the Vocabulary of John Marston." NQ,
    n.s. 5:4-5, 103-4.
       A continuation of 1954.3. For other continuations, see
    1955.6; 1956.8; 1957.8; 1959.2; 1960.5; 1961.8; 1963.3.

8   _____. "An Unrecognized Poem by John Marston?" MLQ 19:
    325-30.
       Suggests that one of the commendatory verses printed with
    John Weever's Epigrammes in the Oldest Cut and Newest Fashion is
    by Marston. The poem is entitled "In Authorem" and is signed
    I.K.

9   _____. "The Vocabulary of Lust's Dominion." NM 59:41-48.
       Points out that the play contains sixty-seven words that
    antedate the Oxford English Dictionary's earliest examples and
    twenty-two words not noted in this compilation.

10 _____. "The Way of All Flesh." NQ, n.s. 5:257.
       Discusses the occurrence of this phrase in The Dutch
    Courtezan.

11 ECCLES, MARK. "Martin Peerson and the Blackfriars." ShS
    11:100-106.
       Discusses the lawsuit concerning Blackfriars and points out
    that for a time Marston was involved in the legal proceedings.

12 HARRISON, G.B. A Second Jacobean Journal: Being a Record of
    Those Things Most Talked of during the Years 1607-1610. Ann
    Arbor: University of Michigan, pp. 92, 181.
       Written as though the author were a Jacobean recording
    events of interest and prominence. The goal is to give the
    student of literature a sense of what living in the time of
    Shakespeare was like. Contains references to Marston's being
    committed to Newgate in 1608 and to his becoming a minister and
    preaching at Oxford.

13 _____. Shakespeare at Work, 1592-1603. Ann Arbor:
    University of Michigan, pp. 192-96, 241-56.
       Reprint of 1933.9.

14 KERNAN, ALVIN. "John Marston's Play Histriomastix." MLQ
    19:134-40.
       Argues that Marston is the sole author of this play.

15   MORRIS, HELEN. Elizabethan Literature. Home University
     Library of Modern Knowledge. London: Oxford University
     Press, pp. 178-79, 184-85, and passim.
          Provides general discussions of Marston.

16   SMITH, JOHN HARRINGTON, LOIS D. PIZER, and EDWARD K. SMITH.
     "Hamlet, Antonio's Revenge, and the Ur-Hamlet." SQ 19:493-98.
          Suggests that neither Shakespeare in writing Hamlet nor
     Marston in writing Antonio's Revenge was drawing upon the fin-
     ished work of the other, but that both authors in constructing
     their revenge plays were drawing upon the Ur-Hamlet.

17   SOELLNER, ROLF. "The Madness of Hercules and the Eliza-
     bethans." CL 10:309-20.
          Suggests that the madness of Hercules was the archetype for
     the portrayal of tragic heroes suffering madness in Elizabethan
     drama. Discusses the madness of Antonio in Antonio's Revenge and
     reveals parallels between Antonio's anguish and behavior and
     those of Hercules.

18   SPIVACK, BERNARD. Shakespeare and the Allegory of Evil: The
     History of a Metaphor in Relation to His Major Villains. New
     York: Columbia University Press, pp. 210, 334-36, 338, 361,
     476.
          Discusses Cocledemoy of The Dutch Courtezan as a reincarna-
     tion of the traditional Vice figure of the medieval morality play,
     and views Piero of Antonio's Revenge as a character whose por-
     trayal is mixed between naturalistic motivations and the tradi-
     tional patterns of dramatizing vice.

19   TURNER, ROBERT Y. "The Composition of The Insatiate Countess,
     Q2." SB 12:198-203.
          Discusses the typesetting of quarto 2 of The Insatiate
     Countess (The Insatiate Countess 1616.1) and points out that it
     is a reprint of quarto 1 (The Insatiate Countess 1613.1) and that
     three compositors had a hand in the preparation. Deduces circum-
     stances that affected the composition and suggests that the book
     was set by formes rather than by serialism.

20   WILLIAMS, GEORGE WALTON. "Setting by Formes in Quarto Print-
     ing." SB 11:39-53.
          Discusses the typesetting of The Insatiate Countess 1613.1
     and The Insatiate Countess 1616.1.

                              1959

1   ARMSTRONG, WILLIAM A. "The Audience of the Elizabethan
     Private Theatres." RES, n.s. 10:235-49.
          Includes passing comments on Marston.

2   CROSS, GUSTAVE. "Some Notes on the Vocabulary of John
     Marston." NQ, n.s. 6:101-2, 137-39, 254-55, 355-56.
         A continuation of 1954.3. For other continuations, see
     1955.6; 1956.8; 1957.8; 1958.7; 1960.5; 1961.8; 1963.3.

3   DONOGHUE, DENIS. The Third Voice: Modern British and Amer-
     ican Verse Drama. Princeton: Princeton University Press,
     p. 254.
         Compares Marston's tragic vision with T.S. Eliot's and
     finds that Marston believed in the values of his age, whereas
     Eliot finds modern man unable to accept traditional wisdom.

4   FORKER, CHARLES R. "Tennyson's 'Tithonus' and Marston's
     Antonio's Revenge." NQ, n.s. 6:445.
         Suggests that a description in "Tithonus" of the dawn as
     horses was taken from Antonio's Revenge.

5   GILBERT, ALLAN. The Principles and Practice of Criticism:
     Othello, The Merry Wives, Hamlet. Detroit: Wayne State
     University Press, pp. 51, 110, 117, 119, 130, 146.
         Provides passing comments upon Antonio's Revenge as an
     example of Senecan revenge tragedy.

6   HOLLAND, NORMAN N. The First Modern Comedies: The Signif-
     icance of Etherege, Wycherley, and Congreve. Cambridge,
     Mass.: Harvard University Press, pp. 216-17.
         Discusses Nahum Tate's Cuckolds-Haven, a Restoration adap-
     tation of Eastward Hoe and points out that in Tate's version the
     villains are unrepentant and that an air of amorality permeates
     the play.

7   KERNAN, ALVIN. The Cankered Muse: Satire of the English
     Renaissance. Yale Studies in English, vol. 142. New Haven:
     Yale University Press, passim. Reprint. 1976.
         Attempts to define the nature of Elizabethan satire not
     only as a technique but also as a way of viewing the world.
     Studies theories of the psychological origins of satire and
     Elizabethan views of its purpose and effectiveness. Provides
     considerable information on Marston's career as a satirist, his
     views of satire, and the satirical elements in his plays.
         Antonio and Mellida, The Fawn, Histriomastix, The
     Malcontent, The Scourge of Villainy, What You Will

8   KINDERMANN, HEINZ. Theatergeschichte Europas. Vol. 3.
     Salzburg: Otto Müller, pp. 104, 110, 130, 140, 142.
         Provides passing comments on Marston.

9   LEVIN, HARRY. The Question of Hamlet. New York: Oxford
     University Press, pp. 114, 117-18, 122.
         Discusses The Malcontent and Hamlet.

10   MILLER, EDWIN HAVILAND. The Professional Writer in Eliza-
     bethan England: A Study of Nondramatic Literature. Cambridge,
     Mass.: Harvard University Press, passim.
         Provides passing comments on Marston.

11   NIVA, WELDON N. "Significant Character Names in English Drama
     to 1603." Ph.D. diss., University of Pennsylvania.
         Studies the use in the drama of significant names, such as
     Lightborn, Pistol, Fastidious Brisk, which suggests the charac-
     ters of their bearers. Points out that this technique began in
     the Middle Ages and that it was widely used in Elizabethan drama
     for such purposes as satire, foreshadowing, and so forth. Points
     out that Marston often used these names ironically for satire.

12   REYBURN, MARJORIE L. "New Facts and Theories about the
     Parnassus Plays." PMLA 74:325-35.
         Suggests that Furor Poeticus represents Marston. Also
     considers the relationship of Satiromastix to the Parnassus plays.

13   SHARPE, ROBERT BOIES. Irony in the Drama: An Essay on Imper-
     sonation, Shock, and Cartharsis. Chapel Hill: University of
     North Carolina Press, pp. 123-34. Reprint. Westport, Conn.:
     Greenwood Press, 1975.
         Suggests that the unexpected happy ending of The Malcontent
     destroys the possibility of a tragic catharsis, which the play's
     action has led the audience to expect.

                                  1960

1   BARISH, JONAS A. Ben Jonson and the Language of Prose Comedy.
     Cambridge, Mass.: Harvard University Press, pp. 126-28, 282-
     83, and passim. Reprint. New York: Norton, 1970.
         Suggests that the language of Tucca in Satiromastix
     barely resembles that of the original Tucca in The Poetaster.
     Sees the language of Cocledemoy in The Dutch Courtezan as inco-
     herent.

2   CROSS, GUSTAV. "The Date of The Malcontent Once More." PQ
     39:104-13.
         Suggests that The Malcontent could not have been written
     later than 1600.

3   _____. "Marston, Montaigne, and Morality: The Dutch
     Courtezan Reconsidered." ELH 27:30-43.
         Argues for the play's essential morality by demonstrating
     that Marston, drawing upon Montaigne's concepts of sexuality,
     upholds the naturalness of sex and the legitimate expression of
     the sexual impulse.

4   _____. "Marston's 'Metamorphosis of Pigmalion's Image': A
     Mock-Epyllion." EA 13:331-36.

Defends Marston from the charge that The Metamorphosis of Pigmalion's Image was written as pornography and upholds the view that the poem is a mock-epyllion, satirizing erotic verse, Petrarchan concepts and conventions, and Elizabethan society. Bases much of the argument upon Marston's intrusions into the narrative and his asides to the reader.

5   _____. "Some Notes on the Vocabulary of John Marston." NQ, n.s. 7:135-36.
       A continuation of 1954.3. For other continuations, see 1955.6; 1956.8; 1957.8; 1958.7; 1959.2; 1961.8; 1963.3.

6   _____. "Webster and Marston: A Note on The White Devil, V. iii. 106." NQ, n.s. 7:337.
       Suggests that Webster borrowed the conception of the devil as a linguist from The Malcontent.

7   DAICHES, DAVID. A Critical History of English Literature. Vol. 1. New York: Ronald Press, pp. 325-26.
       Provides a general discussion of Marston.

8   DENT, R.W. John Webster's Borrowing. Berkeley: University of California Press, passim.
       Discusses Webster's borrowings from Marston.

9   ELLIOTT, ROBERT C. The Power of Satire: Magic, Ritual, Art. Princeton: Princeton University Press, pp. 136-38, 162-65, 261, 263, 277.
       Provides a general discussion of the style and nature of Marston's satires.
       The Malcontent, The Scourge of Villainy

10   ELLRODT, ROBERT. L'Inspiration personnelle et l'esprit du temps chez les poètes métaphysiques anglais: Second partie. 3 vols. Paris: José Corti, passim.
       Provides passing comments on Marston.

11   No entry.

12   HARRIS, BERNARD. "Men Like Satyrs." In Elizabethan Poetry. Stratford-upon-Avon Studies, vol. 2. Edited by John Russell Brown and Bernard Harris. New York: St. Martin's, pp. 175-202.
       Provides a general discussion of Marston.
       The Metamorphosis of Pigmalion's Image, The Scourge of Villainy

13   HUNTER, G.K. "English Folly and Italian Vice: The Moral Landscape of John Marston." In Jacobean Theatre. Stratford-upon-Avon Studies, vol. 1. Edited by by John Russell Brown and Bernard Harris. New York: St. Martin's, pp. 85-111. Reprint. New York: Capricorn Books, 1967.

Credits Marston with popularizing on the Elizabethan stage
the concept of Italy as a hotbed of vice, depravity, and Machiavellianism. Discusses Marston's influence in the use of Italy
upon Tourneur and Webster and other dramatists. Sees Marston as
basically concerned with the evils of human nature and with what
he feels men must inevitably be.
    Antonio and Mellida, Antonio's Revenge, The Dutch
Courtezan, The Malcontent

14   JONES, DAVID E. The Plays of T.S. Eliot. Toronto: Univer-
      sity of Toronto Press, pp. 12-13.
      Discusses Eliot's comment on Sophonisba that a hidden pat-
tern underlies the action and applies this theory to Eliot's
later plays.

15   MAGILL, FRANK N., ed. Masterpieces of World Literature in
      Digest Form, Third Series. New York: Harper, pp. 317-20,
      619-21.
      Provides plot summaries of Eastward Hoe and The Malcontent.

16   ORAS, ANTS. Pause Patterns in Elizabethan and Jacobean Drama.
      University of Florida Monographs, no. 3. Gainsville: Univer-
      sity of Florida Press, p. 81.
      Includes a chart pointing out the number of instances of
internal punctuation in Antonio and Mellida, Antonio's Revenge,
The Insatiate Countess, The Malcontent, Sophonisba, What You
Will.

17   ORNSTEIN, ROBERT. The Moral Vision of Jacobean Tragedy.
      Madison: University of Wisconsin Press, pp. 152-63. Reprint.
      Westport, Conn.: Greenwood Press, 1975.
      Points out strengths and weaknesses in Marston's plays;
concludes that the author is intellectually confused and has
difficulty in seriously dealing with ethical issues.
    Antonio's Revenge, The Dutch Courtezan

18   REIMAN, DONALD H. "Marston, Jonson, and The Spanish Tragedy
      Additions." NQ, n.s. 7:336-37.
      Suggests that Poetaster parodies Antonio's Revenge and that
the additions we now have to The Spanish Tragedy were written
earlier than those Jonson was paid for.

19   ROSEN, WILLIAM. Shakespeare and the Craft of Tragedy.
      Cambridge, Mass.: Harvard University Press, p. 21.
      Quotes Marston on the Machiavel.

20   SABOL, ANDREW J. "Two Unpublished Stage Songs for the 'Aery
      of Children.'" RN 8:222-23.
      Discusses and provides the musical setting for
Franceschina's song, "The Dark Is My Delight" from The Dutch
Courtezan.

21 SEHRT, ERNST. Der dramatische Auftakt in der
    elisabethanischen Tragödie. Göttingen: Vandenbröck &
    Ruprecht, pp. 25, 43, 62, 167, 195.
        Provides passing comments on Marston.

22 SNUGGS, HENRY L. Shakespeare and Five Acts, Studies in
    Dramatic Convention. New York: Vantage, pp. 39, 43-45.
        Cites The Dutch Courtezan, The Malcontent, and Sophonisba
    to furnish evidence that the private theaters included musical
    intervals between the acts of the plays, whereas the public
    theaters did not.

23 TAYLOR, ARCHER. "Proverbs and Proverbial Phrases in the Plays
    of John Marston." SFQ 24:193-216.
        Lists proverbs in all of Marston's plays.
        Antonio and Mellida, Antonio's Revenge, The Dutch
    Courtezan, Eastward Hoe, The Fawn, Histriomastix, The Insatiate
    Countess, Jack Drum's Entertainment, The Malcontent, Sophonisba,
    What You Will

                              1961

1   ADAMS, JOHN CRANFORD. The Globe Playhouse: Its Design and
    Equipment. New York: Barnes & Noble, passim.
        Provides passing comments on Antonio's Revenge.

2   ANON. Annals of English Literature, 1475-1950: The Principal
    Publications of Each Year Together with an Alphabetical Index
    of Authors with Their Works. Oxford: Clarendon Press,
    passim.
        Lists years in which Marston's works were published.

3   BLUMENTHAL, WALTER HART. Paging Mr. Shakespeare: A Critical
    Challenge. New York: University Publishers, passim.
        Provides passing comments on Marston.

4   BROWN, ARTHUR. "Studies in Elizabethan and Jacobean Drama
    Since 1900." ShS 14:1-14.
        Provides passing comments on Marston and books related to
    him.

5   CAPUTI, ANTHONY. John Marston, Satirist. Ithaca: Cornell
    University Press, 280 pp. Reprint. New York: Octagon Books,
    1976.
        Holds that Marston reacted to the intellectual ferment and
    confusion of his age by creating a seriocomic view in his works.
    Suggests that by this means Marston could confront and seek to
    understand the problems of his generation. Sees neo-Stoicism and
    Christianity as shaping forces upon Marston's thought. Stresses
    that as a dramatist Marston utlized the lovers-in-distress and
    disguise plots to communicate his seriocomic vision. Also holds

that the use of boy players to burlesque adults is basic to
Marston's technique. Judges that Marston's works vitally mirror
the doubts and complexities of his era. Based upon Caputi's
dissertation: 1956.4. Reviews: 1963.13, 16.
  Antonio and Mellida, Antonio's Revenge, Certain Satires,
The Dutch Courtezan, Eastward Hoe, The Fawn, Histriomastix, The
Insatiate Countess, Jack Drum's Entertainment, The Malcontent, The
Metamorphosis of Pigmalion's Image, The Scourge of Villainy,
Sophonisba, What You Will

6   CHARNEY, MAURICE. Shakespeare's Roman Plays: The Function of
    Imagery in the Drama. Cambridge, Mass.: Harvard University
    Press, pp. 22-23.
      Discusses diction in The Scourge of Villainy.

7   CROSS, GUSTAV. "The Retrograde Genius of John Marston." REL
    2:19-27.
      Affirms the moral seriousness of Marston and suggests that
    at the end of his dramatic career, Marston began to value Stoi-
    cism, a philosophical position that earlier he had criticized as
    inadequate.
      Antonio and Mellida, Antonio's Revenge, The Dutch
    Courtezan, The Malcontent, Sophonisba

8   _____. "Some Notes on the Vocabulary of John Marston." NQ,
    n.s. 8:123-26, 298-300, 388-91.
      A continuation of 1954.3. For other continuations see
    1955.6; 1956.8; 1957.8; 1958.7; 1959.2; 1960.5; 1963.3.

9   _____. "Tilley's Dictionary of Proverbs in England, H348, and
    Marston's Antonio and Mellida." NQ, n.s. 8:143-44.
      Points out the appearance of the Elizabethan proverb,
    "Heaven is above all," in Antonio and Mellida.

10 GILDERSLEEVE, VIRGINIA CROCHERON. Government Regulation of
    the Elizabethan Drama. New York: Burt Franklin, pp. 101-2,
    103, 104.
      Discusses the controversy involving Eastward Hoe.

11 HALLIDAY, F.E. Shakespeare. New York: Thomas Yoseloff,
    pp. 135, 151, 163-64, 227.
      Provides passing comments on Marston.

12 HENSLOWE, PHILIP. Henslowe's Diary. Edited by R.A. Foakes
    and R.T. Rickert. Cambridge: Cambridge University Press,
    p. 124.
      A more recent edition of 1904.7.

13 HIBBARD, GEORGE R. "The Early Seventeenth Century and the
    Tragic View of Life." Renaissance and Modern Studies 5:5-28.
      Discusses Marston's views of tragedy as provided in the
    prologue to Antonio's Revenge and finds that Marston has no
    concept of tragedy as a moral force.

14   KELLER, HELEN REX. The Reader's Digest of Books. New York:
Macmillan, p. 42.
      Provides plot summaries of Antonio and Mellida and
Antonio's Revenge.

*15   KORNINGER, SIEGFRIED. "John Marston und die Bedeutung des
Malcontent." In Festschrift zum 75, Geburtstag von Theodor
Spira. Heidelburg: Winter, pp. 152-63.
      Cited in the Annual Bibliography of English Language and
Literature, 1961.

16   LONG, JOHN H. Shakespeare's Use of Music: A Study of the
Music and Its Performance in the Original Production of Seven
Comedies. Gainesville: University of Florida Press, passim.
      Provides passing comments on Antonio and Mellida, The
Malcontent, Sophonisba.

17   MacCARDLE, DOROTHY. Shakespeare: Man and Boy. London:
Faber & Faber, pp. 131-32, 159.
      Provides a general discussion of Marston.

18   MAXWELL, J.C. "A Reading in Marston." NQ, n.s. 8:195.
      Suggests a textual emendation to The Fawn. For additional
support for this emendation, see 1961.21.

19   PRAZ, MARIO. Storia della letteratura inglese. Florence:
G.C. Sansoni, pp. 203-5 and passim.
      Provides a general discussion of Marston.

20   ROSSITER, A.P. Angel with Horns and Other Shakespeare
Lectures. London: Longmans, p. 150.
      Suggests that Troilus and Cressida and Antonio and Mellida
are similar in that in both plays ideas are more important than
action.

21   SMITH, GERALD ALFRED. "A Reading in Marston." NQ, n.s.
8:397.
      Supports the textual emendation provided in 1961.18.

1962

1   AKRIGG, G.P.V. Jacobean Pageant: Or the Court of King James.
Cambridge, Mass.: Harvard University Press, p. 50. Reprint.
New York: Atheneum, 1967.
      Discusses the uproar caused by the initial performances of
Eastward Hoe.

2   ANON. "Marston, John." In Everyman's Dictionary of Literary
Biography, English and American. London: Dent, p. 454.
      Provides a general discussion of Marston.

3   BECKERMAN, BERNARD. Shakespeare at the Globe: 1599-1609.
    New York: Macmillan, passim. Reprint. New York: Collier
    Books, 1966.
        Provides passing comments on the way in which The
    Malcontent was probably performed at the Globe.

4   BEVINGTON, DAVID M. From Mankind to Marlowe: Growth and
    Structure in the Popular Drama of Tudor England. Cambridge,
    Mass.: Harvard University Press, p. 112.
        Points to Marston's dislike of the convention of actors
    doubling their roles.

5   BOKLUND, GUNNAR. The Duchess of Malfi, Sources, Themes,
    Characters. Cambridge, Mass.: Harvard University Press,
    pp. 82, 148, 156, 169, 177.
        Provides passing references to Marston.

6   BRADBROOK, M.C. The Rise of the Common Player: A Study of
    Actor and Society in Shakespeare's England. Cambridge, Mass.:
    Harvard University Press, passim.
        Provides passing comments on Marston.

7   BRETTLE, R.E. "Notes on John Marston." RES 13:390-93.
        Discusses extant specimens of Marston's handwriting and
    Marston's relationship with his father-in-law.

8   BUSH, DOUGLAS. English Literature in the Earlier Seventeenth
    Century. 2d ed. Oxford History of English Literature.
    Oxford: Clarendon Press, pp. 60, 108, 125, 550, 577.
        Provides passing comments on Marston. Revised edition of
    1945.2. Includes many rewritten sections and an expanded bibli-
    ography. Some variations appear in references to Marston.

9   FINKELPEARL, PHILIP J. "Henry Walley of the Stationers'
    Company and John Marston." PBSA 56:366-68.
        Sheds light on Marston's friendship with Walley.

10 FOAKES, R.A. "John Marston's Fantastical Plays: Antonio and
    Mellida and Antonio's Revenge." PQ 41:229-39.
        Suggests that Antonio and Mellida and Antonio's Revenge
    were written as parodies of the plays performed by the adult
    companies and thus are not awkwardly constructed melodramas. For
    further treatment of this idea, see 1971.11; 1972.6; 1977.6. For
    Richard Levin's criticism of this view, see 1972.20; 1974.12.

11 HARBAGE, ALFRED. "Intrigue in Elizabethan Tragedy." In
    Essays on Shakespeare and Elizabethan Drama in Honor of Hardin
    Craig. Edited by Richard Hosley. Columbia, Mo.: University
    of Missouri Press, pp. 37-44.
        Discusses Antonio's Revenge and views it as a faulty play.

12   HIBBARD, GEORGE R. <u>Thomas</u> <u>Nashe:</u> <u>A Critical Introduction.</u>
     London: Routledge & Kegan Paul, p. 55.
        Suggests that Marston might have been influenced by Nashe.

13   HUNTER, G.K. <u>John</u> <u>Lyly:</u> <u>The</u> <u>Humanist</u> <u>as</u> <u>Courtier.</u>
     Cambridge, Mass.:   Harvard University Press, passim.
        Provides passing comments on Marston.

14   JONES, ELDRED.   "The Physical Representation of African Char-
     acters on the English Stage during the Sixteenth and Seven-
     teenth Centuries." <u>TN</u> 17:17-21.
        Discusses the treatment of the Negro as villain in <u>Lust's</u>
     <u>Dominion.</u>

15   KNIGHT, G. WILSON. <u>The</u> <u>Golden</u> <u>Labyrinth:</u> <u>A Study of British</u>
     <u>Drama.</u>   New York: Norton, pp. 97-99, 130, 142, 159.
        Provides general discussions of <u>Antonio and Mellida,</u>
     <u>Antonio's</u> <u>Revenge,</u> <u>The</u> <u>Malcontent,</u> and suggests that Marston
     idealizes the person whose makeup contains both male and female
     characteristics.

16   NICOLSON, MARJORIE HOPE. <u>The</u> <u>Breaking</u> <u>of the Circle:</u> Studies
     <u>in the</u> <u>Effect</u> <u>of the</u> <u>"New</u> <u>Science"</u> <u>upon</u> <u>Seventeenth-Century</u>
     <u>Poetry.</u>   New York: Columbia University Press, pp. 47-48.
        Quotes a passage from <u>Histriomastix</u> concerning time.

17   RIBNER, IRVING. <u>Jacobean</u> <u>Tragedy:</u> <u>The</u> <u>Quest</u> <u>for</u> <u>Moral</u> <u>Order.</u>
     London: Methuen, pp. 12-14, 97, 163.   Reprint.   Totowa, N.J.:
     Rowman & Littlefield, 1979.
        Holds that Marston's satiric temperament disqualified him
     as a tragedian and sees <u>Sophonisba</u> as a tragedy limited in scope
     and effectiveness and atypical of the Jacobean age.

18   RIGHTER, ANNE. <u>Shakespeare</u> <u>and the</u> <u>Idea</u> <u>of the</u> <u>Play.</u>   London:
     Chatto & Windus, pp. 171-72.
        Compares Marston's references to actors with Shakespeare's
     comments on the acting profession.

                                 1963

1   ANON.   "Marston, John."   In <u>The</u> <u>Concise</u> <u>Encyclopedia</u> <u>of</u>
     <u>English</u> <u>and</u> <u>American</u> <u>Poets</u> <u>and</u> <u>Poetry.</u>   Edited by Stephen
     Spender and Donald Hall.   New York: Hawthorn Books, p. 196.
        Provides a general article on Marston.

2   BERGQUIST, G. WILLIAM, ed. <u>Three</u> <u>Centuries</u> <u>of</u> <u>English</u> <u>and</u>
     <u>American</u> <u>Plays:</u> <u>A Checklist.</u>   New York: Hafner, p. 169.
        Lists early editions of Marston's plays and masques avail-
     able on microfilm.

3   CROSS, GUSTAV. "Some Notes on the Vocabulary of John
    Marston." NQ, n.s. 10:308-12.
        A continuation of 1954.3. For other continuations, see
    1955.6; 1956.8; 1957.8; 1958.7; 1959.2; 1960.5; 1961.8.

4   DAY, MARTIN S. History of English Literature to 1660. Garden
    City, N.Y.: Doubleday, pp. 340-41, 351-52.
        Provides a general discussion of Marston.
        Antonio's Revenge, The Dutch Courtezan, Eastward Hoe, The
    Malcontent

5   DENT, R.W. "Ovid, Marlowe, and The Insatiate Countess." NQ,
    n.s. 10:334-35.
        Holds that passages in The Insatiate Countess are imita-
    tions of Marlowe's translation of Ovid's Amores.

6   ECCLES, MARK. Shakespeare in Warwickshire. Madison:
    University of Wisconsin Press, pp. 128, 138-39.
        Reprints a letter sent to Marston from the aldermen of
    Stratford-upon-Avon. The letter asks for certain legal documents
    concerning a Thomas Greene.

7   ECKHARDT, EDUARD. Die Dialekt und Ausländertypen des älteren
    englischen Dramas. Materials for the Study of the Old English
    drama, ser. 1, vols. 27, 32. Vaduz: Kraus Reprint, passim.
        A combined reprint of 1910.2 and 1911.4.

8   FINKELPEARL, PHILIP J. "Donne and Everard Gilpin [sic]:
    Additions, Corrections, and Conjectures." RES 14:164-67.
        Suggests that the families of Marston and Guilpin were
    related by marriage.

9   GOLDSMITH, ROBERT HILLIS. Wise Fools in Shakespeare. East
    Lansing: Michigan State University Press, passim.
        Provides passing comments upon the use of satire and treat-
    ment of fools in The Fawn and The Malcontent.

10 KILBY, JAMES A. "'Drinking Danes' in Shakespeare and
    Marston." NQ, n.s. 10:347.
        Suggests that the omission of the remark about drinking
    Danes in the 1616 quarto of Jack Drum's Entertainment supports
    the view that a similar passage was removed from the Hamlet text
    of the First Folio because of political pressures.

11 KLEIN, DAVID. The Elizabethan Dramatists as Critics. New
    York: Philosophical Library, passim. Reprint. Westport,
    Conn.: Greenwood Press, 1968.
        Quotes from plays and writings of Elizabethan dramatists to
    show that these authors had a clear understanding of dramatic and
    aesthetic principles and that these dramatists were not haphazard
    in their use of dramatic theory.

12   LECOCQ, LOUIS. "Travaux récents sur John Marston." EA
     16:351-63.
          Provides a survey of recent writings on Marston and
     includes annotations of these writings.

13   LEECH, CLIFFORD. "Recent Studies in Elizabethan and Jacobean
     Drama." SEL 3:369-85.
          Presents a favorable review of Anthony Caputi's John
     Marston, Satirist (1961.5) and tacit agreement with its findings.
     For another review, see 1963.16.

14   _____. Webster: The Duchess of Malfi. Studies in English
     Literature, no. 8. London: Edward Arnold, p. 8.
          Discusses Marston's plays as ingredients of Webster's
     dramatic background.

15   ORRELL, JOHN. "The Sources of Marston's The Wonder of Women
     or The Tragedie of Sophonisba." NQ, n.s. 10:102-3.
          Suggests that Appian's account of Sophonisba is the major
     source of the play and that Marston used Livy's telling of the
     story to supplement Appian's.

16   PETER, J.D. Review of Anthony Caputi's John Marston,
     Satirist. MLR 58:94-95.
          Disagrees with many of Caputi's findings (1961.5), particu-
     larly with his emphasis upon the burlesque element in Marston's
     writings. Sees the discussion of The Malcontent as faulty.
     Suggests that Marston is a minor writer who scarcely deserves a
     book-length study. For another review, see 1963.13.

17   QUENNELL, PETER. Shakespeare: A Biography. Cleveland:
     World Publishing Co., pp. 36, 188, 214, 263, 264, 270-71.
          Quotes from and comments upon Marston's defense in Jack
     Drum's Entertainment of children's theaters.

18   ROWSE, ALFRED LESLIE. William Shakespeare: A Biography. New
     York: Harper & Row, pp. 316-17. Reprint. New York: Pocket
     Books, 1965.
          Discusses the War of the Theaters.

19   STAGG, LOUIS CHARLES. "An Analysis and Comparison of the
     Imagery in the Tragedies of Chapman, Heywood, Jonson, Marston,
     Webster, Tourneur, and Middleton." Ph.D. diss., University of
     Arkansas.
          Classifies imagery in the tragedies of these authors as to
     subject, that is, beast images and food images, and shows how the
     imagery was used for dramatic purposes and delineation of charac-
     ter and setting of mood.

20   STEINER, GEORGE. The Death of Tragedy. New York: Hill &
     Wang, pp. 145-46.

Discusses the influence of Marston and other Elizabethan-Jacobean dramatists upon the dramatic efforts of the English romantics.

21   THAYER, C.G. Ben Jonson: Studies in the Plays. Norman:
      University of Oklahoma Press, pp. 3, 12, 38, 39.
          Provides passing comments on Marston.

22   TURNER, ROBERT Y. "The Causal Induction in Some Elizabethan
      Plays." SP 50:183-90.
          Discusses the use of allegorical characters in
      Histriomastix to frame and suggest the dramatic action.

                                1964

1   ANDERSON, DONALD K. "The Banquet of Love in English Drama
      (1595-1642)." JEGP 62:422-32.
          Discusses the use of the device of the love banquet in The
      Insatiate Countess.

2   FRIPP, EDGAR. Shakespeare: Man and Artist. Vol. 2. Oxford:
      Oxford University Press, 564-66.
          Suggests that Shakespeare is satirized as the character
      Troilus in Histriomastix.

3   HARBAGE, ALFRED. The Annals of English Drama, 975-1700.
      Revised by S. Schoenbaum. London: Methuen, passim.
          Revised edition of 1940.3. Uses recent findings to update
      Harbage's data.

4   HERRICK, MARVIN T. Comic Theory in the Sixteenth Century.
      Urbana: University of Illinois Press, p. 138.
          Cites The Malcontent as displaying common prejudices
      against foreigners.

5   HOLMES, MARTIN. The Guns of Elsinore. London: Chatto &
      Windus, passim.
          Provides passing comments on Marston.

6   HOY, CYRUS. The Hyacinth Room: An Investigation into the
      Nature of Comedy, Tragedy, and Tragicomedy. New York: Knopf,
      pp. 192-98, 215-16, and passim.
          Discusses the breakdown of reason in Antonio's Revenge and
      the conflict of reason and passion in The Dutch Courtezan.

7   HUNTER, G.K. "The Spoken Dirge in Kyd, Marston, and
      Shakespeare: A Background to Cymbeline." NQ, n.s. 11:146-47.
          Discusses the dirge in Antonio's Revenge.

8   KIMBROUGH, ROBERT. Shakespeare's Troilus and Cressida and Its
      Setting. Cambridge, Mass.: Harvard University Press, passim.

Provides passing comments on the following Marston plays:
Antonio and Mellida, Antonio's Revenge, Histriomastix, Jack
Drum's Entertainment, What You Will.

9   KNOLL, ROBERT E. Ben Jonson's Plays: An Introduction.
     Lincoln: University of Nebraska Press, pp. 61-62 and passim.
          Criticizes Marston's style in Antonio and Mellida as
     extravagant.

10   LEGOUIS, ÉMILE, and LOUIS CAZAMIAN. A History of English
     Literature. New York: Macmillan, pp. 320-21, 456-62.
          Revised edition of 1926.5., combined with Cazamian's second
     volume. Material on Marston is the same.

11   MURRAY, PETER B. A Study of Cyril Tourneur. Philadelphia:
     University of Pennsylvania Press, pp. 54-55, 152-53, 159-60,
     163-64, 249-53, and passim.
          Provides passing comments on Marston. Discusses the
     orthography of The Fawn and What You Will. Compares The
     Malcontent with The Revenger's Tragedy.

12   SMITH, IRWIN. Shakespeare's Blackfriars Playhouse: Its
     History and Design. New York: New York University Press,
     pp. 191-92, 195-96, 520-26, and passim.
          Provides passing comments on Marston and his involvement
     with the theatrical world. Reprints legal documents relating to
     Robert Keyser's suit of Richard Burbage, in which Marston is
     mentioned.
          The Dutch Courtezan, Eastward Hoe, The Fawn, The Malcontent

13   STODDER, JOSEPH HENRY. "Satire in Jacobean Tragedy." Ph.D.
     diss., University of California.
          Investigates the presence of satire in the tragedies of
     major Jacobean dramatists; sees satirical strengths in Marston's
     plays.
          Antonio and Mellida, The Dutch Courtezan, The Fawn, The
     Insatiate Countess, The Malcontent, Sophonisba

14   TOMLINSON, T.B. A Study of Elizabethan and Jacobean Tragedy.
     Cambridge: Cambridge University Press, pp. 218-23, 224, 229,
     237.
          Discusses Marston within the context of changing theatrical
     fashions and emerging dramatic decadence; sees Antonio's Revenge
     as decadent and The Dutch Courtezan and The Malcontent as suc-
     cesses.

1965

1   BALDWIN, T.W. On Act and Scene Division in the Shakspere
     First Folio. Carbondale: Southern Illinois University Press,
     p. 39.
          Discusses cues in Antonio and Mellida.

2   CAZAMIAN, LOUIS. The Development of English Humor. New York:
    AMS Press, pp. 112, 336, 342-44.
        Reprint of 1952.3.

3   COGHILL, NEVILL. Shakespeare's Professional Skills.
    Cambridge: Cambridge University Press, pp. 14-15.
        Criticizes the use of the supernatural in Antonio's Revenge
    and finds it inept.

4   CUNNINGHAM, JOHN E. Elizabethan and Early Stuart Drama.
    London: Evans Brothers, pp. 58-59, 90, 115.
        Provides a general discussion of Marston.

5   DAVIS, GILBERT R. "The Characterization of Mamon in Jack
    Drum's Entertainment." ELN 3:22-24.
        Attacks the view that Mamon is intended to represent a Jew
    and suggests that he is simply a caricature of the Elizabethan
    moneylender.

6   EVANS, IFOR. A Short History of English Drama. Riverside
    Studies in Literature. Boston: Houghton Mifflin Co.,
    pp. 73-75.
        Provides a general discussion of Marston and discusses
    Antonio and Mellida, Antonio's Revenge, The Malcontent.

7   FINKELPEARL, PHILIP J. "From Petrarch to Ovid: Metamorphoses
    in John Marston's Metamorphosis of Pigmalion's Image." ELH
    32:333-48.
        Suggests that the poem is a serious effort to write Ovidian
    verse and a satire.

8   HALLIDAY, F.E. "Marston, John." In A Shakespeare Companion,
    1564-1964. Rev. ed. New York: Schocken Books, pp. 304-5.
        Provides a general discussion of Marston. Revised edition
    of 1952.4.

9   HONIGMANN, E.A.J. The Stability of Shakespeare's Text.
    Lincoln: University of Nebraska Press, pp. 12, 172, 173, 175,
    191.
        Provides passing comments upon the publication of Marston's
    plays.

10 JENSON, EJNER. "Themes and Imagery in the Plays of John
    Marston." Ph.D. diss., Tulane University.
        Suggests that Marston developed his skill in the use of
    imagery and that in his later plays imagery is powerfully
    employed to support themes.

11 LEECH, CLIFFORD. "Shakespeare: Elizabethan and Jacobean."
    QQ 72:5-25.
        Provides passing comments on Marston and Jacobean dramatic
    techniques.

12   LEVIN, RICHARD. "The Eager Queen and the Melancholy Moor."
      AN&Q 4:35-36.
          Suggests that the episode in Act II, Scene iii, of
      Shakespeare's Titus Andronicus in which Tamora tries to entice
      Aaron into making love to her and he refuses her advances was
      written to highlight her lechery. To confirm this point of view,
      the author parallels this scene with one in Lust's Dominion in
      which the queen is refused by Eleazar. Also suggests that the
      author or authors of Lust's Dominion modeled this scene on the
      one in Shakespeare's revenge play.

13   MATCHETTE, WILLIAM H. The Phoenix and the Turtle:
      Shakespeare's Poem and Chester's Loves Martyr. SengL, no. 1.
      The Hague: Mouton, passim.
          Comments upon Marston's contribution to the volume of
poems.

14   NOSWORTHY, J.M. Shakespeare's Occasional Plays: Their Origin
      and Transmission. New York: Barnes & Noble, passim.
          Provides passing comments on Marston and his plays. Sug-
gests that Sophonisba influenced Shakespeare and that Macbeth and
Antony and Cleopatra reveal verbal echoes of Marston's tragedy.

15   REED, ROBERT RENTOUL The Occult on the Tudor and Stuart
      Stage. Boston: Christopher Publishing House, pp. 161-63 and
      passim.
          Analyzes the portrayal of the witch Erictho in Sophonisba
and finds it successful.
          Antonio's Revenge

16   WHITAKER, VIRGIL. The Mirror up to Nature: The Technique of
      Shakespeare's Tragedies. San Marino, Calif.: Huntington
      Library, passim.
          Provides passing comments on Marston.

                                1966

1   ANON. "Marston, John." In The Reader's Encyclopedia of
      Shakespeare. Edited by Oscar James Campbell and Edward G.
      Quinn. New York: Crowell, pp. 503-4.
          Provides a general discussion of Marston and quotes and
comments upon Marston's remarks on Romeo and Juliet from The
Scourge of Villainy.

2   COLE, DOUGLAS. "The Comic Accomplice in Elizabethan Revenge
      Tragedy." RD 9:125-39.
          Discusses Strotzo and Balurdo of Antonio and Mellida and
Antonio's Revenge. Finds that these comic accomplices do not fit
well into the context of the plays and, therefore, reveal the
disjointedness critics have noticed in Marston's works.

3   ENCK, JOHN L. Jonson and the Comic Truth. Madison:
     University of Wisconsin Press, pp. 205-7 and passim.
     Presents a brief discussion of Eastward Hoe.

4   FINKELPEARL, PHILIP J. "John Marston's Histrio-Mastix as an
     Inns of Court Play: A Hypothesis." HLQ 29:223-34.
         Suggests that Histriomastix was written in accord with the
     views of the intellectuals at the inns of Court.

5   GUSS, DONALD L. John Donne, Petrarchist: Italianate Conceits
     and Love Theory in The Songs and Sonets. Detroit: Wayne
     State University Press, p. 176.
         Contrasts Marston's and Dryden's satires to illustrate an
     intellectual and spiritual shift in the seventeenth century.

6   INGRAM, R.W. "Marston, Old or New Elizabethan." HAB 17:
     19-26.
         Attacks the current view that Marston, through the use of
     parody, irony, and satire, was a significant forerunner of the
     theater of the absurd.
         Antonio and Mellida, Antonio's Revenge, The Malcontent

7   JONSON, BEN. Conversations with William Drummond of
     Hawthornden 1619. In Ben Jonson. Discoveries 1641,
     Conversations with William Drummond of Hawthornden 1619.
     Edited by G.B. Harrison. Bodley Head Quartos. New York:
     Barnes & Noble, p. 1-18.
         Reprint of an earlier, undated edition. For other editions
     of Conversations, see 1842.1; 1906.8; 1923.6.

8   LU, FEI-PAI. T.S. Eliot: The Dialectical Structure of His
     Theory of Poetry. Chicago: University of Chicago Press,
     p. 54.
         Discusses and quotes from Eliot's essay on Marston.
         Sophonisba

9   McDONALD, CHARLES OSBORNE. The Rhetoric of Tragedy: Form in
     Stuart Drama. Amherst: University of Massachusetts Press,
     pp. 161-78.
         Studies the use of rhetoric in The Malcontent and
     Sophonisba and finds Sophonisba a weak play, burdened
     with Senecan clichés.

10   MacLURE, MILLAR. George Chapman: A Critical Study. Toronto:
     University of Toronto Press, pp. 19-20, 46, 94, 229, 230.
         Provides passing comments on Eastward Hoe.

11   MEHL, DIETER. The Elizabethan Dumb Show. Cambridge, Mass.:
     Harvard University Press, pp. 123-38.
         Discusses the use of silent action and pantomime in Antonio
     and Mellida, Antonio's Revenge, The Fawn, The Malcontent,
     Sophonisba, and What You Will and finds Marston's blending of

such techniques with dramatic action a hallmark of his art and a contribution to the development of the dumb show.

12   RIBNER, IRVING, ed. Tudor and Stuart Drama. Goldentree
      Bibliographies. New York: Appleton-Century-Crofts,
      pp. 44-45.
          Provides a brief listing of books and articles concerning
      Marston. Presents no annotations, but indicates more important
      items with asterisks.

13   SAINTSBURY, GEORGE. A Short History of English Literature.
      New York: Macmillan, pp. 279, 343.
          Presents a general discussion of Marston. Revised edition
      of 1900.4.

14   SCHÄFER, JÜRGEN. Wort und Begriff Humour in der
      elisabethanischen Komödie. Munich: Verlag Aschendorff,
      passim.
          Provides passing comments upon Histriomastix, Jack Drum's
      Entertainment, The Scourge of Villainy, What You Will.

15   SCHOENBAUM, S. Internal Evidence and Elizabethan Dramatic
      Authorship: An Essay in Literary History and Method.
      Evanston, Ill.: Northwestern University Press, passim.
          Provides general and basic comments upon Marston within the
      contexts of Elizabethan publishing practices, manuscripts, modern
      editions of plays, and questions of authorship.

16   SERPIERI, ALESSANDRO. John Webster. Bari: Adriatica
      Editrice, passim.
          Provides passing comments on Marston.

17   SMITH, MARION BODWELL. Dualities in Shakespeare. Toronto:
      University of Toronto Press, p. 38.
          Discusses Oscar James Campbell's view that Troilus and
      Cressida was influenced by the satirical comedies of Marston and
      Chapman.

18   SPENCER, THEODORE. "The Elizabethan Malcontent." In Theodore
      Spencer: Selected Essays. Edited by Alan C. Purves. New
      Brunswick: Rutgers University Press, pp. 139-50.
          Reprint of 1948.8.

19   _____. "John Marston." In Theodore Spencer: Selected
      Essays. Edited by Alan C. Purves. New Brunswick: Rutgers
      University Press, pp. 123-38.
          Reprint of 1934.8.

20   STRATMAN, CARL J., ed. Bibliography of English Printed Tragedy
      1565-1900. Carbondale: Southern Illinois University Press,
      pp. 399-402.

Provides basic bibliographical data on Marston's tragedies, individual editions of the plays, and the appearance of the plays in collected editions of Marston's works. Lists libraries where manuscripts of Marston's tragedies may be found.

21   TUCKER, MARTIN, ed. "Marston, John." In Moulton's Library of Literary Criticism of English and American Authors. Vol. 1. New York: Frederick Ungar, pp. 351-53.
    Revised edition of 1935.12 with more recent criticism excerpted.

22   WOOD, J.O. "Woman with a Horn." HLQ 29:295-300.
    Discusses the curious case of an elderly Welsh woman who grew a four-inch horn from her forehead. Points out that this affliction resulted from a rare type of bone tumor, but stresses that many Elizabethans interpreted this growth to be the result of God's punishment of sin. Marston refers to this case in The Malcontent.

23   WOODBRIDGE, ELIZABETH. Studies in Jonson's Comedy. New York: Gordian Press, p. 84.
    Reprint of 1898.6.

24   YOUNG, DAVID. Something of Great Constancy: The Art of A Midsummer Night's Dream. New Haven: Yale University Press, pp. 131-32.
    Discusses Marston's defense of the imagination in What You Will and quotes the passage.

1967

1   BRETTLE, R.E. "John Marston and the Duke of Buckingham, 1627-1628." NQ, n.s. 14, 326-30.
    Suggests that Marston, after his retirement from the stage, authored two satirical poems against the duke of Buckingham.

2   BROOKE, C.F. TUCKER. The Renaissance. In A Literary History of England. Edited by Albert C. Baugh. 2d ed. New York: Appleton-Century-Crofts, pp. 563-65, S 563-65.
    Reprint of 1948.3. Prints Brooke's original text with minor corrections. Includes a supplement (S 563-65) by Matthias A. Shaaber listing current editions of Marston's plays and some of the important writings about him that appeared after the first edition of Brooke's work.

3   DAVIS, JOE LEE. The Sons of Ben: Jonsonian Comedy in Caroline England. Detroit: Wayne State University Press, pp. 92-94 and passim.
    Provides passing comments and remarks on Marston.

4   De LUNA, B.N. Jonson's Romish Plot: A Study of Cataline and Its Historical Context. Oxford: Clarendon Press, passim.
    Provides passing comments upon Marston.

5   EVANS, MAURICE. <u>English Poetry in the Sixteenth Century</u>. New
    York: Norton, pp. 158-61.
        Provides a general discussion of Marston and the satirical
    climate of his age.

6   FINKELPEARL, PHILIP J. "The Use of the Middle Temple's
    Christmas Revels in Marston's <u>The Fawne</u>." <u>SP</u> 64:199-209.
        Points out similarities between the Court of Cupid scene in
    <u>The Fawn</u> and the activities at the courts of love trials during
    the Christmas festivities at the Inns of Court. Suggests that
    <u>The Fawn</u> dramatizes this traditional entertainment.

7   FREEMAN, ARTHUR. <u>Thomas Kyd: Facts and Problems</u>. Oxford:
    Clarendon Press, pp. 126-28 and passim.
        Points out and discusses parodies of Kyd's <u>The Spanish
    Tragedy</u> in <u>Antonio and Mellida</u>.

8   GIBBONS, BRIAN, ed. Introduction to <u>The Revenger's Tragedy</u>.
    NMS. London: Benn, pp. xi-xii.
        Discusses Marston's possible influence upon the author of
    <u>The Revenger's Tragedy</u>.

9   HARVEY, Sir PAUL. "Marston, John." In <u>The Oxford Companion
    to English Literature</u>. Revised by Dorothy Eagle. 4th ed.
    Oxford: Clarendon Press, p. 520.
        Revised edition of 1932.5. Revisions mainly concern
    twentieth-century British authors. Material on Marston is
    the same as in earlier editions of this work.

10 JENSEN, EJNER. "Hall and Marston: The Role of the Satirist."
    <u>SNL</u> 4:72-83.
        Stresses that Hall was committed to an asthetic theory as
    to the nature and function of satire: that it should startle and
    shock men from the pursuit of vice. Holds that Marston had no
    clear theory of satire's function and seemed to ignore its impor-
    tant moral purpose. Sees Marston, moreover, weakening his satires
    with several aesthetic flaws, particularly overt didacticism.
    Judges that Hall is the more skilled and more effective practi-
    tioner of satire.

11 JONES, ELDRED. <u>Othello's Countrymen: The African in English
    Renaissance Drama</u>. London: Oxford University Press,
    pp. 72-78 and passim.
        Points out that the black characters in <u>Sophonisba</u> are
    shown to be villainous and suggests that the black servant Vangue
    represents the evil side of his master Syphax.

12 KEYISHIAN, HARRY. "Dekker's <u>Whore</u> and Marston's <u>Courtesan</u>."
    <u>ELN</u> 4:261-66.
        Suggests that <u>The Dutch Courtezan</u> was written in part to
    parody Thomas Dekker's <u>The Honest Whore, Part I</u> and its treatment
    of the heroine, a prostitute with a heart of gold.

13   MUIR, KENNETH. <u>Introduction</u> <u>to</u> <u>Elizabethan</u> <u>Literature</u>. New
     York: Random House, pp. 108, 155, 191.
     Provides basic comments on Marston and his writings.

14   PAULSON, RONALD. <u>The</u> <u>Fictions</u> <u>of</u> <u>Satire</u>. Baltimore: Johns
     Hopkins University Press, pp. 76, 89-92.
     Provides a general discussion of Marston as a verse sati-
     rist; sees Marston as defective in writing true satire.

15   PROSSER, ELEANOR. <u>Hamlet</u> <u>and</u> <u>Revenge</u>. Stanford: Stanford
     University Press, passim.
     Discusses <u>Antonio's</u> <u>Revenge</u> and <u>The</u> <u>Malcontent</u> within the
     context of the tradition of the Elizabethan revenge play; sug-
     gests that Marston wishes us to disapprove of Antonio's violence
     and condemn his murder of Piero.

16   RATHBURN, PAUL A. "Prose in the Plays of John Marston."
     Ph.D. diss., University of Wisconsin.
     Discusses Marston's use of dramatic prose and suggests that
     Marston was a more skilled prose artist than has been recognized.
     Observes that Marston experimented with different prose styles in
     his plays for purposes of satire, delineating character, and
     setting mood.
          <u>Antonio</u> <u>and</u> <u>Mellida</u>, <u>Antonio's</u> <u>Revenge</u>, <u>The</u> <u>Dutch</u>
     <u>Courtezan</u>, <u>The</u> <u>Fawn</u>, <u>Jack</u> <u>Drum's</u> <u>Entertainment</u>, <u>The</u> <u>Malcontent</u>,
     <u>What</u> <u>You</u> <u>Will</u>

17   SCHWEITZER, FREDERICK M., and HARRY E. WEDECK, eds. "Marston,
     John." In <u>Dictionary</u> <u>of</u> <u>the</u> <u>Renaissance</u>. New York:
     Philosophical Library, pp. 391-92.
     Provides a general discussion of Marston.

18   SENG, PETER J. <u>The</u> <u>Vocal</u> <u>Songs</u> <u>in</u> <u>the</u> <u>Plays</u> <u>of</u> <u>Shakespeare</u>.
     Cambridge, Mass.: Harvard University Press, pp. 19, 51, 153.
     Uses Marston's plays to illustrate musical terms.

19   SHEAVYN, PHOEBE. <u>The</u> <u>Literary</u> <u>Profession</u> <u>in</u> <u>the</u> <u>Elizabethan</u>
     <u>Age</u>. Revised by J.W. Saunders. New York: Barnes & Noble,
     passim.
     Revised edition of 1909.8. Alterations, based on recent
     scholarship, made with Sheavyn's approval. Provides a similar
     treatment of Marston.

20   SILVETTE, HERBERT. <u>The</u> <u>Doctor</u> <u>on</u> <u>the</u> <u>Stage:</u> <u>Medicine</u> <u>and</u>
     <u>Medical</u> <u>Men</u> <u>in</u> <u>Seventeenth-Century</u> <u>England</u>. Knoxville:
     University of Tennessee Press, passim.
     Cites passages in Marston's plays to illustrate
     seventeenth-century concepts of disease, medicines, and
     human nature.

21   SPIVACK, CHARLOTTE. <u>George</u> <u>Chapman</u>. TEAS, no. 60. New York:
     Twayne, pp. 99-103 and passim.
     Provides a general discussion of Marston and <u>Eastward</u> <u>Hoe</u>.

22   SUTHERLAND, JAMES. English Satire. Cambridge: Cambridge
      University Press, pp. 32-33, 141-42, and passim.
         Provides general discussions of Marston and the satirical
      climate of his age.

23   WHITER, WALTER. A Specimen of a Commentary on Shakespeare:
      Being the Text of the First (1794) Edition Revised by the
      Author and Never Previously Published. Edited by Alan Over
      and Mary Bell. London: Methuen, pp. 77, 83, 92.
         Cites Marston's plays to illustrate and define Elizabethan
      terms and usages.

24   WILSON, JOHN DOVER. What Happens in Hamlet. Cambridge:
      Cambridge University Press, p. 55.
         Revised edition of 1935.18. Contains additional material
      dealing with Hamlet criticism since the original edition. Com-
      ments on Marston remain the same.

                                    1968

1   ANON. "Marston, John." In Chamber's Biographical Dictionary.
      Edited by J.O. Thorne. New York: St. Martin's, p. 855.
         Provides a general discussion of Marston.

2   BERGSON, ALLEN. "A Study of the Ironic Tragedies of Marston
      and Chapman." Ph.D. diss., University of California at
      Berkeley.
         Suggests that in the tragedies of Marston and Chapman the
      protagonist sets out to do good but becomes immersed in evil and
      suffers a degeneration and fragmentation of personality.
      Antonio and Mellida, Antonio's Revenge

3   BEVINGTON, DAVID M. Tudor Drama and Politics: A Critical
      Approach to Topical Meaning. Cambridge, Mass.: Harvard
      University Press, pp. 25, 265-66, 279-80, 282-85.
         Discusses Antonio's Revenge, Histriomastix, and
      Satiromastix. Emphasizes ways in which they reflect upon
      theories of responsible social and political conduct.

4   COURTNEY, WINIFRED, ed. The Reader's Advisor: A Guide to the
      Best in Literature. Vol. 1. New York: Bowker, pp. 898-99.
         Lists currently available writings by and about Marston.
      Current editions of this book should be consulted for up-to-date
      offerings.

5   FISK, VIVA K. "Court Satire in the Dramas of John Webster,
      Thomas Middleton, and John Marston." Ph.D. diss., University
      of New Mexico.
         Suggests that the court dramas of these dramatists and
      other playwrights derive their violence, savagery, and bitterness
      from a conviction that courts no longer abide by the ideal of the

good commonwealth, but have become schools of vice, affecting the
entire nation.

6   FROST, DAVID L. The School of Shakespeare: The Influence of
    Shakespeare on English Drama, 1600-42. Cambridge: Cambridge
    University Press, pp. 39-41, 174-88, and passim.
        Discusses parallels between the works of Marston and
    Shakespeare and concludes that Shakespeare influenced Marston.
        Antonio and Mellida, Antonio's Revenge, The Malcontent

7   GIBBONS, BRIAN. Jacobean City Comedy: A Study of Satiric
    Plays by Jonson, Marston, and Middleton. Cambridge:
    Cambridge University Press, pp. 83-104.
        Suggests that Marston successfully learned to use the
    Jonsonian form of satirical drama and, making it his own, pro-
    duced an art based on parody and the portrayal of violent, dis-
    cordant emotions.
        Antonio and Mellida, Antonio's Revenge, The Fawn, The
    Malcontent, Satiromastix

8   HEILMAN, ROBERT BECHTOLD. Tragedy and Melodrama: Versions of
    Experience. Seattle: University of Washington Press,
    pp. 136, 190, 191, 202, 212, 225.
        Provides passing comments on Marston. Discusses the por-
    trayal of emotions in Antonio and Mellida and Antonio's Revenge,
    and suggests that it provides evidence of emerging decadence in
    the drama.

9   JACQUOT, JEAN, ed. Dramaturgie et société: rapports entre
    l'oeuvre théâtrale, son interprétation et son public aux XVIe
    et XVIIe siècles. Vol. 2. Paris: Éditions du Centre
    National de la Recherche Scientifique, passim.
        Includes a number of articles on Elizabethan drama that
    make passing comments on Marston.

10 LANDA, M.J. The Jew in Drama. Port Washington, N.Y.:
    Kennikat Press, pp. 77, 91, 94-95, 96.
        Discusses Mizaldus, a character meant to be a Jew in The
    Insatiate Countess, and shows that he is presented as evil.

11 NICOLL, ALLARDYCE. English Drama: A Modern Viewpoint.
    London: Harrap, pp. 4-15 and passim.
        Defends Marston's integrity as a playwright by pointing out
    that his techniques resemble those of the modern theater of the
    absurd.
        Antonio and Mellida, Antonio's Revenge

12 PENNELL, C.A., and W.P. WILLIAMS. "Marston, 1939-65." In
    Elizabethan Bibliography Supplements IV. London: Nether
    Press, pp. 33-43.
        Presents a supplement to Tannenbaum's bibliography of
    Marston (1940.5) and lists books and articles on Marston by year
    rather than author. Does not annotate these entries.

13   RHODES, ERNEST L. "Me Thinks This Stage Shews Like a Tennis
     Court." RenP 21-28.
        Uses Eleazar's comparison of the stage to a tennis court to
     suggest the structural influence of tennis courts upon the Eliza-
     bethan stage and to suggest some stages, instead of being plat-
     forms, were basically rectangular and contained five doors in
     three abutting walls.

14   ROBBINS, MARTIN L. "Shakespeare's Sweet Music: A Glossary of
     Musical Terms in the Work of Shakespeare (with Additional
     Examples from the Plays of Lyly, Marston, and Jonson)." Ph.D.
     diss., Brandeis University.
        Includes musical terms from Marston's plays.

15   ROSTON, MURRAY. Biblical Drama in England: From the Middle
     Ages to the Present Day. Evanston, Ill.: Northwestern
     University Press, p. 84.
        Briefly discusses The Dutch Courtezan as part of an anti-
     Puritan theatrical movement.

16   SANDERS, WILBUR. The Dramatist and Received Idea: Studies in
     the Plays of Marlowe and Shakespeare. Cambridge: Cambridge
     University Press, pp. 115, 342, 362, 382.
        Provides passing comments on Marston.

17   SIEGEL, PAUL N. Shakespeare in His Time and Ours. Notre
     Dame: University of Notre Dame Press, p. 240.
        Quotes satirical comments of Marston on Puritans.

18   STAVIG, MARK. John Ford and the Traditional Moral Order.
     Madison: University of Wisconsin Press, pp. 133-34.
        Compares the murder of Ferentes in Ford's Love's Sacrifice
     to that of Piero in Antonio's Revenge.

19   TRUAX, ELIZABETH. "Preview of the Vanishing Hero: A Study of
     the Protagonists in Jacobean Drama." Ph.D. diss., University
     of Southern California.
        Suggests that the dramatic heroes of the Jacobean period
     show a progressive diminishment in stature from the heroes of the
     epic and high tragedy. Stresses that instead of performing
     heroic action, these men sink into a morass of thwarted emotions,
     baffled reasoning, petty crimes, and senseless murder. Studies
     Antonio in Antonio's Revenge from this perspective.

20   VICKERS, BRIAN. The Artistry of Shakespeare's Prose. London:
     Methuen, p. 7.
        Comments upon Malevole's use of prose in The Malcontent.

1969

1   ALLEN, RICHARD OTTAWAY.   "Jacobean Drama and the Literature of
     Decay: A Study of Conservative Reaction in Literature."
     Ph.D. diss., University of Michigan.
          Suggests that a central element in the Jacobean literature
     of decay is anomie, a sense of alienation and loss of selfhood,
     brought about by disorienting social change.   Stresses that indi-
     viduals afflicted with this condition suffer from hysteria, sense
     of abandonment and apocalypse, retreats into inactivity, and
     outbursts of violence.   Such feelings produce central features of
     the writings of Webster, Tourneur, Chapman, Marston, and others.

2   ANSARI, K.H.   John Webster: Image Patterns and Canon.
     Kerala, India: Jalaluddin Rumi Publications, passim.
          Provides passing comments upon Antonio's Revenge.

3   BATTENHOUSE, ROY W.   Shakespearean Tragedy: Its Art and
     Christian Premises.   Bloomington: Indiana University Press,
     p. 309.
          Suggests that Sophonisba might have influenced Shakespeare
     in the choice of writing Roman plays.

4   BERLAND, ELLEN.   "The Function of Irony in Marston's Antonio
     and Mellida."   SP 66:739-55.
          Suggests that the dramatic structure of Antonio and Mellida
     is based upon an irony that points up the discrepancy between
     appearance and reality, but that does not attempt to reform the
     world as satire does.   Views the play as a parody of romantic
     comedy presenting an ironical view of life.

5   BRADBROOK, M.C.   Shakespeare, the Craftsman: The Clark
     Lectures 1968.   London: Chatto & Windus, pp. 127-29, 130-32.
          Discusses Antonio's Revenge and The Malcontent as absurdist
     black comedies.

6   CHARNEY, MAURICE.   Style in Hamlet.   Princeton: Princeton
     University Press, p. 290.
          Compares Malevole's shifts in mood in The Malcontent with
     those of Hamlet.

7   DAVIS, WALTER R.   Idea and Act in Elizabethan Fiction.
     Princeton: Princeton University Press, p. 195.
          Comments upon Marston's charge that Hall abandoned fiction
     for truth.

8   FINKELPEARL, PHILIP J.   John Marston of the Middle Temple.
     Cambridge, Mass.:   Harvard University Press, 284 pp.
          Suggests that the Inns of Court, where Marston resided,
     created a profound seminal influence upon his dramatic style and
     thought.   Devotes the book's first section to a discussion of the

Inns of Court, their residents, the ways of living and intellectual traditions of the students, and the dramatic festivities and
entertainments. Sees the atmosphere of the Middle Temple foster-
ing an ambiguous outlook, a fusion of cynicism and idealism and
other contrarieties that influenced Marston. Devotes the book's
second portion to the influence of the Inns on Marston's works.
Also gives attention to such topics as contemporary allusions and
persons satirized by Marston. Though not elevating Marston to
the ranks of the greatest writers, concludes by judging him an
author worthy of attention. Reviews: 1970.4, 13, 16; 1971.29.
Reprint of chapter on The Malcontent: 1970.7.

Antonio and Mellida, Antonio's Revenge, Certain Satires,
The Dutch Courtezan, Eastward Hoe, The Fawn, Histriomastix, The
Insatiate Countess, Jack Drum's Entertainment, The Malcontent,
The Metamorphosis of Pigmalion's Image, The Scourge of Villainy,
Sophonisba, What You Will

9   GENTILI, VANNA. Le Figure della pazzia nel teatro
     elisabettiano. Lecca: Edizione Milella, passim.
          Provides passing comments on Antonio and Mellida, Antonio's
     Revenge, The Fawn, and The Malcontent.

10   GOTTWALD, MARIA. Satirical Elements in Ben Jonson's Comedies.
     Wroclaw: La Société des Sciences et des Lettres de Wroclaw,
     pp. 50-60.
          Discusses Jonson's attack upon Marston in Poetaster.

11   GREENFIELD, THELMA. The Induction in Elizabethan Drama.
     Eugene: University of Oregon Press, pp. 83-87 and passim.
          Discusses inductions in Antonio and Mellida, The
     Malcontent, Sophonisba, and What You Will.

12   GREENMAN, DAVID J. "The Soul of Lively Action: Dramatic
     Activity in the Plays of John Marston." Ph.D. diss., Indiana
     University.
          Defends Marston from the charge of dramatic ineptitude and
     suggests that he was a skilled theatrical craftsman who employed
     a variety of techniques--pageantry, symbols, dumb shows--to give
     unity to his plays and delight to his audiences.

13   GRUNDY, JOAN. The Spenserian Poets: A Study in Elizabethan
     and Jacobean Poetry. London: Edward Arnold, pp. 165, 166,
     171, 176.
          Provides passing comments on Marston. Suggests that George
     Wither in writing the dedication to his satires might have imi-
     tated Marston.

14   HEATH-STUBBS, JOHN. The Verse Satire. London: Oxford
     University Press, pp. 25-28.
          Provides a general discussion of The Scourge of Villainy.

15   HODGART, MATTHEW. <u>Satire</u>. Home University Library. New
      York: McGraw-Hill, pp. 141-42, 191.
           Provides a general discussion of Marston.

16   LEECH, CLIFFORD. <u>Tragedy</u>. Critical Idiom, no. 1. London:
      Methuen, pp. 3-4, 67.
           Quotes from the prologue to <u>Antonio's Revenge</u> to provide
      one of many comments upon the nature of tragedy.

17   LEVIN, RICHARD. "The Elizabethan 'Three-Level' Play." <u>RenD</u>,
      n.s. 2:23-37.
           Discusses levels of action in <u>Eastward Hoe</u>.

18   McPEEK, JAMES A.S. <u>The Black Book of Knaves and Unthrifts in
      Shakespeare and Other Renaissance Authors</u>. Storrs:
      University of Connecticut Press, pp. 195-96.
           Points out villainous behavior described in <u>The Scourge of
      Villainy</u>.

19   MEHL, DIETER. "Emblems in English Renaissance Drama." <u>RenD</u>,
      n.s. 2:39-57.
           Comments upon the burlesquing of emblems in <u>Antonio and
      Mellida</u>.

20   OMANS, STUART E. "The War of the Theaters: An Approach to
      Its Origins, Development, and Meaning." Ph.D. diss., North-
      western University.
           Criticizes past studies of the War of the Theaters and
      suggests that the central issue was not clashes of personalities
      but the nature of the theater and dramatic satire. Points out
      that some personal satire appears, but holds that it is direct
      and explicit. Looked at from this perspective, the plays in-
      volved can be seen as valid works of art in their own right, not
      as mere vehicles of personal diatribe.
           <u>Jack Drum's Entertainment</u>, <u>Histriomastix</u>, <u>Satiromastix</u>,
      <u>What You Will</u>

21   PRICE, GEORGE R. <u>Thomas Dekker</u>. TEAS, no. 71. New York:
      Twayne, passim.
           Provides passing comments on Marston.

22   QUINN, EDWARD. "Marston, John." In <u>The Reader's Encyclopedia
      of World Drama</u>. Edited by John Gassner and Edward Quinn. New
      York: Crowell, pp. 549-50.
           Provides a general article on Marston.

23   RIBNER, IRVING, ed. "John Marston, 1576-1634." In <u>The
      Critical Temper: A Survey of Modern Criticism on English and
      American Literature from Its Beginnings to the Twentieth
      Century</u>. Edited by Martin Tucker. Vol. 1. New York:
      Frederick Ungar, pp. 404-9.
           Provides excerpts from criticism of Marston.

24   RUTHVEN, K.K. The Conceit. Critical Idiom, no. 4. London:
     Methuen, p. 21.
          Comments upon Marston's contempt for certain conceits of
     amorous poetry.

25   WEST, HERBERT F., Jr. "Unifying Devices in Four Globe Plays."
     Ph.D. diss., University of Georgia.
          Studies such unifying devices as foreshadowing, tone, echo
     scenes, balance, and contrast in four Globe plays and suggests
     that each of the plays, including The Malcontent, is more care-
     fully constructed than many critics have realized.

                              1970

1   AGGELER, GEOFFREY D. "Stoicism and Revenge in Marston." ES
     51:507-17.
          Suggests that Antonio's Revenge and The Malcontent explore
     the problem of revenge from a Stoical point of view derived from
     Seneca's essays, Epictetus, and Plutarch and that Marston opposes
     blood vengeance.

2   BERGSON, ALLEN. "The Ironic Tragedies of Marston and Chapman:
     Notes on Jacobean Tragic Form." JEGP 69:613-30.
          Suggests that an underlying ironic pattern exists in
     Antonio and Mellida and Antonio's Revenge, which unfolds
     as Antonio degenerates morally and loses the noble standards he once
     held.

3   BRENNAN, ELIZABETH M. "'An Understanding Auditory': An
     Audience for John Webster." In John Webster. Edited by
     Brian Morris. Mermaid Critical Commentaries. London: Benn,
     pp. 1-19.
          Discusses Marston's influence upon Webster.

4   COLE, DOUGLAS. "Recent Studies in Elizabethan and Jacobean
     Drama." SEL 10:425-38.
          Reviews Finkelpearl's John Marston of the Middle Temple
     (1969.8). Outlines Finkelpearl's thesis that Marston was influ-
     enced by the Middle Temple. Praises Finkelpearl for maintaining
     a balanced view of Marston and not letting his enthusiasm for a
     minor writer override critical judgment. Suggests that on the
     whole Finkelpearl's book is a valid contribution to the study of
     Marston.

5   DONNO, ELIZABETH STORY. "The Epyllion." In English Poetry
     and Prose, 1540-1674. Edited by by Christopher Ricks. History
     of Literature in the English language, no. 2. London: Barrie
     & Jenkins, pp. 82-95.
          Provides a basic discussion of The Metamorphosis of
     Pigmalion's Image.

6 FABER, J. ARTHUR. "Rhetorical Strategy in John Marston's <u>The</u> <u>Malcontent</u>." <u>HussR</u> 4:18-24.
   Suggests that Marston was a skilled dramatist who made effective use of the rhetorical training of his time and uses <u>The</u> <u>Malcontent</u> to illustrate this idea. Observes that Marston uses the rhetorical concepts of ethos (the nature of the speaker) and pathos (the emotional response of the audience) to characterize Malevole and win for him the spectator's approval. Furthermore, suggests that Acts I and II make use of deliberative rhetoric (the rhetoric of politics), Acts III and IV make use of forensic rhetoric (the rhetoric of law), and Act V makes use of epideictic rhetoric (the rhetoric of ceremony and praise).

7 FINKELPEARL, PHILIP J. "<u>The</u> <u>Malcontent</u>: Virtuous Machiavellianism." In <u>Shakespeare's</u> <u>Contemporaries</u>. Edited by Max Bluestone and Norman Rabkin. 2d ed. Englewood Cliffs, N.J.: Prentice-Hall, pp. 255-69.
   Discusses the major characters, then centers attention upon Malevole-Altofronto and his Machiavellian conduct; sees the question of how a virtuous man can behave morally in a corrupt world as a central concern of the play. Suggests that Marston sees a resolution to this problem in the view that the virtuous ruler or man must conceal his virtue and pretend to take part in the corruption of the world, even at times participating in it, but ever keeping his ideals in sight. Reprints the chapter on <u>The</u> <u>Malcontent</u> from 1969.8.

8 FRASER, RUSSELL. <u>The</u> <u>War</u> <u>against</u> <u>Poetry</u>. Princeton: Princeton University Press, p. 84.
   Quotes Marston from <u>Eastward</u> <u>Hoe</u> to illustrate Jacobean attitudes toward the nobles' lack of thrift.

9 GURR, ANDREW. <u>The</u> <u>Shakespearean</u> <u>Stage,</u> <u>1574-1664</u>. Cambridge: Cambridge University Press, passim.
   Provides passing comments on Marston and his plays.

10 HERNDL, GEORGE C. <u>The</u> <u>High</u> <u>Design</u>: <u>English</u> <u>Renaissance</u> <u>Tragedy</u> <u>and</u> <u>the</u> <u>Natural</u> <u>Law</u>. Lexington: University Press of Kentucky, pp. 125-26.
   Suggests that Calvinism forms the intellectual core of <u>The</u> <u>Scourge</u> <u>of</u> <u>Villainy</u>.

11 HIRST, DÉSIRÉE. "The Enigmatic Mr. Marston." <u>AntigR</u> 1:97-99.
   Speculates upon Marston's obsession with evil and raises the question as to whether <u>Antonio's</u> <u>Revenge,</u> more than any other of Marston's plays, expresses the author's view of life.
   <u>Antonio</u> <u>and</u> <u>Mellida</u>, <u>Antonio's</u> <u>Revenge</u>, <u>The</u> <u>Fawn</u>, <u>The</u> <u>Malcontent</u>

12 HOLMES, DAVID M. <u>The</u> <u>Art</u> <u>of</u> <u>Thomas</u> <u>Middleton</u>: <u>A</u> <u>Critical</u> <u>Study</u>. Oxford: Clarendon Press, p. 43.

Contrasts Middleton's detached style of writing with
Marston's didacticism.

13   JENSEN, EJNER. Review of Philip J. Finkelpearl's John Marston
      of the Middle Temple. JEGP 69:174-77.
            Views Finkelpearl's study (1969.8) as the best to date on
      Marston, but believes that Finkelpearl overestimates the influ-
      ence of the Inns of Court on Marston's dramatic style. Disagrees
      with some of the individual analyses of the plays, but feels that
      on the whole the book is a helpful work of scholarship, one that
      takes Marston as a serious writer and makes a helpful, though not
      entirely adequate, attempt to understand the essence of Marston's
      art and outlook.

14   _____. "Theme and Imagery in The Malcontent." SEL 10:367-84.
            Suggests that the imagery performs a central role in the
      play in depicting a world of corruption and evil.

15   JONES, ROBERT C. "Italian Settings and the 'World' of Eliza-
      bethan Tragedy." SEL 10:251-68.
            Points out that the Italy of Elizabethan dramatists was an
      Italy of the Elizabethan imagination rather than actuality and
      comments upon Antonio and Mellida, Antonio's Revenge, and The
      Malcontent in this context.

16   LEVENSON, JILL. Review of Philip J. Finkelpearl's John
      Marston of the Middle Temple. MP 68:199-201.
            Presents a detailed report on Finkelpearl's findings and
      gives a favorable response to the book (1969.8). Faults it only
      in being too brief and not giving full development to some of the
      ideas and theories presented.

17   McDONALD, ELMER MILTON. "John Day's Coterie Comedy." Ph.D.
      diss., University of Virginia.
            Studies Day's comedies in the light of comic conventions in
      the plays of Marston and others.

18   MYERS, ROBIN, ed. A Dictionary of Literature in the English
      Language from Chaucer to 1940. Vol. 1. Oxford: Pergamon
      Press, 559.
            Provides a brief bibliography of Marston, listing first
      editions of his plays and collected editions of his works.

19   PARKES, HENRY BAMFORD. The Divine Order: Western Culture in
      the Middle Ages and the Renaissance. London: Gollancz,
      pp. 456-58.
            Sees Marston's pessimism influencing Shakespeare.

20   PATTERSON, ANNABEL. Hermogenes and the Renaissance: Seven
      Ideas of Style. Princeton: Princeton University Press,
      passim.
            Provides passing comments on The Scourge of Villainy.

21 POVIACS, JOYCE THERESA. "Actor as Character and Structure in the Plays of John Marston." Ph.D. diss., University of Minnesota.

Suggests that Marston's art is based upon an awareness that the stage world is an illusion, a fantasy realm, and that he uses actors to remind the audience of this truth and to unify the plays. These techniques lead to a tragiabsurd portrayal of life. Antonio and Mellida, Antonio's Revenge, The Dutch Courtezan, The Fawn, Jack Drum's Entertainment, The Malcontent, What You Will

22 PUTT, S. GORLEY. "The Relevance of Jacobean Drama." E&S 23:18-33.

Discusses Marston's pessimism.

23 SAMPSON, GEORGE. The Concise Cambridge History of English Literature. 3d ed. Cambridge: Cambridge University Press, pp. 251, 254-55, 268, 280.

Provides a general discussion of Marston.

24 SCHOENBAUM, S. Shakespeare's Lives. Oxford: Clarendon Press, pp. 566, 584, 596, 605, 678, 698.

Provides passing comments on Marston.

25 STAGG, LOUIS CHARLES. An Index to the Figurative Language of John Marston's Tragedies. Charlottesville: Bibliographical Society of the University of Virginia, 86 pp.

Cited in the 1970 MLA International Bibliography.

26 STARTZMAN, LOUIS E. "Images of Evil in the Formal Verse Satires of Joseph Hall, John Marston, John Donne, and Alexander Pope." Ph.D. diss., Ohio University.

Concerns each of these satirist's perceptions of evil as a means of understanding the individual writer's concept of the world and human nature; finds Marston presenting the view that man, basically a rational being, has forsaken reason and yielded himself up to base appetites. The Scourge of Villainy

27 TOKSON, ELLIOT HARVEY. "The Popular Image of the Black Man in English Drama, 1550-1688." Ph.D. diss., Columbia University.

Discusses the treatment of Eleazar as villain in Lust's Dominion.

1971

1 ANDREWS, MICHAEL C. "Jack Drum's Entertainment as Burlesque." RenQ 24:226-31.

Suggests that Jack Drum's Entertainment burlesques romantic plays of the public stage in general and in particular a contemporary play entitled The Trial of Chivalry.

2   AUSTIN, ALLEN. <u>T.S.</u> <u>Eliot:</u> <u>The</u> <u>Literary</u> <u>and</u> <u>Social</u>
     <u>Criticism.</u> Bloomington: Indiana University Press, p. 115.
         Quotes from and comments upon Eliot's essay on Marston
     (1934.2-3; 1951.5; 1956.11).
         <u>Sophonisba</u>

3   BERGSON, ALLEN. "Dramatic Style as Parody in Marston's <u>Antonio</u>
     <u>and</u> <u>Mellida.</u>" SEL 11:307-25.
         Suggests that <u>Antonio</u> <u>and</u> <u>Mellida</u> and <u>Antonio's</u> <u>Revenge</u>
     should be viewed as one ten-act play whose dramatic style is
     based upon literary parody. Suggests that such an approach sheds
     light upon concerns such as the work's tone, characterization,
     and use of violence.

4   BRODWIN, LEONORA LEET. <u>Elizabethan</u> <u>Love</u> <u>Tragedy,</u> <u>1587-1625.</u>
     New York: New York University Press, pp. 68-86 and passim.
         Discusses Marston's plays as representing a breakdown in
     the use of courtly love traditions as a basis of love tragedy.
     Sees Marston experimenting with new types of love tragedy, to
     which the old standards and traditions do not apply.
         <u>Antonio</u> <u>and</u> <u>Mellida</u>, <u>Antonio's</u> <u>Revenge</u>, <u>The</u> <u>Insatiate</u>
     <u>Countess</u>, <u>Sophonisba</u>

5   BROWER, REUBEN A. <u>Hero</u> <u>and</u> <u>Saint:</u> <u>Shakespeare</u> <u>and</u> <u>the</u> <u>Graeco-</u>
     <u>Roman</u> <u>Heroic</u> <u>Tradition.</u> Oxford: Clarendon Press, p. 240.
         Discusses Marston's ideas and <u>Troilus</u> <u>and</u> <u>Cressida.</u>

6   CALDWELL, HARRY B., and DAVID L. MIDDLETON, eds. <u>English</u>
     <u>Tragedy,</u> <u>1370-1600:</u> <u>Fifty</u> <u>Years</u> <u>of</u> <u>Criticism.</u> San Antonio,
     Texas: Trinity University Press, pp. 52-54.
         Provides a brief listing of some of the more important
     items concerning <u>Antonio</u> <u>and</u> <u>Mellida</u> and <u>Antonio's</u> <u>Revenge.</u>

7   COWPER, J.M., ed. Introduction to <u>The</u> <u>Times</u> <u>Whistle,</u> <u>or</u> <u>A</u> <u>New</u>
     <u>Daunce</u> <u>of</u> <u>Seven</u> <u>Satires</u> <u>and</u> <u>Other</u> <u>Poems.</u> EETS. London:
     Published for the Early English Texts Society by N. Trübner,
     pp. ix, xx.
         Raises the possibility that Marston wrote this work, but
     rejects the idea.

8   DESSEN, ALAN C. <u>Jonson's</u> <u>Moral</u> <u>Comedy.</u> Evanston, Ill.:
     Northwestern University Press, pp. 31-32, 35, 66, 67.
         Includes a basic discussion of <u>Histriomastix.</u>

9   FOAKES, R.A. <u>Shakespeare,</u> <u>The</u> <u>Dark</u> <u>Comedies</u> <u>to</u> <u>the</u> <u>Last</u>
     <u>Plays:</u> <u>From</u> <u>Satire</u> <u>to</u> <u>Celebration.</u> Charlottesville:
     University Press of Virginia, pp. 39-43, 63-75, and passim.
         Defends Marston as an artist and sees the essence of his
     art residing in caricature and burlesque. For further treatment
     of this idea, see 1962.10; 1972.5; 1977.6. For criticism of this
     idea, see 1972.16; 1974.12.

Antonio and Mellida, Antonio's Revenge, Eastward Hoe, The
Malcontent, The Scourge of Villainy

10   GECKLE, GEORGE L. "Fortune in Marston's The Malcontent."
     PMLA 86:202-9.
        Suggests that the concept of the wheel of fortune is a
     central symbol in the play and informs the drama's action. Holds
     that Malevole overcomes his adversaries because he approaches
     fortune with a Stoical fortitude and Christian faith. Reprinted:
     1980.5.

11   GUNBY, D.C. Webster: The White Devil. Studies in English
     Literature, no. 45. London: Edward Arnold, p. 18.
        Discusses the use of sententiae in Marston's plays.

12   HORWICH, RICHARD. "Hamlet and Eastward Hoe." SEL 11:223-33.
        Points out various parallels, such as those in the names of
     characters and attitudes toward wealth, between Hamlet and
     Eastward Hoe and suggests that Eastward Hoe derives much of
     its force from parodying and imitating Shakespeare's play.

13   JAMIESON, MICHAEL. "Marston, John." In The Penguin Companion
     to English Literature. Edited by David Daiches. New York:
     McGraw-Hill, p. 351.
        Provides a general article on Marston.

14   JOHNSON, LEMUEL A. The Devil, the Gargoyle, and the Buffoon:
     The Negro as Metaphor in Western Literature. Port Washington,
     N.Y.: Kennikat Press, p. 37.
        Discusses the Negro as villain in Sophonisba.

15   JONES, EMRYS. Scenic Form in Shakespeare. Oxford: Clarendon
     Press, p. 264.
        Suggests that Shakespeare might have been influenced by
     Sophonisba.

16   JORGENSEN, PAUL N. Our Naked Frailties: Sensational Art and
     Meaning in Macbeth. Berkeley: University of California
     Press, p. 127.
        Quotes from The Insatiate Countess to illustrate an
     Elizabethan conventional creation of a tragic atmosphere.

17   KERMODE, FRANK. "Shakespeare's Learning." In Shakespeare,
     Spenser, and Donne. New York: Viking, pp. 181-99.
        Discusses Marston's contribution to Robert Chester's Love's
     Martyr.

18   KRIEGER, MURRAY. The Classic Vision: The Retreat from
     Extremity in Modern Literature. Baltimore: Johns Hopkins
     University Press, p. 54.
        Suggests that Marston's plays reveal a split in the
     Nietzschean Apollonian-Dionysian unity--a unity maintained
     in Shakespeare's plays.

19   LAWSON, ANITA S. "In Dispraise of Folly: Satiric Themes and
     Techniques in Selected Plays of Chapman, Jonson, and Marston,
     1597-1606." Ph.D. diss., Tulane University.
          Analyzes the ways in which these dramatists use and modify
     traditional dramatic conventions to present their satirical por-
     traits of vices and follies. Finds that Marston used familiar
     genres and conventions as satirical techniques as well as employ-
     ing traditional techniques in nontraditional ways. Suggests that
     Marston had a cautious faith in neo-Stoicism as a means by which
     man could confront evil.
          Antonio and Mellida, The Dutch Courtezan, The Malcontent

20   LEVER, J.W. The Tragedy of State. London: Methuen,
     pp. 20-28.
          Sympathetically assesses Antonio's Revenge as a revenge
     play and sees Marston as aware of moral ambiguities in the play
     and in life. Points out a historical parallel to the behavior of
     Piero's assassins.
          Antonio and Mellida

21   LEVIN, RICHARD. The Multiple Plot in English Renaissance
     Drama. Chicago: University of Chicago Press, pp. 88-90.
          Suggests that Eastward Hoe satirizes both the vices of the
     reprobates and the traditional middle-class values upheld by the
     "good characters."

22   LYONS, BRIDGET GELLERT. Voices of Melancholy: Studies in
     Literary Treatments of Melancholy in Renaissance England. New
     York: Barnes & Noble, pp. 58-76, 117-20, and passim.
          Discusses the influence of the concept of melancholy as a
     physiological disorder upon literature. Devotes a chapter to
     Marston, discussing him as a writer obsessed with portraying
     melancholy in various forms. Suggests that Marston's treatments
     of melancholy shed light on other works of the period.

23   MAXWELL, J.C. "An Echo of Tacitus in Marston." NQ, n.s.
     18:13-14.
          Suggests that Marston in writing Act I, Scene ii, 11. 319-
     23 of The Fawn was following the words of the opening paragraph
     of Tacitus's Histories.

24   MORRIS, BRIAN. "Elizabethan and Jacobean Drama." English
     Drama to 1710. Edited by Christopher Ricks. History of
     Literature in the English Language, no. 3. London: Barrie &
     Jenkins, pp. 65-117.
          Provides a general discussion of Marston.
          The Fawn, The Malcontent, Sophonisba

25   O'NEILL, DAVID. "The Commencement of Marston's Career as a
     Dramatist." RES 22:442-45.
          Suggests that Marston was interested in playwriting and
     turned to it before the ban on satire was enacted and that,

therefore, the burning of his satires cannot be considered the sole factor that made him a dramatist.

26   PERRY, GEORGE FRANCIS. "A Study of the Image of Man in
      Jacobean City Comedy." Ph.D. diss., Fordham University.
           Suggests that the writers of Jacobean city comedy base
      their satirical portraits of the citizens and their wives upon
      classical and medieval character types and, therefore, present a
      limited view of human nature.

27   POWELL, ANTHONY. "Marston and Jorrocks." TLS, 2 April,
      p. 396.
           Suggests that Robert Surtees, the creator of Mr. Jorrocks,
      knew The Dutch Courtezan and was influenced by it, particularly
      in the choices of the names of some of his characters.

28   [PUTT, S. GORLEY.] "Theatre of Cruelty in the Middle Temple."
      TLS, 5 February, pp. 155-57.
           Reviews Finkelpearl's John Marston of the Middle Temple
      (1969.8). Comments briefly on Finkelpearl's main argument, then
      presents a discussion and evaluation of Marston. Sees Marston as
      a serious and worthy artist whose plays are better understood
      from the standpoint of the 1970s than from those of the nine-
      teenth century and the early decades of the twentieth. Finds
      Marston a mannerist artist, employing such diverse styles as
      parody, satire, violent melodrama, and verbal experimentation to
      portray a dark and distressed vision of human experience, com-
      parable to that of the modern theater of the absurd.

29   RONK, BRUCE A. "John Marston, the Growth of a Satirist."
      Ph.D. diss., University of Nebraska.
           Suggests that Marston's use of satirical techniques was not
      static but developed throughout his career. Points out that in
      the early nondramatic satires Marston adopts a bitter, vindictive
      stance, but suggests that in the plays, while still writing
      satire, he reveals a more sympathetic and understanding attitude
      toward human foibles and vices. Argues that a cautious optimism
      based upon a new awareness of good as well as evil emerges in the
      world of the plays.
           Certain Satires, The Scourge of Villainy, What You Will

30   SCHÄFER, JÜRGEN. "Huarte: A Marston Source." NQ, n.s.
      18:16-17.
           Sees Juan Huarte's Examen de Ingenios para las ciencias as
      the source of Hercules's speech on procreation in The Fawn.

31   SCHNEIDER, BEN ROSS. The Ethos of Restoration Comedy.
      Urbana: University of Illinois Press, pp. 29, 63-64, 112.
           Briefly discusses Betterton's The Revenge, a Restoration
      adaptation of The Dutch Courtezan.

32   SLIGHTS, WILLIAM. "Political Morality and the Ending of The
      Malcontent." MP 69:138-39.
         Discusses the problematic concluding speech of Malevole in
      the 1604 version of The Malcontent and interprets it to mean that
      Marston upholds traditional views of political order.

33   STALLINGS, WALTON DEES. "The Decline of Debate: Changing
      Attitudes Towards Rhetoric in English Renaissance Drama."
      Ph.D. diss., University of South Carolina.
         Studies the use of rhetoric by four Elizabethan dramatists--
      Lyly, Shakespeare, Jonson, and Marston--and finds that although
      Marston appears to rebel against the practices of traditional
      rhetoric, he is essentially an experimenter with language and
      reveals a knowledge of traditional rhetorical craft.

34   STRATTON, JOHN D. "The Dramatic Structures of the Plays in
      the King's Men's Repertory, 1604-1608." Ph.D. diss., Univer-
      sity of Nebraska.
         Selects seventeen plays produced by the King's Men between
      1604 and 1608 and studies the basis of these dramas' emotional
      impact. Finds two basic patterns of plot development: a rejec-
      tion pattern, in which the protagonist rejects a person he has
      loved, and a manipulative pattern, in which the hero, like
      Marston's Malevole, manipulates others to achieve an end.
      Suggests that the audience's emotional responses grow out
      of the unfolding of these patterns.
         The Malcontent

35   THOMPSON, KARL F. Modesty and Cunning: Shakespeare's Use of
      Literary Traditions. Ann Arbor: University of Michigan
      Press, p. 128.
         Sees The Malcontent as a trite, slipshod play.

36   WAITH, EUGENE. Ideas of Greatness: Heroic Drama in England.
      New York: Barnes & Noble, pp. 142-44 and passim.
         Discusses Sophonisba's glorification of a heroic woman.

                                    1972

1   ANDERSON, DONALD K. John Ford. TEAS, no. 129. New York:
      Twayne, p. 64.
         Upholds William Hazlitt's theory (1931.7) that Calantha's
      interrupted dance in John Ford's The Broken Heart was influenced
      by a similar one in The Malcontent.

2   ANON. "Marston, John." In The McGraw-Hill Encyclopedia of
      World Drama. Edited by David Eggenberger. Vol. 3. New York:
      McGraw-Hill, pp. 108-11.
         Provides a general discussion of Marston.

3 AYRES, PHILIP J. "Marston's <u>Antonio's Revenge</u>: The Morality of the Revenging Hero." <u>SEL</u> 12:359-74.
    Sees the play as treating Antonio ironically so that, although Antonio believes in the rightness of his cause, the audience perceives him as depraved and monstrous.

4 BERRY, RALPH. <u>The Art of John Webster</u>. Oxford: Clarendon Press, passim.
    Provides passing comments on Marston.

5 FOAKES, R.A. "Mr. Levin and 'Good Bad Drama.'" <u>EIC</u> 22: 327-29.
    Replies to Levin's article (1972.16) criticizing Foakes's earlier interpretations of <u>Antonio and Mellida</u> as a parody (1962.10; 1971.9). Defends his earlier position. For Levin's reply to Foakes's reply, see 1974.12. See also 1977.6 for Foakes's later defense of his position.

6 GECKLE, GEORGE. "John Marston's <u>Histriomastix</u> and the Golden Age." <u>CompD</u> 6:205-22.
    Suggests that Marston uses the concept of the golden age to give thematic focus to the play by presenting a standard against which the vices and follies of the characters are to be contrasted. Reprinted: 1980.5.

7 GILLIE, CHRISTOPHER. "Marston, John (1575?-1634)." In <u>Longman Companion to English Literature</u>. London: Longman, pp. 632-33.
    Provides a general discussion of Marston.

8 GOLDMAN, MICHAEL. <u>Shakespeare and the Energies of Drama</u>. Princeton: Princeton University Press, p. 164.
    Compares <u>The Malcontent</u> and <u>Measure for Measure</u>.

9 GOTTSCHALK, PAUL <u>The Meanings of Hamlet: Modes of Literary Interpretation since Bradley</u>. Albuquerque: University of New Mexico Press, pp. 46, 51, 56, 60, 162.
    Provides passing comments upon <u>Antonio's Revenge</u>.

10 GOWDA, H.H. ANNIAH. <u>Dramatic Poetry: From Medieval to Modern Times</u>. Madras: Macmillan Co. of India, passim.
    Provides passing comments on Marston.

11 HARBAGE, ALFRED. <u>Shakespeare without Words and Other Essays</u>. Cambridge, Mass.: Harvard University Press, passim.
    Provides passing comments on Marston.

12 HAWKINS, HARRIETT. <u>Likenesses of Truth in Elizabethan and Restoration Drama</u>. Oxford: Clarendon Press, pp. 52-54, 56-57, 75-77, and passim.
    Discusses <u>The Malcontent</u> as a tragicomedy and compares it to <u>Measure for Measure</u>.

13   HUNTER, G.K. "Further Borrowings in Webster and Marston."
     NQ, n.s. 19:452-53.
          Points out various borrowings in Webster and Marston from
     other sources.

14   KIRSCH, ARTHUR C. Jacobean Dramatic Perspectives.
     Charlottesville: University Press of Virginia, pp. 25-37.
          Sees Marston as an inept dramatist, unable on the whole to
     dramatize his dramatic sensibility in a coherent form. Considers
     The Malcontent to be his one successful play.
          Antonio and Mellida, Antonio's Revenge

15   LEVIN, RICHARD. "A Marston-Wilkins Borrowing." NQ, n.s.
     19:453.
          Suggests that Marston in The Fawn borrowed a line from
     George Wilkins's The Miseries of Enforced Marriage.

16   _____. "The New New Inn and the Proliferation of Good Bad
     Drama." EIC 22:41-47.
          Attacks the current critical trend of finding aesthetic and
     intellectual values in plays deemed second- or third-rate by
     previous generations of scholars. Criticizes Foakes's interpre-
     tation of Antonio and Mellida as burlesque and parody (1962.10;
     1971.9). For a further statement of Levin's views, see 1974.12.
     For Foakes's replies, see 1972.5; 1977.6.

17   MADELAINE, R.E.R. "'When Griffon Saw the Reconciled Quean':
     Marston, Ariosto and Haydocke." NQ, n.s. 19:453-54.
          Points out Marston's use in The Malcontent of a passage
     from Ariosto's Orlando Furioso.

18   MORRIS, IVOR. Shakespeare's God: The Role of Religion in the
     Tragedies. New York: St. Martin's, p. 186.
          Quotes Marston's views on tragedy from Antonio's Revenge.

19   POHL, FREDERICK J. Like to the Lark: The Early Years of
     Shakespeare. New York: Clarkson N. Potter, pp. 160-68.
          Suggests that Shakespeare was part author of Satiromastix
     and that Captain Tucca represents Dekker and Crispinus
     Shakespeare.

20   ROWSE, ALFRED LESLIE. The Elizabethan Renaissance: The
     Cultural Achievement. New York: Scribner's, pp. 29, 138.
          Provides comments on Marston's relationship to his age.

21   SIMMONS, J.L. "Lust's Dominion: A Showpiece for the Globe."
     TSE 20:11-12.
          Discusses the original staging of the play and supports
     Cross's view (1958.6) that the play is in part Marston's.

22   WEISS, ADRIAN. "Rhetoric and Satire: New Light on John
     Marston's Pigmalion and the Satires." JEGP 71:22-35.

Suggests that W. K[insayder] is a persona, not Marston himself, and that the preoccupation with vice, sin, and monstrous caricatures of humanity in the nondramatic satires should not be identified with Marston's views and feelings.
Certain Satires, The Metamorphosis of Pigmalion's Image, The Scourge of Villainy

23   WICKHAM, GLYNNE. Early English Stages, Vol. 2, 1576-1660, Part 2. London: Routledge & Kegan Paul, passim.
Provides passing comments on Marston's plays.

24   WILSON, ALICE C. "The Concept of Wealth in the Works of John Marston." Ph.D. diss., University of Notre Dame.
Sees the inordinate desire for riches as one of the major sources of evil in the world of Marston's plays and suggests that Marston's ideal man is one who can use wealth or any gift or good without becoming obsessed with it.
Antonio and Mellida, Antonio's Revenge, The Dutch Courtezan, The Fawn, Jack Drum's Entertainment, The Malcontent, Sophonisba, What You Will

25   YOUNG, DAVID. The Heart's Forest: A Study of Shakespeare's Pastoral Plays. New Haven: Yale University Press, p. 104.
Quotes Marston's comments on time from The Insatiate Countess.

1973

1   COLLEY, JOHN S. "Opinion and the Reader in John Marston's The Metamorphosis of Pigmalion's Image." ELR 3:221-31.
Suggests that the poem is indeed a satire and that Marston uses pornography to indict the reader as a fool. Also suggests that the poem sees the forces of opinion as the fountainhead of folly.

2   COVATTA, ANTHONY. "A Marston-Middleton Parallel: New Light on the Growth of City Comedy." NQ, n.s. 20:459-60.
Suggests that The Dutch Courtezan influenced Middleton in the writing of A Mad World, My Masters.

3   _____. Thomas Middleton's City Comedies. Lewisburg: Bucknell University Press, passim.
Provides passing comments on Marston.

4   FLANAGAN, JAMES D. "The Satirist-Intriguer in Elizabethan and Jacobean Comedy." Ph.D. diss., University of Minnesota.
Discusses the function of the satirist who is also a main character in the drama. Sees the device of this character type as a means of combining comedy and satire within a play. Centers attention on the ways that writers used this type and sees

Marston's Malevole in <u>The</u> <u>Malcontent</u> as the most successful
example of this character type.

5   GECKLE, GEORGE L.   "Antonio's Revenge: 'Never more woe in
     lesser plot was found.'"   <u>CompD</u> 6:323-35.
         Studies <u>Antonio's</u> <u>Revenge</u> within the context of the tradi-
     tions of the Elizabethan revenge play and Senecan drama and
     suggests that Marston's play justifies vengeance.   Sees the play
     as ethically sound and artistically successful within the frame-
     work of Renaissance philosophical and aesthetic thought.
     Reprinted: 1980.5.

6   HUNTER, G.K.   "Italian Tragicomedy on the English Stage."
     <u>RenD</u>, n.s. 6:123-48.
         Discusses the development of tragicomedy in Elizabethan
     England; sheds light on Marston's adapting this Italian dramatic
     form to the English stage in <u>The</u> <u>Malcontent</u>.

7   KERNODLE, GEORGE R.   "The Mannerist Stage of Comic Detach-
     ment."   In <u>The</u> <u>Elizabethan</u> <u>Theatre</u> <u>III</u>.   Edited by David
     Galloway.   Hamden, Conn.:   Archon Books, pp. 119-34.
         Sees Malevole's detached stance in <u>The</u> <u>Malcontent</u> as char-
     acteristic of mannerist drama.

8   KNIGHT, W. NICHOLAS.   <u>Shakespeare's</u> <u>Hidden</u> <u>Life:</u>   <u>Shakespeare</u>
     <u>at</u> <u>Law,</u> <u>1585-1595</u>.   New York: Mason & Lipscomb, passim.
         Provides passing comments on Marston.

9   LEECH, CLIFFORD.   "Three Times Ho and a Brace of Widows:
     Some Plays for the Private Theatre."   In <u>The</u> <u>Elizabethan</u>
     <u>Theatre</u> <u>III</u>.   Edited by David Galloway.   Hamden, Conn.:
     Archon Books, pp. 14-32.
         Discusses <u>Eastward</u> <u>Hoe</u> along with <u>Westward</u> <u>Ho</u> and <u>Northward</u>
     <u>Ho</u> and points out similarities in structure, staging, and outlook
     among the three plays.

10   LEGGATT, ALEXANDER.   <u>Citizen</u> <u>Comedy</u> <u>in</u> <u>the</u> <u>Age</u> <u>of</u> <u>Shakespeare</u>.
     Toronto: University of Toronto Press, pp. 120-24 and passim.
         Discusses <u>The</u> <u>Dutch</u> <u>Courtezan</u> and <u>Jack</u> <u>Drum's</u> <u>Entertainment</u>
     as examples of Jacobean city comedy.

*11 NOZAKI, MUTSUMI.   "John Marston the Dramatist."   <u>SELit</u>,
     (English no.), 187-88.
         Cited in the <u>MLA</u> <u>International</u> <u>Bibliography</u>.

12   PEARSALL, L.E.   "Marston, John."   In <u>Webster's</u> <u>New</u> <u>World</u>
     <u>Companion</u> <u>to</u> <u>English</u> <u>and</u> <u>American</u> <u>Literature</u>.   New York:
     World Publishing, pp. 439-41.
         Provides a general discussion of Marston.

13   PEARSE, NANCY COTTON.   <u>John</u> <u>Fletcher's</u> <u>Chastity</u> <u>Plays</u>.
     Lewisburg, Pa.:   Bucknell University Press, pp. 101, 200, 236.
         Provides passing comments upon <u>The</u> <u>Insatiate</u> <u>Countess</u>.

14   PENDLETON, THOMAS A.   "The Reciprocal Relationship between
     Shakespeare and John Marston."   Ph.D. diss., Fordham University.
        Investigates the complex relationship between Marston
     and Shakespeare and suggests that Marston borrowed less from
     Shakespeare than has hitherto been supposed and that during his
     career Marston passed from a relative unawareness of Shakespeare
     to a reliance upon him. Also suggests that Shakespeare upon
     occasion borrowed from Marston.
        Antonio and Mellida, Antonio's Revenge,The Fawn, The
     Malcontent, The Metamorphosis of Pigmalion's Image, Sophonisba

15   QUENNELL, PETER. "Marston, John." In A History of English
     Literature. Springfield, Mass.: G. & C. Merriam, pp. 96-97.
        Provides a general article on Marston.

16   SHAPIRO, MICHAEL. "Audience vs. Dramatist in Jonson's
     Epicoene and Other Plays of the Children's Troupes." ELR
     3:400-417.
        Discusses the comments made on staging in the induction to
     What You Will.

17   SLIGHTS, WILLIAM. "'Elder in a deform'd church.': The
     Function of Marston's Malcontent." SEL 13:360-73.
        Argues that Altofronto's disguising himself as Malevole
     serves to bring about the moral and political redemption of most
     of the characters.

                                1974

1   BERRY, HERBERT. "Italian Definitions of Tragedy and Comedy
     Arrive in England." SEL 14:179-87.
        Discusses Marston's views of comedy.

2   BLUESTONE, MAX. From Story to Stage: The Dramatic Adaptation
     of Prose Fiction in the Period of Shakespeare and His Contem-
     poraries. SengL, no. 70. The Hague: Mouton, passim.
        Provides passing comments upon The Dutch Courtezan, The
     Insatiate Countess, and The Malcontent.

3   BORDEN, ALLEN B. "The Philosophical and Political Meaning
     of the Hall-Marston Poetomachia." Ph.D. diss., Boston
     University.
        Suggests that Hall and Marston carried on certain features
     of the Gabriel Harvey-Thomas Nashe quarrel with Hall upholding a
     Puritan-Anglican, Christian-neoplatonic tradition and Marston a
     skeptic and Epicurean viewpoint.

4   CARROLL, D. ALLEN, ed. Introduction to The Skialetheia.
     Chapel Hill: University of North Carolina Press, p. vii.
        Discusses Marston's influence upon Guilpin. Other
     editions: 1598.1; 1878.2; 1931.5.

                                163

5   COHEN, RALPH A.   "The Functional Setting in Eastward Hoe."
     RenP, 83-96.
         Sees Eastward Hoe as a topographical comedy in which the
     Thames influences the action and acts as a moral agent by depos-
     iting the wastrels and social climbers after the shipwreck at
     thematically approprite locations along its banks.

6   COLLEY, JOHN S.   John Marston's Theatrical Drama.   JDS,
     no. 33.   Salzburg: Institut für Englische Sprache und
     Literatur, University of Salzburg, 202 pp.
         Sees Marston as a serious theatrical experimenter whose
     plays are based upon "scene units" rather than an overall artis-
     tic structure.   Emphasizes the use of stage action in his plays.
     Sees Marston upholding a Christian world view and attempting to
     educate the audience.
         Antonio and Mellida, Antonio's Revenge, The Dutch
     Courtezan, Eastward Hoe, The Fawn, Histriomastix, The Insatiate
     Countess, Jack Drum's Entertainment, The Malcontent,
     Satiromastix, Sophonisba, What You Will

7   _____.   "Music in the Elizabethan Private Theatres."   YES
     4:62-69.
         Attacks the widely held view that the children's dramatic
     companies specialized in including songs in plays, whereas the
     adult companies used few songs.   Suggests that the authors'
     interest in music and the dramatic needs of the play determined
     the frequency of songs in the plays of both kinds of companies.
     Includes numerous incidental comments on Marston's use of songs.

8   COLMAN, E.A.M.   The Dramatic Use of Bawdy in Shakespeare.
     London: Longman, passim.
         Uses phrases and words from Antonio and Mellida, The Dutch
     Courtezan, and The Malcontent to illustrate and define Eliza-
     bethan uses of bawdy language.

9   GARBER, MARJORIE.   Dream in Shakespeare.   New Haven: Yale
     University Press, pp. 26-27.
         Discusses the purpose of the induction John Webster wrote
     for The Malcontent.

10   HEDRICK, DONALD K.   "The Elizabethan Satiric-Heroic Mode:
     Jonson, Shakespeare, and Marston."   Ph.D. diss., Cornell
     University.
         Studies the backgrounds and sources of the use of the
     satirist as hero in Elizabethan-Jacobean drama.   Also gives
     attention to techniques used in portraying the satirist in the
     drama.   Discusses Malevole in The Malcontent as an example of a
     satirist whose nobility is revealed despite his lowly disguise.

11   HOUSER, DAVID J.   "Purging the Commonwealth: Marston's Dis-
     guised Dukes and A Knack to Know a Knave."   PMLA 89:993-1004.

Points out similarities in form shared by A Knack to Know a
Knave and The Fawn and The Malcontent.

12   LEVIN, RICHARD. "The Proof of the Parody." EIC 24:312-16.
Replies to Foakes's reply (1972.5) to Levin's earlier essay
(1972.16) and criticizes Foakes's theory that the performances of
the boy actors parodied adult behavior. Holds that no parodic
elements are in Antonio and Mellida. Also voices the view that
Elizabethan-Jacobean dramas should be read as "straight" plays--
plays that mean what they appear to be saying--unless the critic
can produce strong and numerous proofs that the author's inten-
tion is ironic or parodical. For Foakes's other statements of
this idea, see 1962.10; 1971.9; 1977.6.

13   MacDONALD, ALLISTER I. "John Marston's Stoicism." Ph.D.
diss., University of Toronto.
Studies some of Marston's plays in accord with the light
that Seneca and other Stoic writers shed on them. Sees Antonio
and Mellida and Antonio's Revenge as showing the inability of
Antonio and Andrugio to live in accord with Stoical ideals. Sees
Malevole in The Malcontent playing a Stoical role as "surgeon-
satirist." Sees Sophonisba as Marston's attempt to write a true
Stoical tragedy and sees Sophonisba as a heroine upholding
Senecan ideals.

14   SALOMON, BROWNELL. "The Theological Basis of Imagery and
Structure in The Malcontent." SEL 14:271-84.
Argues that Calvinism is central to Marston's world view
and that it influences the diction and structure of The Malcontent.

15   URE, PETER. "John Marston's Sophonisba: A Reconsideration."
In Elizabethan and Jacobean Drama: Critical Essays by Peter
Ure. Edited by J.C. Maxwell. New York: Barnes & Noble,
pp. 75-92.
Reprint of 1949.7.

16   WHARTON, T.F. "The Malcontent and 'Dreams, Visions,
Fantasies.'" EIC 24:261-74.
Reverses some common interpretations of the play and views
Piero, the usurper, as one of the more noble characters; sees
Malevole not as a wholly virtuous prince who simply seeks to
restore his throne to himself but also as a schemer delighting in
discord and anguish. Suggests that Marston, however, intended
Malevole to represent the virtuous ruler and was unaware of the
sinister implications of his protagonist's behavior. Judges the
play an artistic failure because it fails to acknowledge the
irony implicit in Malevole's plotting.

17   YAE, YOUNG S. "Moral Growth through Contrived Experience in
Selected Plays of John Marston." Ph.D. diss., University of
Oregon.

Argues that Marston's major plays are based upon a Renaissance belief that only harsh experience can awaken men to their
follies and base natures and that these plays feature a con-
triver, who arranges an educating and reforming experience for
other characters.
Antonio and Mellida, Antonio's Revenge, The Dutch
Courtezan, The Fawn, Histriomastix, The Malcontent, The
Metamorphosis of Pigmalion's Image, The Scourge of Villainy

*18   YAGI, TSUYOSHI. "Fushigeki The Malcontent." EigoS 19:696-98.
      Cited in the MLA International Bibliography.

                                1975

1   BUCKRIDGE, PATRICK JAMES. "Play and Recreation in the Poems
      and Early Dramas of John Marston." Ph.D. diss., University of
      Pennsylvania.
         Suggests that Marston's purpose as a writer was not to
      persuade readers to adopt a certain type of conduct but to
      "recreate" them; that is, to provide them with an escape from the
      workaday world and everyday pattern of thinking and to enable
      them to seek truth on an intuitive level, a process by which they
      could improve morally. Suggests, however, that according to
      Marston's theory, such improvement was dependent upon the grace
      of God.
         Certain Satires, Jack Drum's Entertainment, Histriomastix,
      The Metamorphosis of Pigmalion's Image, The Scourge of Villainy

2   ELLRODT, ROBERT. "Self-Consciousness in Montaigne and
      Shakespeare." ShS 28:37-50.
         Mentions the influence of Montaigne's essay "We Taste Noth-
      ing Purely" on Marston.

3   FLEISSNER, ROBERT F. "Shakespeare's Carte Blanche--
      Appropriated by Marston." ES 56:390-92.
         Suggests that What You Will was the original title of
      Twelfth Night and that Marston wrote his What You Will as a
      takeoff on Shakespeare's play.

4   GILL, R.B. "A Purchase of Glory: The Persona of Late
      Elizabethan Satire." SP 72:408-18.
         Discusses the use of the persona in Marston's satires.
      Sees Marston's persona not only intensifying the satirist's con-
      ventional sense of outrage but embodying Marston's own dislikes
      and moral judgments. Suggests that, therefore, some confusion
      about the nature and purpose of his satires arises and that those
      who would interpret these writings must be aware of the problem.

5   GREENMAN, DAVID. "Atmosphere, Contrast, and Control in
      Marston's The Malcontent." SJW, pp. 134-44.

                                166

Judges the portrayal of Malevole an artistic success and
sees him as the thematic and dramatic center of the play. Points
out how such techniques as set speeches, confrontations between
characters, and contrasts in action contribute to his effective-
ness and shape the world and meaning of the play.

6   HALL, ANNE DRURY. "Coined Words and Elizabethan Satiric
     Forms: Farthings into Double Pistols." Ph.D. diss., Stanford
     University.
        Discusses the use of coined words as vehicles of satire in
the writings of several Renaissance authors. Sees Marston using
coined words for their satiric vehemency and satiric austerity.
Holds that these uses help define his satiric picture and create
a sense of aesthetic distance in the work's relationship to the
reader.

*7   MINOR, EARL, ed. Illustrious Evidence: Appraoches to English
     Literature of the Early Seventeenth Century. Berkeley:
     University of California Press, 135 pp.
        Cited in the MLA International Bibliography.

8   PALUMBO, RONALD J. "Volpone, III, vii, 100-105: A Mocking
     Allusion." AN&Q 13:98-99.
        Believes that Corvino's threat to hang his wife bound to a
corpse from his window derives from Piero's desire in Antonio's
Revenge to treat Mellida in a similar way. Holds that Marston's
use of this grotesquerie is awkward since Piero's command for
this to happen is not carried out, whereas Jonson's succeeds, for
it is used to underscore the satirical treatment of Corvino.

9   ROBERTS, GARETH. "The 'Beasts of Death' in Marston's
     Sophonisba." NQ, n.s. 22:248.
        Points out that the expression "beasts of death" was bor-
rowed from Lucan's De Bello Civili, Book VI, and faults Wood
(Collected edition 1938.1) for emending the term to "heastes of
death," in accord with the 1606 quarto.

10   RUOFF, JAMES. Crowell's Handbook of Elizabethan and Stuart
     Literature. New York: Crowell, pp. 125-26, 267-68, 272-73.
        Provides plot summaries of and critical comments upon The
Dutch Courtezan and The Malcontent. Also provides a general
article on Marston.

11   SCHOENBAUM, S. "Marston, Middleton, and Massinger." In
     English Drama (Excluding Shakespeare). Edited by Stanley
     Wells. Select Bibliographical Guides. London: Oxford
     University Press, pp. 69-92.
        Provides a bibliographical essay on Marston, discusses the
collected editions, highlights virtues and faults, and turns
attention to single editions. Then surveys Marston criticism,
commenting upon substance and value of the books and some of the
more important articles written on Marston.

12   SIEMON, JAMES EDWARD. "Disguise in Marston and Shakespeare."
      HLQ 38:105-23.
           Suggests that in some Elizabethan plays, particularly The
      Malcontent, the disguise assumed by the character serves to
      objectify certain elements in or sides of his personality.

13   WELD, JOHN. Meaning in Comedy: Studies in Elizabethan
      Romantic Comedy. Albany: State University of New York Press,
      pp. 59-60.
           Cites evidence in Histriomastix to indicate that old-style
      moralities were losing prestige among the intellectuals.

14   WHARTON, T.F. "Old Marston or New Marston: The Antonio
      Plays." EIC 25:357-69.
           Attacks the current favorable view of Marston, which seeks
      to elevate his dramatic skills by viewing him as a master of
      irony and parody.
           Antonio and Mellida, Antonio's Revenge

                                   1976

1   COURSEN, HERBERT R. Christian Ritual and the World of
      Shakespeare's Tragedies. Lewisburg, Pa.: Bucknell University
      Press, passim.
           Provides passing comments on Marston.

2   FLY, RICHARD. Shakespeare's Mediated World. Amherst:
      University of Massachusetts Press, p. 48.
           Argues against the view of Campbell (1938.2) and others
      that in writing Troilus and Cressida, Shakespeare was imitating
      Marston's satirical writings.

3   GUNBY, D.C. "Marston, Mecho, and Supererogation." ELN 14:
      98-99.
           Suggests that Mecho in the fourth satire of The Scourge of
      Villainy is a Puritan, who, upon occasion, embraces the Catholic
      belief in good works to salve his conscience.

4   HEDRICK, DONALD K. "Marston's Antonio and Mellida, V. i. 54."
      Expl 35:15-16.
           Suggests that Feliche's remarks on Alberto's hanging him-
      self refer to a well-known tale in which Archilochus, the sati-
      rist, caused the woman who spurned him and her father to kill
      themselves because of the bitterness of the verses he wrote about
      them. Also suggests that the remarks refer to a legendary tale
      that poets with their verses could kill rats.

5   HUNTER, G.K. "Were There Act-Pauses on Shakespeare's Stage?"
      In English Renaissance Drama: Essays in Honor of Madeleine
      Doran and Mark Eccles. Edited by Standish Henning, Robert

Kimbrough, and Richard Knowles. Carbondale: Southern
Illinois University Press, pp. 15-35.
Argues that the induction to The Malcontent cannot be used
to prove that there were no musical interludes between the acts
at adult theaters.

6 _____. "'Virtue in Labour with Eternal Chaos': The Plays of
Chapman, Marston, and Tourneur." In The Revels History of
Drama in English. Edited by J. Leeds Barroll, Alexander
Leggatt, Richard Hosley, and Alvin Kernan. Vol. 3. London:
Methuen, pp. 387-94.
Provides a general discussion of Marston.

7 McGRATH, LYNETTE. "John Marston's Mismanaged Irony: The
Poetic Satires." TSLL 18:393-408.
Sees Marston's chief problems in Certain Satires, The
Metamorphosis of Pigmalion's Image, and The Scourge of Villainy
as his inability to manage irony in order to suggest a moral
norm. Stresses that Marston's persona tends to be static,
unchanging in his feelings and attitudes, and that this stance
along with other difficulties makes it difficult for Marston to
treat the persona so as to suggest moral improvement.

8 MANNINGHAM, JOHN. The Diary of John Manningham of the Middle
Temple, 1602-1603. Edited by Robert Parker. Hanover, N.H.:
Published for the University of Rhode Island by the University
Press of New England, p. 133 and passim.
Newly edited edition of 1868.1. Contains passing comments
on Marston in the introduction and in the notes.

9 MILES, ROSALIND. The Problem of Measure for Measure. New
York: Barnes & Noble, pp. 142-53 and passim.
Discusses Marston's use of the device of the disguised duke
in The Fawn and The Malcontent and points out dramatic and the-
matic advantages Marston gains from this technique. Finds
Marston successful in portraying these character types.

10 PALUMBO, RONALD J. "From Melodrama to Burlesque: A Theatrical
Gesture in Kyd, Shakespeare, and Marston." ThS 17:220-23.
Discusses the use in Elizabethan drama of the device of a
person, overcome with grief, falling to the ground. Points out
that in Kyd's The Spanish Tragedy this technique was used seriously, but that by the time of Marston it was treated with burlesque.
Antonio and Mellida

11 PENNINGER, FRIEDA ELAINE, ed. English Drama to 1660
(Excluding Shakespeare). Detroit: Gale Research Co.,
pp. 301-3.
Lists Marston bibliographies, collected editions of his
works, and seven of the more important secondary works. Provides
brief annotations.

12   STILLING, ROGER. Love and Death in Renaissance Tragedy.
      Baton Rouge: Louisiana State University Press, pp. 82-100.
         Suggests that idealized romantic love, love leading to
      marriage, is the central thematic thread in Antonio and Mellida
      and that Antonio's Revenge reveals the frustration and destruc-
      tion of this ideal in Antonio and Mellida's doomed love and the
      consequent violence and death such frustration leads to.

13   WILSON, ROBERT BENJAMIN. "A Survey of Stoicism and Neo-
      stoicism in the Dramatic Works of Chapman, Marston, and
      Shakespeare." Ph.D. diss., Southern Illinois University.
         Discusses the influence of Stoicism via Renaissance theo-
      rists upon Marston, Chapman, and Shakespeare and points out
      various Stoical character types in Marston's plays. Also gives
      attention to Marston's sense of the world's being evil and his
      view that providence controls destiny.
         Antonio's Revenge, Jack Drum's Entertainment, The Fawn,
      What You Will

                              1977

1   ARTHOS, JOHN. Shakespeare's Use of Dream and Vision. Totowa,
      N.J.: Rowman & Littlefield, pp. 20-24, 45-46, and passim.
         Points out and discusses Senecan and Platonic elements in
      the poems Marston contributed to Robert Chester's Love's Martyr.
      Sees Marston as upholding the idea of the couple celebrated by
      the poems gaining immortality through their children.

2   BABULA, WILLIAM. "The Avenger and the Satirist: John
      Marston's Malevole." In Elizabethan Theatre VI. Edited by
      G.R. Hibbard. Hamden, Conn.:   Archon Books, pp. 48-58.
         Emphasizes the function of satire in the play and sees
      Malevole more as a satirist than an avenger. Suggests that the
      play sees the world as redeemable and views man as capable of
      moral reformation.
         Antonio's Revenge

3   BUCKRIDGE, PATRICK. "Elements of an Anti-Rhetorical Poetic in
      the Satires of John Marston." Parergon 19:11-12.
         Suggests that Marston doubted the classical theory that
      satire could reform mankind and that, therefore, he conceived of
      The Scourge of Villainy as a form of recreation in which he
      assumed the role of a melancholy poet. Holds that to Marston
      satire was also a means of gaining self-knowledge.

4   CHAMPION, LARRY S. Tragic Patterns in Jacobean and Caroline
      Drama. Knoxville: University of Tennessee Press, passim.
         Provides passing comments on Marston.

5   DESSEN, ALAN C. Elizabethan Drama and the Viewer's Eye.
      Chapel Hill: University of North Carolina Press, pp. 61-63
      and passim.

Points out a symbolic analogue between Piero and Antonio in
Antonio's Revenge that suggests that Antonio is lowered to
Piero's bloodthirsty level.

6   FOAKES, R.A. "On Marston, The Malcontent, and The Revenger's
     Tragedy." In Elizabethan Theater VI. Edited by R.G. Hibbard.
     Hamden, Conn.: Archon Books, pp. 59-75.
         Discusses the technique of juxtaposing the serious and the
     comical in The Revenger's Tragedy and in The Malcontent. Finds
     that the former play uses the technique to support the play's
     informing moral seriousness, whereas The Malcontent employs the
     device to make the "evil" characters appear frivolous and inane.
     Does not suggest that the use of the device in The Malcontent
     destroys the play's ability to comment on evil, but sees The
     Malcontent as a lesser achievement than The Revenger's Tragedy.
     Also defends the author's earlier view (1962.10; 1971.9: 1972.5)
     that our understanding of Elizabethan plays can be enhanced by
     our comprehending Renaissance stage conditions and noting ele-
     ments of parody and burlesque in Marston's plays. For Levin's
     criticisms of these views, see 1972.16; 1974.12.

7   GAIR, REAVLEY. "The Presentation of Plays at Second Paul's:
     The Early Phase (1599-1602)." In Elizabethan Theatre VI.
     Edited by G.R. Hibbard. Hamden, Conn.: Archon Books,
     pp. 21-47.
         Discusses the staging of Marston's plays at Paul's and
     comments upon such topics as Marston's use of the stage and
     theatrical resources of the boys' company, his relationship with
     the audience, and his controversies with various critics. Also
     draws upon the texts of Marston's plays and other dramas per-
     formed by this company to decide upon the physical makeup of the
     stage and the props of the actors. Concludes by locating the
     stage within the Chapter House precinct.
         Antonio and Mellida, Antonio's Revenge, Jack Drum's
     Entertainment, What You Will

8   HALLETT, CHARLES A. "Andrea, Andrugio, and King Hamlet: The
     Ghost as Spirit of Revenge." PQ 56:43-64.
         Studies the ghost of the revenge plays as a powerful symbol
     both of a mysterious power that influences the protagonist of the
     revenge play and of the impulse that drives him to violence.
     Suggests that in Antonio's Revenge the ghost serves as a symbol
     of bloody vengeance as well as a messenger of divine will and
     that these two functions produce much of the play's thematic
     confusion.

9   HOTSON, LESLIE. Shakespeare by Hilliard. Berkeley:
     University of California Press, passim.
         Provides passing comments on Marston.

10   KEACH, WILLIAM. Elizabethan Erotic Narratives: Irony and
     Pathos in the Ovidian Poetry of Shakespeare, Marlowe, and

Their Contemporaries. New Brunswick: Rutgers University
Press, pp. 134-36.
    Sees The Metamorphosis of Pigmalion's Image as a neophyte's
attempt to write Ovidian poetry in which the author includes both
satirical thrusts and explicit eroticism. Sees the result as an
important fusion of diverse elements, which leads to ambiguities
in tone, theme, and poetic technique.

11 KING, ROBERT PETER. "Theatrical Playmaking in Elizabethan
    Revenge Tragedy." Ph.D. diss., New York University.
    Discusses the use of the play-within-a-play technique and
role-playing in revenge tragedy and concludes that these devices
by their very nature inhibit absolute moral judgments.
Antonio's Revenge

12 KNIGHT, G. WILSON. Shakespeare's Dramatic Challenge: On the
    Rise of Shakespeare's Tragic Heroes. New York: Barnes &
    Noble, p. 88.
    Compares Macbeth's degeneration to that of Antonio in
Antonio's Revenge.

13 McCULLEY, CECIL M. "John Marston." In The New Intellectuals.
    Edited by Terence P. Logan and Denzil S. Smith. Lincoln:
    University of Nebraska Press, pp. 171-247.
    Provides a bibliographical essay covering scholarship on
Marston from 1923 to 1974; comments upon editions of Marston's
plays, biographical and general studies of Marston, and discussions of his plays.

*14 RICHARDS, BERNARD. "John Marston." Brazen Nose (Brasenose
    College, Oxford University) 16:51-55.
    Cited in the MLA International Bibliography.

15 SCOTT, MICHAEL. "Marston's Early Contribution to The
    Insatiate Countess." NQ, n.s. 24:116-17.
    Suggests that instead of being a late play that Marston
abandoned in the midst of composition around 1608, the work is
really an early unfinished piece, written before 1603.

16 SHAPIRO, MICHAEL. Children of the Revels: The Boy Companies
    of Shakespeare's Time. New York: Columbia University Press,
    passim.
    Discusses the boy companies, their composition, audience,
acting style, use of music, and so forth. Provides numerous
comments upon and discussions of Marston in regard to these
topics.
    Antonio and Mellida, Antonio's Revenge, Eastward Hoe,
Histriomastix, The Fawn, Jack Drum's Entertainment, Satiromastix,
Sophonisba, What You Will

17 TRICOMI, ALBERT. "Identifying Sir Gervase Clifton, the
    Addressee of Marston's Letter, 1607." NQ, n.s. 24:202-3.

Supplies additional information to support Brettle's iden-
tification (1928.2) of Sir Gervase Clifton and provides data on
Clifton's life.

1978

1   ALTMAN, JOEL B. The Tudor Play of Mind: Rhetorical Inquiry
    and the Development of Elizabethan Drama. Berkeley:
    University of California Press, passim.
        Provides passing comments on Marston.

2   BEAURLINE, L.A. Jonson and Elizabethan Comedy: Essays in
    Dramatic Rhetoric. San Marino, Calif.: Huntington Library,
    passim.
        Provides passing comments on Marston.

3   BRADBROOK, M.C. Shakespeare: The Poet in His World. New
    York: Columbia University Press, pp. 134-35 and passim.
        Discusses Marston's early career and his quarrels with Hall
    and Jonson.

4   CORNELIA, MARIE. "Dramatic Style and Dramatic Language in
    Marston's Antonio and Mellida." ArielE 9:21-29.
        Suggests that many of the verbal idiosyncrasies in Antonio
    and Mellida result from Marston's attempts to discover a linguis-
    tic medium by which he could dramatize tragic emotions. Adds
    that Marston also experimented with ritual and other forms of
    stage action in order to realize these emotions in the audience.

5   INGRAM, R.W. John Marston. TEAS, no. 216. Boston: Twayne,
    180 pp.
        Provides a sympatheitc view of Marston. Views him as a man
    of the theater, an experimenter with dramatic techniques who had
    a profound influence upon the drama of his age. Finds his dra-
    matic style "intimately bound up with his presentation of an
    uneasily questioning, insecure, dangerously deceptive world."
    Thus finds him deeply involved with the intellectual problems of
    his era. Sees his works, though often faulty, as an achievement
    in their own right. Gives some attention to Marston's minor
    works.
        Antonio and Mellida, Antonio's Revenge, Certain Satires,
    The Dutch Courtezan, Eastward Hoe, The Fawn, Histriomastix, The
    Insatiate Countess, Jack Drum's Entertainment, The Malcontent,
    The Metamorphosis of Pigmalion's Image, Satiromastix, The Scourge
    of Villainy, Sophonisba, What You Will

6   LEECH, CLIFFORD. "Masking and Unmasking in the Last Plays."
    In Shakespeare's Romances Reconsidered. Edited by Carol
    McGinnis Kay and Henry E. Jacobs. Lincoln: University of
    Nebraska Press, pp. 40-59.

Discusses the masque in The Malcontent as a variation
of the standard stage device in which assassins masquerade as
revelers.

7   LITTLE, MATTHEW. "Marston's Kinsayder and the Cure of Folly."
     ELN 15:271-74.
          Suggests that Marston's pen name W. Kinsayder may derive
     from Keisnijder, a Dutch word meaning "stonecutter." Links the
     name to the tradition of a physician removing stones—the causes
     of follies and madness—from the head.

8   PALUMBO, RONALD J. "Philosophic Wordplay: A Note on
     Marston's Quadratus." AN&Q 16:102-3.
          Judges Quadratus's name ironical since it is derived from
     quadrato, meaning "square," a geometrical figure associated with
     steadfastness in Renaissance thought.

9   ROSENBERG, MARVIN. The Masks of Macbeth. Berkeley:
     University of California Press, passim.
          Provides passing comments on Marston.

10   SCOTT, MICHAEL. John Marston's Plays. New York: Barnes &
     Noble, 129 pp.
          Considers Marston's plays as works written for performance,
     not for reading, and concludes that Marston is a vital dramatist
     who was a tireless experimenter and whose works reveal an affinity
     with the theater of the absurd and surrealistic drama. Gives
     attention to dramatic techniques used by Marston and suggests
     that his plays derive much of their power and significance from
     their resemblance to dreams. Provides information upon adapta-
     tions of his plays and modern productions of his dramas.
          Antonio and Mellida, Antonio's Revenge, The Dutch
     Courtezan, The Fawn, Histriomastix, The Insatiate Countess, Jack
     Drum's Entertainment, The Malcontent, Sophonisba, What You Will

11   SPIVACK, CHARLOTTE. The Comedy of Evil on Shakespeare's
     Stage. Cranbury, N.J.: Associated University Presses,
     pp. 123-25.
          Discusses the depiction of evil in The Dutch Courtezan and
     The Malcontent.

12   THOMPSON, ANN. Shakespeare's Chaucer: A Study in Literary
     Origins. New York: Barnes & Noble, pp. 32-33.
          Discusses the Troilus and Cressida episode in Histriomastix
     and suggests that it is an attack upon a lost play by Thomas
     Dekker using this story.

13   WARD, JAMES XENOPHON. "A Computer Concordance to John
     Marston's The Malcontent." Ph.D. diss., University of
     South Carolina.
          Provides a two-part dissertation, the first a study of
     Marston, his career, style, influences, and so forth; the second,

the concordance itself based upon the Revels edition of <u>The
Malcontent</u> (<u>The Malcontent</u> 1975.1). Holds that this concordance
is the most complete of any Renaissance text. Points out that it
lists every word in the text in variant spellings and gives the
number of times the word appears.

1979

1   BROOKE, NICHOLAS. <u>Horrid Laughter in Jacobean Tragedy</u>. New
    York: Barnes & Noble, p. 6.
        In discussing the use of laughter in tragedy, points out
    that Marston's Antonio plays include "tragic rhetoric and blatant
    farce, moral sententiae and apparent self-parody," but sees no
    clear purpose in Marston's use of these devices.

*2 CHAUCHAIX, JACQUELINE. "<u>Un Personnage et ses origines</u>: <u>Le
    Gelosso de la Sophonisbe de Marston</u>." <u>Confluents</u>, 5, 19-26.
        Cited in <u>MLA International Bibliography</u>.

3   HALLETT, CHARLES A., and ELAINE S. HALLETT. "<u>Antonio's
    Revenge</u> and the Integrity of the Revenge Tragedy Motifs." <u>SP</u>
    76: 366-86.
        Suggests that <u>Antonio's Revenge</u> fails because Marston tried
    unsuccessfully to fuse two irreconcilable dramatic modes: the
    Kydian revenge play and the play of retribution befalling a hero-
    villain, that is, Shakespeare's <u>Richard III</u>. Suggests that,
    therefore, Marston ineptly treats such fundamental motifs of the
    revenge play as the avenger's madness, the ghost, the play-
    within-a-play, and the avenger's death. Also provides much
    information on the function of these motifs in the revenge play.

4   JENSEN, EJNER J. <u>John Marston Dramatist</u>: <u>Themes and Imagery
    in the Plays</u>. Salzburg Studies in English Literature, JDS 20.
    Salzburg: Institut für Anglistik and Amerikanistik,
    Universität Salzburg, 152 pp.
        Rejects the concept that the essence of Marston's dramatic
    art lies in parody. Rather sees imagery as the basic means by
    which Marston "establishes his claim to our critical attention."
    Sees Marston as a pessimistic writer, who distrusts government
    and believes man inhabits a hostile world. Judges Marston's
    authorial career as one of development in which he refined his
    skills until he wrote his final plays, his best works.
        <u>Antonio's Revenge</u>, <u>Antonio and Mellida</u>, <u>The Dutch
    Courtezan</u>, <u>Eastward Hoe</u>, <u>The Fawn</u>, <u>Histriomastix</u>, <u>Jack Drum's
    Entertainment</u>, <u>The Malcontent</u>, <u>Sophonisba</u>, <u>What You Will</u>

5   KERNAN, ALVIN B. <u>The Playwright as Magician, Shakespeare's
    Image of the Poet in English Public Theater</u>. New Haven: Yale
    University Press, pp. 54-55.
        Discusses Marston's satiric treatment of a professional
    acting company, Sir Oliver Owlet's men, in <u>Histriomastix</u>.

6   LEVIN, RICHARD. New Readings vs. Old Plays. Chicago:
     University of Chicago Press, p. 128.
         Reiterates his skepticism of views that see Antonio and
     Mellida and Antonio's Revenge as burlesque and satire. Applies
     same criticism to similar interpretations of Jack Drum's Enter-
     tainment. For earlier statements of Levin's views, see 1972.16;
     1974.12. For the opposing views of Foakes, see 1962.10; 1971.9;
     1972.5; 1977.6.

7   McELROY, BERNARD P., Jr. "Recent Studies in Elizabethan and
     Jacobean Drama." SEL 19:327-54.
         Presents a basically favorable view of Scott's John
     Marston's Plays (1978.10). Finds that the author's theatrical
     approach to interpreting the plays clarifies "some of the often
     inexplicable dramaturgy of Marston."

8   MATHIESON, BARBARA JEAN OFFUT. "Patterns of Misogyny in
     Jacobean Tragedy." Ph.D. diss., Stanford University.
         Suggests that misogyny frequently voiced by characters in
     Jacobean tragedy does not necessarily express the dramatists' own
     feelings. Argues that most of the tragedies use fear and hatred
     of women to portray a deranged or evil personality. Discusses
     The Malcontent within this context.

*9   MELCHIORI, GIORGIO. "The Insatiate Countess (1613)." In Le
     forme del teatro. Edited by Giorgio Melchiori. Rome: Ed. di
     Storia e Lett, pp. 81-142.
         Cited in the MLA International Bibliography.

10   MIRABELLA, BELLA MARYANNE. "Part I--Rhetoric: Dance in
     Shakespeare and Marston. Part II--The Machine in the Garden:
     The Theme of Work in Tess of the D'Urbervilles. Part III--Art
     and Imagination in Edith Wharton's The House of Mirth." Ph.D.
     diss., Rutgers University.
         The first part of this dissertation discusses the use of
     dance in Elizabethan plays as a means of "illuminating and illus-
     trating plot and character." Holds that The Malcontent employs
     dance to suggest the decadence of the court.

11   PALUMBO, RONALD J. "Emblematic Characters in Marston's
     Antonio Plays." AN&Q 18:35-37.
         Suggests that the Antonio plays present a fourfold pattern
     of symbolic characters who represent aspects of Renaissance hero-
     ism, ranging from the passionate (Antonio) through the Stoical
     (Feliche, Pandulpho) to the Machiavellian (Piero). Argues that
     the plays reveal both Stoicism and Machiavellianism as insuf-
     ficient, subject to the blows of fortune. Sees Balurdo, the
     fool, as completing the quartet of types in that he satirizes the
     others. In his idiocy he is free from their turmoil.

12   SHOAP, JEFFREY. "The Children's Plays of Marston, Chapman,
     and Middleton, 1600-1605." Ph.D. diss., University of
     Massachusetts.

Suggests that the plays of these dramatists reveal an awareness of the chaos of their era. Holds that Marston and Chapman include a surrogate dramatist among their characters who expresses the feelings and convictions of the playwright.

13   UNGERER, GUSTAV. "'My Lady's a Catayan, We are Politicians, Maluolios a Peg-A-Ramsie.'" ShS 32:104.
       Draws upon What You Will to suggest that the expression "a kind of Puritane" applied to Malvolio in Twelfth Night accuses him of sexual immorality.

                              1980

1   BRADBROOK, M.C. John Webster, Citizen and Dramatist. New York: Columbia University Press, pp. 113-17 and passim.
      Provides passing comments on Marston. Discusses the induction to The Malcontent. Also discusses Eastward Hoe.

2   COUSINS, A.D. "The Protean Nature of Man in Marston's Verse Satires." JEGP 79:517-29.
      Argues that the dominant motif of Certain Satires and The Scourge of Villainy is an attack upon the Christian humanist view that man's Protean nature allows him to rise in moral stature toward excellence. Suggests that Marston also sees man as Protean, but that he sees mankind's changeability directed toward moral degradation and nothingness.

3   DIEHL, HUSTON. "The Iconography of Violence in English Renaissance Tragedy." RD, n.s. 11:27-44.
      Suggests that English Renaissance tragedy, drawing upon iconography, used scenes of violence and horror for moral ends to make men shun such behavior. Discusses Marston's use of the emblem of the bloody dagger in Antonio's Revenge. Sees Marston using the device to blur ethical distinctions between Piero and Antonio.

*4   GARLICK, HARRY. "Two Aspects of John Marston's Sophonisba." Parergon 27:39-41.
      Cited in the MLA International Bibliography.

5   GECKLE, GEORGE. John Marston's Drama, Theme, Imagery, Sources. Cranbury, N.J.: Associated University Presses, 217 pp.
      Drawing upon the views of Wood (Collected edition (1939.1), Eliot (1934.2-3; 1951.5; 1956.11), and Ellis-Fermor (1936.4), sees Marston as a serious dramatist concerned with moral issues. However, studies the plays "as plays written and produced within the years 1598 to 1606 by a man deeply imbued with the principles of a Christian upbringing, rhetorical education, and humanistic culture. Reprints 1971.10; 1972.6; 1973.5.

Antonio and Mellida, Antonio's Revenge, The Dutch
Courtezan, The Fawn, Histriomastix, Jack Drum's Entertainment,
The Malcontent, Sophonisba, What You Will

6   ORNSTEIN, ROBERT. "Recent Studies in Elizabethan and Jacobean
    Drama." SEL 20:345-63.
        Reviews Ingram's John Marston (1978.5), as balanced, in-
    sightful. Discusses Scott's John Marston's Plays (1978.10).
    Praises the author's enthusiasm and some insights, yet feels that
    other observations are strained.

7   PEARSON, JACQUELINE. Tragedy and Tragicomedy in the Plays of
    John Webster. Totowa, N.J.: Barnes & Noble, passim.
        Discusses Jack Drum's Entertainment and The Malcontent in
    some depth.

8   SINFIELD, ALAN. "Hamlet's Special Providence." SHS 33:90-91.
        Observes that Marston in Antonio and Mellida and Antonio's
    Revenge questions the supposed self-sufficiency of the Stoical
    hero and suggests that these plays might have influenced
    Shakespeare's view of Stoicism.

9   TRICOMI, ALBERT H. "John Marston's Manuscripts." HLQ 43:
    87-102.
        Discusses the reputed autograph manuscripts of Marston's
    works, particularly The Montebank's Masque and the two satirical
    poems on the duke of Buckingham. On the basis of known Marston
    autographs and a supposedly lost manuscript of The Montebank's
    Masque concludes that Marston did not write this work. Also
    concludes that John Marston, the dramatist, did not write the two
    satires on the duke of Buckingham (see 1967.1). Posits that
    these poems were written by another John Marston, a Canterbury
    clergyman.

10 WEST, MICHAEL, and MARILYN THORSON. "Observations on the Text
    of John Marston's Sophonisba." Anglia 98:348-56.
        Observes that the play's obscure, elliptical style has
    created numerous obscurities that have baffled editors. Supplies
    emendations for some of these passages.

11 YEARLING, ELIZABETH M. "'Mount Tufty Tamburlaine': Marston
    and Linguistic Excess." SEL 20:257-69.
        Discusses the charges of Marston's ineptitude with diction
    and suggests that despite some stylistic awkwardnesses, Marston
    was well aware of linguistic excesses and in fact burlesqued them
    in his plays. Points out that his heroes realize the insuffi-
    ciency of tragic rant and that his fools are guilty of extrava-
    gant diction. Suggests that Marston was attracted to the plain
    style of writing that was in vogue, but concludes that Marston's
    own faults result from his inability to find a linguistic medium
    for conveying tragic emotions. Holds that he was more acutely

aware of the stylistic problems tragedy presents than many of his
successors were.
     Antonio and Mellida, Antonio's Revenge, The Fawn, Jack
Drum's Entertainment, The Malcontent, Sophonisba, What You Will

*12   ZYNGIER, SONIA. "John Marston: Objeto de Estudo?" EAA
      1979-80:44-55.
         Cited in the MLA Annual Bibliography.

                                 1981

*1   DINNEEN, MARCIA B.   "An Annotated Bibliography of Criticism of
      John Marston's Antonio Plays." BB 38:71-81, 91.
         Cited in the MLA International Bibliography.

2   FREER, COBURN. The Politics of Jacobean Drama. Baltimore:
      Johns Hopkins University Press, pp. 17, 26, 31, 41, 224.
         Provides passing comments on Marston. Suggests that the
      speeches of his characters are often at odds with their actual
      feelings and with those of Marston himself.

3   GRAVES, R.B. "Elizabethan Dramatic Conventions and
      Elizabethan Reality." RenD, n.s. 12:51-70.
         Points out Marston's use of torches in What You Will to
      indicate the approach of night.

4   LAKE, J.D. "Eastward Hoe: Linguistic Evidence for
      Authorship." NQ, n.s. 28:158-66.
         Studies stylistic patterns to decide the shares of Chapman,
      Marston, and Jonson and agrees substantially with earlier attri-
      butions of the authors' respective portions. Holds that Chapman
      had the largest share (1,461 lines), Jonson the next largest (974
      lines), and Marston the least (328).

5   _____. "Histriomastix: Linguistic Evidence for Authorship."
      NQ, n.s. 28:148-52.
         Uses the text's stylistic pattern to suggest that
      Histriomastix is a collaboration of two authors, with Marston
      writing from part of Act III into Act V. Also suggests that the
      unknown collaborator recopied Marston's portion and did some
      revising.

6   _____. "The Insatiate Countess: Linguistic Evidence for
      Authorship." NQ, n.s. 28:166-70.
         Holds to the theory that William Barksted and Lewis Machin
      completed Marston's text and compares Marston's linguistic pat-
      terns with those of the play to argue that the text we have has
      been substantially rewritten. Adds that the collaborators could
      have copied Marstonian passages and unconsciously could have
      translated them into their own stylistic patterns. Hence, we can
      never be certain how much of the play is Marston's.

7   _____. "Webster's Additions to The Malcontent: Linguistic
      Evidence." NQ, n.s. 28:153-58.
           Argues against the theory that John Webster wrote only the
      induction to The Malcontent and supports Hunter's theory (The
      Malcontent 1975.1) that possibly both Marston and Webster wrote
      additions to the play itself. Suggests that Webster's are addi-
      tions 4, 6, 7, 8, and 10. Concludes by stating that these addi-
      tions and Webster's character Passarello slow the play's movement
      and stresses that a sound production will omit them.

8   LEGGATT, ALEXANDER. "Recent Studies in Elizabethan and
      Jacobean Drama." SEL 21:332-62.
           Reviews Jensen's John Marston Dramatist: Themes and
      Imagery in the Plays (1979.4). Sympathizes with the author's
      basic approach, feels that good insights are offered, but judges
      the book's treatment of Marston somewhat thin.

9   PUTT, S. GORLEY. The Golden Age of English Drama: Enjoyment
      of Elizabethan and Jacobean Plays. Totowa, N.J.: Rowman &
      Littlefield, pp. 69-83.
           Justifies Marston's dramaturgy by seeing him as a mannerist
      author, employing farce, satire, irony, horror, and other seem-
      ingly incompatible techniques to create his forceful dramas.
      Sees the Antonio plays as forming a mannerist diptych, with
      Antonio and Mellida as a satirical farce attacking court life and
      Antonio's Revenge as a farcical, yet serious treatment of re-
      venge. Also discusses The Malcontent as a kind of "Mannerist
      black farce." Suggests modern pessimism and the techniques of
      the theater of the absurd have enabled us to appreciate Marston
      better than readers of past generations.

10   SHEPHERD, SIMON. Amazons and Warrior Women: Varieties
      of Feminism in Seventeenth-Century Drama. New York:
      St. Martin's, pp. 102-4, 153-54, and passim.
           Provides passing comments upon the treatment of women in
      Marston's plays. Discusses Mrs. Mulligrub and Crispinella, both
      characters in The Dutch Courtezan.

Index

Included are authors and editors of writings concerning Marston, editors of Marston texts, title of book-length studies of Marston, and editions and discussions of Marston's writings. Also included are literary works and persons cited in the annotations as well as selected subject headings. Literary works of known authorship are listed under the author's name; material in anonymously written works is listed under subject headings. The index does not include titles of articles or journals given in the bibliography.

Ford, John, 1871.1; 1954.4;
  1968.18; 1972.1
Foreign characters on the
  Elizabethan stage, 1910.1;
  1911.4; 1933.2; 1963.7
Forker, Charles R., 1959.4
Forsythe, Robert Stanley, 1914.4
Foster, Frances A., 1912.2
Fraser, Russell A., Dutch
  Courtezan 1976.1; 1970.8
Fratricide Punished, 1902.4
Freeburg, Victor Oscar, 1915.1
Freeman, Arthur, 1967.7
Freer, Coburn, 1981.2
Friedland, Louis Sigmund, 1911.5
Friedman, Lila H., 1955.9
Friedrich, Ernst, 1913.3
Fries, Carl, 1904.6
Fripp, Edgar, 1964.2
Frost, David L. 1968.6
Frye, Northrop, 1957.11
Furnivall, F.J., 1886.2

Gair, Reavley, Antonio's Revenge
  1978.1; 1977.7
Galloway, David, 1973.7, 9
Garber, Marjorie, 1974.9
Garlick, Harry, 1980.4
Garnett, Richard, 1903.3
Gassner, John, 1954.7; 1969.22
Gayley, Charles Mills, Eastward
  Hoe 1913.1
Geckle, George L., 1971.10;
  1972.6; 1973.5; 1980.5
Geddie, Liddell J., 1902.1
Genest, John, 1832.1
Gentile, Vanna, 1969.9
George J., 1957.12
Gerrard, Ernest A., 1928.5
Gibbons, Brian, 1967.8; 1968.7
Gibbs, Henry, 1884.5
Gifford, William, 1860.1
Gilbert, Allan, 1959.5
Gildersleeve, Virginia
  Crocheron, 1961.11
Gill, R.B., 1975.4
Gillard, Julia, 1895.1
Gillie, Christopher, 1972.8
Goetz, Hermann Josef, 1913.4
Goffe, Thomas, 1953.4
Golding, Arthur, 1956.6-7
Golding, S.R., 1928.6

Goldman, Michael, 1972.8
Goldsmith, Robert Hillis, 1963.9
Gomme, A.H., Malcontent 1969.1
Gordon, George, 1944.1
Gosse, Edmund, 1894.1; 1903.3
Gottschalk, Paul, 1972.9
Gottwald, Maria, 1969.10
Gowda, H.H. Anniah, 1972.10
Grant, Allan, Eastward Hoe
  1968.1
Grässe, Johann George Theodor,
  1863.1
Graves, R.B., 1981.3
Graves, Robert, 1925.3; 1949.3
Graves, T.S., 1922.6
Gray, Henry David, 1947.1
Gray, Joseph William, 1905.3
Green, A. Wigfall, 1931.4
Greene, Robert 1908.8
Greenfield, Thelma, 1969.11
Greenman, David J., 1969.12;
  1975.5
Greg, W.W., Antonio's Revenge
  1921.1; Antonio and Mellida
  1921.1; 1900.1; 1904.7;
  1907.5; 1921.2; 1922.7;
  1928.7; 1932.3; 1957.13;
  1968.8
Grieben, Ernst, 1906.5
Grierson, Herbert J.C., 1906.6;
  1944.2
Griffiths, L.M., 1881.1; 1888.2;
  1890.1-2
Grosart, A.B., Collected Edition
  1879.1; Love's Martyr
  1878.1; 1876.1; 1878.1-2
Grossman, Rudolf, 1920.3
Grundy, Joan, 1969.13
Guilpin, Everard
  -as author, 1598.1; 1601.2;
    1878.2; 1951.6; 1974.4
  -and Skialetheia, 1598.1;
    1878.2; 1951.6; 1974.4
  -as subject, 1932.1; 1963.8;
    1974.4
Gunby, D.C., 1971.11; 1976.3
Gurr, Andrew, 1970.9
Guss, Donald L., 1966.5

Hall, Anne Drury, 1975.6
Hall, Donald, 1963.1